THE
ARCHITECTURE
OF
MODERN EMPIRE

ABOUT THE AUTHORS

Arundhati Roy is the author of *The God of Small Things*, which won the Booker Prize in 1997, and *The Ministry of Utmost Happiness*, which was longlisted for the Man Booker Prize 2017. Both novels have been translated into more than forty languages.

My Seditious Heart, published in 2019, collects the work of a two-decade period when Arundhati Roy devoted herself to the political essay as a way of opening up space for justice, rights and freedoms in an increasingly hostile environment.

Azadi, published in 2020 and in an expanded edition in 2022, collects the writing that followed and focuses on the meaning of freedom in a world of growing authoritarianism.

David Barsamian has altered the independent media landscape, both with his weekly radio programme, Alternative Radio (www.alternativeradio.org), and his books with Noam Chomsky, Eqbal Ahmad, Howard Zinn, Tariq Ali, Richard Wolff, Arundhati Roy and Edward W. Said. Barsamian is the winner of the Media Education Award, the ACLU'S Upton Sinclair Award for independent journalism and the Cultural Freedom Fellowship from the Lannan Foundation. The Institute for Alternative Journalism named him one of its Top Ten Media Heroes. He is the recipient of Lifetime Achievement Awards from the Democracy Alliance of Vancouver, the Rocky Mountain Peace and Justice Center and Radical Desi.

THE ARCHITECTURE OF MODERN EMPIRE

ARUNDHATI ROY

CONVERSATIONS WITH

DAVID BARSAMIAN

AFTERWORD BY

NAOMI KLEIN

PENGUIN BOOKS

PENGUIN BOOKS

UK | USA | Canada | Ireland | Australia
India | New Zealand | South Africa

Penguin Books is part of the Penguin Random House group of companies
whose addresses can be found at global.penguinrandomhouse.com.

First published in the United States of America by Haymarket Books 2023
First published in Great Britain by Penguin Books 2024
001

This book was published with the generous support of Lannan Foundation,
Wallace Action Fund and Marguerite Casey Foundation

The moral right of the authors has been asserted

Typeset by Jouve (UK), Milton Keynes
Printed and bound in Great Britain by Clays Ltd, Elcograf S.p.A.

The authorized representative in the EEA is Penguin Random House Ireland,
Morrison Chambers, 32 Nassau Street, Dublin D02 YH68

A CIP catalogue record for this book is available from the British Library

ISBN: 978–1–405–96681–8

www.greenpenguin.co.uk

MIX
Paper | Supporting
responsible forestry
FSC® C018179

Penguin Random House is committed to a
sustainable future for our business, our readers
and our planet. This book is made from Forest
Stewardship Council® certified paper.

Contents

Note on the Text

The first four interviews here, as well as Naomi Klein's afterword, were published by South End Press in 2004 as *The Checkbook and the Cruise Missile: Conversations with Arundhati Roy*. This book adds eight additional interviews. Endnotes for the four original interviews have been updated here to reflect more recent publications. All the interviews have been edited from their original form. Transcripts and audio of the original interviews are available from Alternative Radio (www.alternativeradio.org).

CHAPTER 1

Knowledge and Power

David Barsamian: Tell me about Kerala, where you grew up. It's a singular place in India for many reasons. It's multireligious, has a high rate of literacy, and has been relatively free from the kinds of sectarian violence that plague other parts of the country.

Arundhati Roy: Kerala is a place where great religions coincide. You have Christianity, Hinduism, Islam, and Marxism [laughs]. They all rub each other down and metamorphize into something new. Politically Kerala is quite volatile. This might mean a clash between the Marxists and the right-wing Hindu nationalist Rashtriya Swayamsevak Sangh (RSS) or between different Communist parties, though it's relatively free of the kind of caste killing that you have in states like Bihar or Uttar Pradesh.

When I first came to North India, it was almost like visiting a different century. Still, Kerala is a complex society because it's progressive and parochial simultaneously. Even among the Syrian Christians—who are the oldest, most orthodox Christians in India—you have caste issues. If you look at the Communist parties, most of their leaders are upper-caste. When they fight elections, candidates are carefully chosen to represent the dominant caste of their respective "vote bank"—an example of how communism will harness the traditional caste system in its quest for power in a "representative" democracy.

This interview was conducted while driving from Amherst to Boston, Massachusetts, February 16, 2001.

1

Kerala is known for its high literacy rate, but the quality of the education itself is execrable. Kerala University is among the worst universities in India.

I don't think that something like the Narmada Valley Development Project could easily happen in Kerala. That kind of mass injustice—the eviction of hundreds of thousands of people—might be hard to pull off. On the other hand, the first thing E. M. S. Namboodiripad did when he came to power as head of the first democratically elected Communist government in the world was to get Birla, the big industrial group, to set up a huge rayon factory in Calicut.

In the last thirty years that factory has denuded the bamboo forest, poisoned the Chaliyar River, and polluted the air. There is a high incidence of cancer among the local people and the factory workers. The factory is Kerala's biggest private industry, and Kerala, being Kerala, has thirteen trade unions. In the name of employing three thousand people it destroyed the livelihood of hundreds of thousands who lived on these natural resources, fishermen, bamboo workers, sand quarriers. (They don't qualify as "workers" in the Communist dictionary.) The government and courts did nothing about it. Eventually the factory closed down on its own because it had finished off all the raw material there and wanted to move elsewhere.

Because Kerala is so riven with internecine politics, everybody disagrees with everybody else. There are hundreds of factions, and eventually everything remains frozen in a sort of political rigor mortis.

What's the status of women generally in Kerala? Is it different from the rest of India given the high levels of education?

I know that people say that fertility rates have dropped in Kerala because of literacy. It's probably true. But you have only to watch Malayalam cinema to feel sick to your stomach at the way women are treated and the way women behave. When I was a child, every film I saw had the heroine being raped. Until I was about fifteen,

I believed that every woman gets raped. It was just a question of waiting for yours to happen. That was the kind of terror that was inculcated in young girls.

My mother is very well known in Kerala because in 1986 she won a public interest litigation case. She challenged the Syrian Christian inheritance law that said that a woman can inherit one-fourth of her father's property or five thousand rupees, whichever is less. The Supreme Court ruling in her case gave women equal inheritance with retrospective effect from 1956. But actually no women go to court to claim this right. Everyone said, "You can't have it going back to 1956 because the courts will be flooded with complaints." It didn't happen. The churches had will-making classes. They taught fathers how to disinherit their daughters.

It's a very strange kind of oppression that happens there. Women from Kerala work all over India and all over the world. Many of the world's nuns and nurses are from Kerala. They send all the money they earn back home to support their families. And yet the nurses, who earn comparatively huge salaries, will get married, pay a dowry, and end up having the most bizarrely subservient relationships with their husbands.

Growing up in a little village in Kerala was a nightmare for me. All I wanted to do was to escape, to get out, to never have to marry somebody there. Not that people were queuing to marry me [laughs]. I was the worst thing a girl could be: thin, Black, and clever. No looks, no dowry, no good.

Your mother, Mary, also broke the unofficial love laws.

She married a Bengali Hindu and then, what's worse, divorced him, which meant that everyone was confirmed in their opinion that it was a terrible thing to marry for love—outside the community.

What was it like growing up without a father at home?

In Kerala everyone has what is called a *tharavad,* your ancestral home. If you don't have a father, you don't have a *tharavad.* You're a person without an address. "No address," that's what they call you. I grew up in Ayemenem, the village in which *The God of Small Things* is set. Given the way things have turned out, it's easy for me to say that I thank God that I had none of the conditioning that a normal middle-class Indian girl would have. I had no father, no presence of this man "looking after" us and beating or humiliating our mother occasionally in exchange. I had no caste, no religion, no supervision.

It was made very clear to me early on by everyone around me that I would not be given the protection that other children around me had. Anything could have happened to me. I could have gone under. But because I didn't, I have a vantage point from which to watch what's going on now. I'm not rural, not urban, not completely "traditional" nor wholeheartedly "modern." I grew up in a village. I saw rural India at work. And yet I had the advantage of having an education. It's like being at the top of the bottom of the heap—without the blinkered singlemindedness of the completely oppressed nor the flabby self-indulgence of the well-to-do.

There must be very few girls in India whose mothers say, "Whatever you do, don't get married. And don't sleep with a man until you're financially independent." It was sound advice—not that I listened [laughs]. When I see brides all dressed up for the sacrifice, it gives me a rash. I find them ghoulish, almost. I find what that whole thing means in India so frightening—to see this decorated, bejeweled creature willingly, happily entering a life of permanent subjugation.

You're close to your mother today?

I left home when I was sixteen, for all sorts of reasons, and didn't see her for many years. Like many mothers and daughters, we had a complicated relationship—nothing to do with our politics, though. My mother is like someone who strayed off the set of a Fellini film. But to have been brought up by a woman who never made it her mission in life to find another partner to entwine herself around is a wonderful thing.

My mother runs a school in the town of Kottayam. It's phenomenally successful. People try to book their children into it before they are even born. Yet folks in town don't know quite what to make of her. Or me. The problem is that we are both women who are unconventional. The least we could have done was to be unhappy. But we aren't. That's what bothers people: the fact that you can make these choices and be happy—like a pair of witches.

My mother's school is very unconventional. She started it with five or six students when I was about four or five. She managed to persuade the Rotary Club of Kottayam to rent us their premises in the daytime. In the morning we would put up tables and be taught how to read and write. In the evening the men would meet and smoke and leave all their cigarette butts and teacups and whisky glasses all over. Middle-class Indian men leave their rubbish everywhere for others to clean up. The next morning we would clean it all up and then it would be the school. I used to call it a sliding, folding school. People know that the education children get from my mother's school is invaluable. And yet it makes them uncomfortable because she's not amenable to all the rules and regulations of their society.

Now it's complicated even further by what has happened to me since *The God of Small Things* was published. I was the first student from her school. In a way she's vindicated—it's like a B-grade film script. Suffering, belief, and hard work, then beautiful retribution. You can't imagine that something like this could happen: the way we were treated by that town, the way things were when I was a child, compared to now. Even the book, people don't know how to deal with it. They want to embrace me and to say that this is "our woman," and yet they don't want to address what the book is about, which is their society and its intrinsic, callous brutality. They have to find ways of filtering out the parts they don't want to address. They have to say it's a book about children, something like that.

You were the target of a criminal case in Kerala because someone said The God of Small Things *was obscene.*

I was charged with corrupting public morality [laughs]. As though public morality was pure until I came along. I was at the high court in Kochi a year or two ago. I had appealed to have the case quashed, saying that for a number of reasons it wasn't legally valid. The lawyers of both sides were ready to argue but the judge came on and said, "I don't want to hear this case. Every time it comes up before me I get chest pains" [laughs]. He postponed the hearings, and the case still sits there in court.

Since you wrote your novel, you've produced some remarkable political essays. What was that transition like, from writing in the world of fiction and imagination to writing about concrete things, like dams, people being displaced in the Narmada valley, globalization, and Enron?

It's only to other people that it appears to be a transition. When I was in fourth year in architecture school, I already knew that I would never practice architecture because it involves being a part of a chain of such ugly exploitation. I couldn't do it. I was very interested in urbanization and town planning, in how a city comes to be what it is and what it does to those who live in it.

I've been doing this kind of work since I was twenty-one. It's only to the outside world, those who came to know me after *The God of Small Things*, that it seems like a transition. I wrote political essays before I wrote the novel. I wrote three essays called "The Great Indian Rape Trick" (in two parts) and "The Naughty Lady of Shady Lane" about the way the film *Bandit Queen* exploited Phoolan Devi and whether or not somebody should have the right to restage the rape of a living woman without her consent.

I don't see a great difference between *The God of Small Things* and my nonfiction. In fact, I keep saying, fiction is the truest thing there ever was. Today's world of specialization is bizarre. Specialists and experts end up severing the links between things, isolating them, actually creating barriers that prevent ordinary people from understanding what's happening to them. I try to do the opposite: to create links, to join the dots, to tell politics like a story, to communicate it, to make it real. To make the connection between a man with his child telling you about life in the village he lived in before it was submerged by a reservoir, and the World Trade Organization (WTO), the International Monetary Fund (IMF), and the World Bank. *The God of Small Things* is a book which connects the very smallest things to the very biggest. Whether it's the dent that a baby spider makes on the surface of water in a pond or the quality of the moonlight on a river or how history and politics intrude into your life, your house, your bedroom, your bed, into the most intimate relationships between people—parents and children, siblings and so on.

If you lose these connections, everything becomes noise, meaningless, a career plan to be on track for tenure. It's a bit like the difference between allopathy and homeopathy or any other form of indigenous medicine. You don't just treat the symptoms. You don't just say, "Oh, you've got a patch on your skin, so let me give you some steroids." You ask, "Why do you have it? How has it come there? What does it mean? What are you thinking about today? Are you happy? Why has your body produced this?" You can't just be a skin expert. You must understand the human body and the human mind.

You've talked about the colonization of knowledge and its control and a Brahmin-like caste that builds walls around it. What do you think the relationship should be between knowledge and power and politics?

All over the world today people are fighting for a right to information. The organizations that control the world today—the WTO, the IMF, the World Bank—operate in complete secrecy. Contracts that governments sign with multinationals, which affect people's lives so intimately, are secret documents. For example, I think that the contract between Enron, the giant Houston-based energy corporation, and the government of Maharashtra should be a public document. It is the biggest contract ever signed by the Indian government. It guarantees this one corporation profits that add up to more than 60 percent of India's rural development budget. Why is it a secret document? Who is the government to sign away its public buildings as collateral? The government holds everything, whether it's the natural resources or the Rashtrapati Bhavan, the president's residence in New Delhi, in trust for the people that it represents. It cannot sign these things away. That contract must be a public document. That's one aspect of the relationship between knowledge and power.

But there is a more insidious aspect. It isn't a coincidence that four hundred million Indian people are illiterate. When I say "illiterate," I don't want to imply that the kind of education that is being imparted is literacy. Education sometimes makes people float even further away from things they ought to know about. It seems to actually obscure their vision. The kind of ignorance that people with PhDs display is unbelievable. When the Supreme Court judgment about the Narmada valley came out in October 2000, I wrote an analysis of what it meant. Then I went to the valley. People were marching. They were so angry, they desecrated a copy of the judgment and buried it. There was a public meeting at which many Adivasis and farmers spoke. A friend of mine said, "Isn't it amazing that there isn't a single point that you have brought up that they're not already talking about with the same sophistication?" I said, "No, we're the ones who have to make the leap of faith. For them, it's their lives."

The Supreme Court judgment transforms their lives. It's not an intellectual exercise. It's not research. If you see how far away people who are educated and have become consultants or experts or whatever have floated from what's happening, I think you'll see the entire "development" debate is a scam. The biggest problem is that what they say in their project reports and what actually happens are two completely different things. They've perfected the art of getting it right on paper, but that has nothing to do with what is happening on the ground.

The distance between power and powerlessness, between those who take decisions and those who have to suffer those decisions, has increased enormously. It's a perilous journey for the poor—it's a pitfall filled to overflowing with lies, brutality, and injustice. Sitting in Washington or Geneva in the offices of the World Bank or the WTO, bureaucrats have the power to decide the fate of millions. It's not only their decisions that we are contesting. It's the fact that they have the power to make those decisions. No one elected them. No one said they could control our lives. Even if they made great decisions, it's politically unacceptable.

Those men in pin-striped suits addressing the peasants of India and other poor countries all over again—assuring them that they're being robbed for their own good, like long ago they were colonized for their own good—what's the difference? What's changed? The further and further away geographically decisions are taken, the more scope you have for incredible injustice. That is the primary issue.

The power of the World Bank is not only its money, but its ability to accumulate and manipulate knowledge. It probably employs more PhDs than any university in the world. It funds studies that suit its purpose. Then it disseminates them and produces a particular kind of worldview that is supposedly based on neutral facts. But it's not. It's not at all. How do you deal with that? What is the difference between that and the Vishwa Hindu Parishad (VHP) or the Bharatiya Janata Party (BJP) openly rewriting history texts and saying that we will now give you the Hindu version of history? The World Bank version of development is the same thing.

The Narmada valley project envisions the construction of something like three thousand large and medium dams along the course of the Narmada River and its tributaries. It covers three states: Maharashtra, Gujarat, and Madhya Pradesh. There's been a resistance movement to what was originally a World Bank scheme. The World Bank has now withdrawn from the project, and the government of

India has taken it over. Tell me about the Narmada Bachao Andolan (NBA), the Save the Narmada Movement.

The remarkable thing about the NBA is that it is a cross-section of India. It is the Adivasis, the upper-caste big farmers, the Dalits, and the urban middle class. It's a forging of links between the urban and the rural, between farmers, fishermen, writers, painters, and lawyers. That's what gives it such phenomenal strength.

When dam proponents in India say, "You know, these middle-class people, they are against development and they're exploiting illiterate farmers and Adivasis," it makes me furious. After all, the whole Narmada Valley Development Project was dreamed up by the middle-class mind. Middle-class urban engineers designed it. You can't expect the critique to be just rural or Adivasi. People try to delegitimize the involvement of the middle class, saying, "How can you speak on behalf of these people?" No one is speaking on behalf of anyone. The criticism of middle-class dam opponents is an attempt to isolate the Adivasis, the farmers, and then crush them. After all, government policy documents aren't in Hindi or Bhilali, and the Indian Supreme Court doesn't work in Hindi or Bhilali.

The NBA is a fantastic example of a resistance movement in which people link hands across caste and class. It is India's biggest, finest, most magnificent resistance movement since the independence struggle succeeded in the 1940s. There are other resistance movements in India. It's a miracle that they exist. But I fear for their future.

When you travel from India to the West, you see that the Western notion of "development" has to do with a lack of imagination. A taming of the wilderness, of the human soul. An inability to understand that there is another way to live. In India, the anarchy and the wilderness still exist (though they're under the hammer). But still, how are you going to persuade a *Naga sadhu*—whose life mission has been to stand naked on one leg for twenty years or to tow a car with his penis—that he can't live without Coca-Cola? It's an uphill task.

Estha, one of the characters in your novel, walks "along the banks of the river that smelled of shit and pesticides bought with World Bank loans."

When I first met activists from the NBA, they told me, "We knew that you would be against big dams and the World Bank when we read *The God of Small Things*." I've never had that kind of a reading before [laughs].

In India, the whole pesticide issue is just unbelievable. The Green Revolution, bringing canal irrigation, bore wells, and chemical pesticides and fertilizer, has now led to serious problems. After a point, the productivity of the land begins to diminish. That has started happening in places like Andhra Pradesh, where farmers have been forced to abandon traditional farming and grow cash crops. Now that move has backfired because of the import of food grains under new WTO rules. Hundreds of farmers in Punjab and Andhra Pradesh are committing suicide because of their growing debt. They have to invest more and more in pesticides and fertilizers. Pests have grown resistant to the chemicals. The farmers have to make large capital investments to force a little bit of productivity out of these dead lands. They end up killing themselves by drinking pesticide.

Arrogant interventions in ecosystems that you don't understand can be ruinous. In the northeast of India, some states started exporting frog legs to France. It became a big earner of foreign exchange. As the frogs began to disappear, the pests they used to eat began to destroy crops. The states started having to buy pesticides (with World Bank loans), which eventually cost more than the money they made by exporting frog legs. I think it was in Tanzania that farmers began to shoot hippos because they were raiding and destroying the crops. When the hippos disappeared, so did the fish in the river. Later they discovered that these fish used to lay their eggs in the shit of the hippos. When human beings don't respect something that they don't understand, they end up with consequences that you cannot possibly foretell.

The Western notion of thinking that you must understand everything can also be destructive. Why can't we just be satisfied with not understanding something? It's all right. It's wonderful to not understand something. To respect and revere the earth's secrets.

There was a particular mountain in the Himalayas that hadn't ever been climbed. Some climbers wanted to climb it. I had a friend who led a campaign to allow that one peak to remain unclimbed. There's a kind of humility in that. I don't mean to take an extreme position and say that science is bad. But there ought to be a balance between curiosity, grace, humility, and letting things be. Must everything be poked at and prodded and intervened in and understood?

Proponents of the Narmada valley project say that it will bring water to the thirsty and crops to the parched land of three states. What's wrong with that?

I've written about this extensively in my essay "The Greater Common Good." They say the Sardar Sarovar Dam is going to take water to Kutch and Saurashtra, the regions of Gujarat which were the hardest hit by the earthquake in January 2001. They have a terrible drought in these areas. But if you look at the government's own plans, you'll see there is no possibility that the water will get to these regions, even if everything that they say were to work. For example, they arbitrarily assume an irrigation efficiency of 60 percent. No irrigation project has ever been more than 35 percent efficient in India. Kutch and Saurashtra are right at the tail end of this big canal system, but all the politically powerful areas are right up at the head of the canal. They will take away all the water. Already big sugar factories have been licensed before the dam has been built. According to the project, sugar was not going to be allowed to be planted. Huge five-star hotels and golf courses have been built.

Even if all this hadn't happened, according to the Gujarat government's own plan, the Sardar Sarovar Dam will irrigate 1.2

percent of the cultivable area of Kutch and 9 percent of Saurashtra. That's forgetting about the irrigation efficiency and the sugar factories, about the fact that rivers close to Kutch and Saurashtra are being dammed and the water is being taken to central Gujarat.

In fact, when the Supreme Court judgment came and the Gujarat BJP government had a huge ceremony to inaugurate the beginning of the construction of the dam, Kutch and Saurashtra boycotted it. They said, "You are just using us to mop up 85 percent of Gujarat's irrigation budget—and in the process not leaving any money for local water harvesting or for more local solutions to this problem."

That's one thing. The second is that they don't even ask, "Why is there a drought in Kutch and Saurashtra?" The reason is that the government has systematically cut down all the mangrove forests. They have mined groundwater indiscriminately and so there's an ingress of seawater from the coast. They have big industrial complexes that poison whatever groundwater remains. The Gujarat government will do nothing, nothing at all to control this kind of thing.

If they want to take water from the Narmada to Kutch just to make a political statement, of course they can, but it will be as a circus—an economically unviable political circus—like taking red wine or champagne to Kutch. Narmada is so far away from Kutch and Saurashtra that it's a joke to take all that water all the way up through Gujarat. For the price of the Sardar Sarovar Dam, you could finance local water harvesting schemes in every single village in the state of Gujarat.

What prompted the World Bank to pull out of the project?

The peoples' resistance movement in 1993 and 1994. The World Bank was forced to set up an independent review. They sent out a committee under a man named Bradford Morse. The Morse Report, which is now a kind of landmark, said in no uncertain terms that the bank should pull out. Of course the bank tried to cover up the report. It sent another committee, the

Pamela Cox Committee, which tried to say everything's fine. But Morse had agreed that he would do this study only provided it was an independent report. Finally the World Bank was forced to pull out. This is unprecedented in the murky history of the World Bank.

The government of India seems to be determined to complete the Narmada project. What's driving it?

First of all, you must understand that in India the myth of big dams is sold to us from the time we're three years old. In every school textbook, we learn that Pandit Nehru said "dams are the temples of modern India." Criticizing dams is equated with being anti-national.

The thing about dams and the struggle against them is that people have to understand that they're just monuments to corruption and they are undemocratic. They centralize natural resources, snatch them away from people, and then redistribute them to a favored few.

The first dam built on the Narmada was in Madhya Pradesh, the Bargi Dam, which was completed in 1990. They said it would displace seventy thousand people and submerge 101 villages. One day they just filled the reservoir. One hundred and fourteen thousand people, almost twice the government's projection, were displaced and 162 villages were submerged. They were just driven from their homes when the waters rose. They had to run up the hill with their cattle and children. Ten years later, that dam irrigates 5 percent of the land that they said it would. It irrigates less land than it submerged.

In Gujarat, the Sardar Sarovar Dam has been used by every political party as a campaign issue for years. The amount of disinformation about this dam is extraordinary. For contractors and politicians, just the building of the dam makes them a lot of money.

Forty percent of the big dams that are being built in the world today are in India. Tens of millions of Indians have already been displaced by many of the dam projects. What happens to these people? What kind of resettlement or compensation is provided by the government?

Nobody knows. When I was writing "The Greater Common Good," what shocked me more than the figures that do exist and are thrown around and fought over by pro-dam and anti-dam activists are the figures that don't exist. The Indian government does not have any estimate of how many people have been displaced by big dams. I think that's not just a failure of the state, but a failure of the intellectual community. The reason that these figures don't exist is that most of the displaced are the nonpeople, the Adivasis and the Dalits.

I did a sanity check based on a study of fifty-four dams done by the Indian Institute of Public Administration. According to that study, the number of reservoir-displaced, which is only one kind of displacement, came to an average of something like forty-four thousand people per dam. I said, "Let's assume that these fifty-four dams are the bigger of the big dams. Let's quarter this average, and say each dam displaced ten thousand people. We know that India has built thirty-three hundred big dams in the last fifty years. So just a sanity check says that it's thirty-three million people displaced." At the time I wrote this, people mocked this figure. Now, the India Country Study done by the World Commission on Dams puts that figure at as much as fifty-six million.

Today, India doesn't have a national resettlement policy. The government of Madhya Pradesh, where eighty percent of Sardar Sarovar–displaced people are from, gave a written affidavit in court saying it did not have enough land to resettle people. The Supreme Court still ordered the construction of the dam to go ahead.

What happens to the people who are driven out from their villages by these development projects and by the general garroting of India's rural economy? They all migrate to the cities. And there, again, they are noncitizens, living in slums. They are subject to being evicted at a moment's notice, any time a new office complex or a five-star hotel chain covets the land they live on.

You compare the uprooting of these people to a kind of garbage disposal.

That's exactly what it is. The Indian government has managed to turn the concept of nonviolence on its head. Nonviolent repression. Unlike, say, China or Turkey or Indonesia, the government of India doesn't mow down its people. It doesn't kill people who refuse to move. It just continues to pursue the brutal path of this particular model of "development" and to ignore the consequences. Because of the caste system, because of the fact that there is no social link between the people who make the decisions and the people who suffer the decisions, it just goes ahead and does what it wants. It's quite an efficient way of doing things.

India has a very good reputation in the world as a democracy, as a government that cares. But that's just not true.

But you say about your own politics that you're "not an anti-development junkie, nor a proselytizer for the eternal upholding of custom and tradition."

How can I be? As a woman who grew up in a village in India, I've spent my whole life fighting tradition. There's no way that I want to be a traditional Indian woman. So I'm not talking about being against development. I'm talking about the politics of development. I'm talking about more development, not less. More democracy, not less. More modernization, not less. How do you break down this completely centralized, undemocratic process of decision making? How do you make sure that it's decentralized and that people have power over their lives and their natural resources?

I don't even believe in the modern business-like notion of "efficiency." It dovetails with totalitarianism, fascism. People say, "If it's decentralized it will be inefficient." I think that's fine. Let it be inefficient.

Today the Indian government is trying to present privatization as the alternative to the state, to public enterprise. But privatization is only a further evolution of the centralized state, where the state says that they have the right to give the entire power production in Maharashtra to Enron. They don't have the right. The infrastructure of the public sector in India has been built up over the last fifty years with public money. They don't have the right to sell it to Enron. They cannot do that.

You say private enterprise is going to be more efficient? Look at what Enron is doing. Is that efficient? The same thing is happening in the telecom sector.

Three-quarters of our country lives on the edge of the market economy. You can't tell them that only those who can afford water can have it.

Talk about the material you covered in your essay, "The End of Imagination": the nuclear testing in India, followed by Pakistan. You say in India the official reasons given for the testing are threats from China and Pakistan and exposing Western hypocrisy.

When India carried out the nuclear tests in May 1998, within weeks the Pakistani infiltration of Kargil in Kashmir began. The Indian government didn't do anything about it because they knew how embarrassing it would be to actually admit that the nuclear tests triggered a war. So they allowed it to happen. Hundreds of soldiers got killed. The Indian government and the mainstream media used the Kargil War to whip up more patriotism. It's so frightening, the nationalism in the air in India. I'm terrified by it. It can be used to do anything.

Some of the cheering young Hindu men who were thrilled with the destruction of the Babri mosque in Ayodhya in the northern state of Uttar Pradesh were also celebrating the nuclear tests.

And the same ones were protesting about Coke. The same Bal Thackeray of Shiv Sena who met Rebecca Mark of Enron and signed the thirty-billion-dollar deal wants to ban birthday parties and Valentine's Day because they are an attack on Indian culture.

Indian intellectuals today feel radical when they condemn communalism, but not many people are talking about the link between privatization, globalization, and communalism. Globalization suits the Indian elite. Communalism doesn't. It doesn't create a good "investment climate." I think they have to be addressed together, not separately. They are both two sides of the same coin. Growing religious fundamentalism is directly linked to globalization and to privatization. The Indian government is talking about selling its entire power sector to foreign multinationals, but when the consequences of that become hard to manage, the government immediately starts saying, "Should we build the Ram temple in Ayodhya?" Everyone goes baying off in that direction. Meanwhile, contracts are signed.

It's like a game. That's something we have to understand. It's like a pincer action. With one hand they're selling the country out to multinationals. With the other they're orchestrating this howling cultural nationalism. On the one hand you're saying that the world is a global village. On the other hand governments spend millions and millions patrolling their borders with nuclear weapons.

You use a metaphor of two convoys of trucks, one very large one with many people going off in the darkness and another, much smaller, going into the digital promised land.

Every night outside my house in New Delhi I pass this road gang of emaciated laborers digging a trench to lay fiber optic cables to speed up our digital revolution. They work by the light of a few candles. That is what is happening in India today. The convoy that melts into the darkness and disappears doesn't have a voice. It doesn't exist on TV. It doesn't have a place in the national newspapers. And so it doesn't exist. The people that are in the little convoy on their way to this glittering destination at the top of the world don't care to see or even acknowledge the larger convoy heading into the darkness.

In Delhi, the city I live in, the cars are getting bigger and sleeker, the hotels are getting posher, the gates higher. The guards outside houses are no longer the old chowkidars, watchmen, they are young fellows with uniforms. And yet everywhere the poor are packed like lice into every crevice in the city. People don't see that anymore. It's as if you shine a light very brightly in one place, the darkness deepens around it. They don't want to know what's happening. The people who benefit from this situation can't imagine that the world is not a better place.

It's part of that regular diet of contradictions that Indians live with. You made a decision, or the decision was made for you, to identify with, or to be part of, that large convoy.

I can't be a part of the large convoy because it's not a choice that you can make. It's a choice that's made by your circumstances. The fact that I'm an educated person means that I can't be on that convoy. I'm too privileged. Besides, I don't want to be on it. I don't want to be a victim. I don't want to disappear into the darkness. I don't want anyone to disappear into the darkness.

You talk passionately about taking sides, about not being a neutral observer reporting on events in a distant way.

Once you've seen certain things, you can't unsee them, and saying nothing is as political an act as speaking out. There is no innocence. That I'm sure about. There's no innocence and there isn't any sense in which any of us is perfect or not invested in the system. If I put money in a bank it's going to fund the bombs and the dams. When I pay tax, I'm investing in projects I disagree with. I'm not a completely blameless person campaigning for the good of mankind. But from that un-pristine position, is it better to say nothing or to say something? One is not powerful enough nor powerless enough not to be invested in the process. Most of us are completely enmeshed in the way the world works. All our hands are dirty.

I read somewhere that you once lived in a squatter's colony within the walls of Delhi's Feroz Shah Kotla in a small hut with a tin roof, scrounging beer bottles to sell.

That's true. But it's not tragic. It was fun [laughs]. As I said, I left home when I was sixteen. I had to put myself through college.

So I used to live there because the mess manager of the canteen in the school of architecture hostel had this little hut. Feroz Shah Kotla was right next to my college. I used to live there with my boyfriend and a whole lot of other people who could not afford to live in the hostel.

What was your experience working in the film industry in India?

I worked on a few films that were a part of the lunatic fringe, films that no one really wanted to see. It wasn't at all part of the film industry. It was very marginal.

Some of these stories that you're telling about resistance and the NBA would seem to be grist for a film or a television series. Is anything like that going on in India?

No. There are a lot of documentary films. Few of them transcend the boundaries between activism and art. I think there are tremendous stories for making film, like the Bhopal tragedy that Union Carbide was responsible for. But I'm a loner. I can't bear the idea of working with a film crew, negotiating with the producer, actors and all the rest of it. I've done it—it's not my thing.

You could write a screenplay.

But then they'll fuck it up [laughs]. One of the things about writing *The God of Small Things* was that I negotiated with nobody. It was just me and my book. A fantastic way to spend four and a half years of my life. No negotiations.

In January 2000, in a village on the banks of the Narmada, there was a protest against the Maheshwar Dam. You were among many who were arrested there.

The Maheshwar Dam, which is the dam upstream from the Sardar Sarovar, is India's first private hydroelectric project. Its chief promoter is a textile company called S. Kumars. The resistance managed to kick out a whole host of private companies, starting with US companies like Pacgen and Ogden, then German firms like Siemens and HypoVereinsbank. Last year, the villagers decided that they were going to take over the dam site.

I was in the valley in a village called Sulgaon. All night, people were arriving from the surrounding villages, by tractor, by jeep, on foot. By three in the morning there were about five thousand of us. We started walking in the dark to the dam site. The police knew that the dam site would be captured, but they didn't know from where the people would come.

It was unforgettable. Five thousand people, mostly villagers, but also people from the cities, lawyers, architects, journalists, walking through these byways and crossing streams in absolute silence. There was not a person that lit a bidi or coughed or cleared their throats. Occasionally a whole group of women would sit down and pee and then keep walking. Finally, at dawn, we arrived and took over the dam site. For hours, the police surrounded us. Then there was a *lathi*, baton, charge. They arrested thousands of people, including me. They dumped me in a private car that belonged to S. Kumars. It was so humiliating.

The jails were full. Because I was there at that time, there was a lot of press and less violence than usual. But people have captured the Maheshwar Dam site so many times before, and it doesn't even make it to the news.

What is the status of the Narmada valley project now that the Supreme Court decision of October 2000 has granted permission for the completion of the Sardar Sarovar Dam in the state of Gujarat?

The status is totally uncertain. Gujarat is in shambles from the earthquake last month. What is happening there is ugly. The Gujarat government, and its goon squad, the VHP, is commandeering all the relief money. There are reports of how Muslims, Christians, and Dalits are being left out of the reconstruction efforts. In Bhuj, one of the worst-hit towns, they have seventeen different categories of tents for the seventeen different castes. It's infuriating to think of how much money these guys must have received from international donors and what they will end up using it for.

Everyone is keeping very quiet about what effect the earthquake will have on the dam. Sardar Sarovar is on a fault line. This is a point that's been brought up again and again. Everybody's ignored it.

The Vishwa Hindu Parishad, or VHP, is the religious arm of the ruling party, the BJP.

It's a sort of extreme right wing. There's the RSS, and even more right-wing than the RSS is the VHP. Even further to the right is the Bajrang Dal. They are the ones burning churches, destroying mosques, and killing priests.

You make the connection between the rise of extreme Hindu–based nationalism and globalization. Are there any local factors at work here?

There are plenty of local factors, but for me this connection explains how disempowerment works. When you have dispossession and disempowerment on this scale as a result of corporate globalization, the anger that it creates can be channeled in bizarre and dangerous ways. India's nuclear tests were conducted to shore up people's flagging self-esteem. India is still flinching from the cultural insult of British colonialism, still looking for its identity. It's about all that.

Are you thinking about writing any more fiction?

I need to write fiction like you need to eat or exercise, but right now it's so difficult. At the moment, I don't know how to manage my life. Just one writer who says quite simply to the people in the Narmada valley "I'm on your side" leads to so much love and so much affection and so many people asking you to join them. Just the fact that you're known as somebody who's willing to speak out opens you to a universe of conflict and pain and incredible suffering. It's impossible to avert your eyes. Sometimes, of course, it becomes ludicrous. A woman rang me up and said, "Oh, darling, I thought that piece on the Narmada was fantastic. Now could you do one for me on child abuse?" I said, "Sure. For or against?"

People just assume you're a gun for hire, you can write about anything. I don't know how I'll ever be able to make the space to say, "I'm writing a book now, and I'm not going to be able to do x or y." I would love to.

You are a celebrity within India and also outside. How do you handle this?

As a rule I never do things because I'm a celebrity. Also I never avoid doing things because I'm a celebrity. I try to ignore that whole noisy production. Of course I have the whole business of people asking me to inaugurate this or that. I never do that. I stand by what I write. That's what I am—a writer. If I began to believe the publicity about myself, whether for or against, it would give me a very absurd idea of myself. I know that there's a very fine balance between accepting your own power with grace and misusing it.

When I say my own power, I don't mean as a celebrity. Everybody, from the smallest person to the biggest, has some kind of power, and even the most powerless person has a responsibility. I don't feel responsible for everybody. Everybody also is responsible for themselves. I don't ever want to portray myself as a representative of the voiceless or anything like that. I'm scared of that.

You were attacked from the left for The God of Small Things *and from the right for "The End of Imagination." There's a little cottage industry of anger springing up around you.*

The pillars of society can't decide whether I'm extreme left, extreme right, extreme Green, or an extremely bad writer.

Gandhi called India's independence "a wooden loaf." Many of the issues plaguing the Subcontinent are rooted in its partition. What's your perspective on relations between India and Pakistan? India is a multicultural, multilayered country and has one of the largest Muslim populations in the world.

Partition has left a huge and bloody legacy between India and Pakistan. I think both countries are doing their best to keep it alive. The reasons for this range from actual communal hatred and religious suspicion to governments and bureaucrats making money off arms deals. They use this manufactured conflict and hypernationalism to gain political mileage in their own countries.

I sense some optimism on your part on what you call the "inherent anarchy" of India to resist the tide of globalization.

I don't know whether to be optimistic or not. When I'm outside the cities, I do feel optimistic. In India, unlike perhaps many other countries which are being broken by these new forms of colonialism, there is such grandeur. Ultimately, people prefer to eat roti and idlis and dosas rather than McDonald's burgers. Whether it's Indian food or textiles, there's so much beauty. I don't know whether they can kill it. I want to think they can't. I don't think that there is anything as beautiful as a sari. Can you kill it? Can you corporatize a sari?

Just before I came here, I went to a market in Delhi. There was a whole plate of different kinds of rajma dal, lentils. Today, that's all it takes to bring tears to your eyes, to look at all the kinds of rajma that there are, all the kinds of rice, and think that they don't want this to exist.

They want to privatize it and control the seeds.

They want to do the same to cultures and people and languages and songs. Globalization means standardization. The very rich and the very poor must want the same things, but only the rich can have them.

CHAPTER 2

Terror and the
Maddened King

It's been nineteen months since our last interview. Can you update me on the criminal case filed against you in a district magistrate's court in Kerala for your book The God of Small Things. *The charge was "corrupting public morality." What has been the outcome of that particular case?*

Well, it hasn't had an outcome. It's still pending in court, but every six months or so the lawyer says, "There's going to be a hearing; can you please come?"

This is one of the ways in which the state controls people. Having to pay a lawyer, or having a criminal case in court, never knowing what's going to happen. It's not about whether you get sentenced eventually or not. It's the harassment. It's about having it on your head, about not knowing what will happen.

More recently you've been charged and found guilty of contempt of court by India's Supreme Court, apparently in response to your criticism of its decision to allow construction to proceed on the Narmada Valley Dam Project. You could have been sentenced to six months in jail, but they gave you only a symbolic one-day sentence and a small fine.

This text is based on two interviews conducted in Albuquerque, New Mexico, and Las Vegas, Nevada, on September 19 and 29, 2002.

It's McCarthyism—a warning to people that criticizing the Supreme Court could jeopardize your career. You'd have to hire lawyers, make court appearances—and eventually you may or may not be sentenced. Who can afford to risk it?

Tell me about Aradhana Seth's film, called DAM/AGE.

Usually when people ask me to make films with them, I refuse. The request to do *DAM/AGE* came just after the final Supreme Court hearing, when it became pretty obvious to me that I was going to be sentenced, one way or another. I didn't know for how long. I was pretty rattled, and thought that if I was going to be in jail for any length of time, at least my point of view ought to be out in the world.

In India, the press is terrified of the court. So there wasn't any real discussion of the issues. It was discussed in a "Cheeky Bitch Taken to Court" sort of cheap, sensationalist way, but not seriously. After all, what is contempt of court? What does this law mean to ordinary citizens? None of these things had been discussed at all. So I agreed to do the film simply because I was nervous and wanted people to know what this debate was about.

In a very moving segment of the film, you discuss a man named Bhaiji Bhai. Can you talk about him?

Bhaiji Bhai is a farmer in Gujarat, from a little village called Undava. When I first met him, I remember thinking, "I know this man from somewhere." I had never met him before. Then I remembered that a friend of mine who had made a film on the Narmada years before had done an interview with Bhaiji Bhai. He had lost something like seventeen of his nineteen acres to the irrigation canal in Gujarat. And because he had lost it to the canal, as opposed to submergence in the reservoir area, he didn't count as a project-affected person, and wasn't compensated. So he was pauperized, and had spent I-don't-know-how-many years telling strangers his story. I was just another stranger that he told his story to, hoping that someday someone would intervene and right this great wrong that had been done to him.

Women seem to be central to the struggle in the Narmada valley. Why do you think women are so actively engaged there?

Women are actually actively engaged in many struggles in India. And especially in the Narmada valley. In the Maheshwar Dam submergence villages, the women of the valley are particularly effective. Women are more adversely affected by uprootment than men. Among the Adivasi people, it is not the case that men own the land and women don't. But when Adivasis are displaced from their ancestral lands, the meager cash compensation is given by the government to the men. The women are completely disempowered. Many are reduced to offering themselves as daily laborers on construction sites, and they are exploited terribly. Women often realize that if they're displaced, they are more vulnerable, and therefore they understand the issues in a more visceral and deeper sense than the men do.

You write in your latest essay, "Come September," that the theme of much of what you talk about is the relationship between power and powerlessness. And you write about "the physics of power." I'm interested that you use that term, physics. It kind of connects with the mathematical term you used in another of your essays, "The Algebra of Infinite Justice." What do you have in mind there?

Unfettered power results in excesses such as the ones we're talking about now. And eventually, that has to lead to structural damage. I am interested in the physics of history. Historically, we know that every empire overreaches itself and eventually implodes. Then another one rises to take its place.

But do you see those excesses as inherent in the structure of power? Are we talking about something inevitable here?

Inevitable would be too fatalistic a term. But I think unfettered power does have its own behavioral patterns, its own DNA. When you listen to George Bush speak, it's as though he has no perspective because he's driven by the crazed impulse of a maddened king. He can't hear the murmuring in the servants' quarters. He can't hear the words of the world's subjects. He's driving himself into a situation and he cannot turn back.

Yet, just as inevitable as the journey that the powerful undertake is the journey undertaken by those who are engaged in the business of resisting power. Just as power has a physics, those of us who are opposed to power also have a physics. Sometimes I think the world is divided into those who have a comfortable relationship with power and those who have a naturally adversarial relationship with power.

You've just spent a couple of weeks in the United States. You spoke in New York and Santa Fe, then took a driving trip through parts of New Mexico. What do you think about the incredible standard of living that Americans enjoy, and the price that is exacted from the developing world to maintain that standard of living?

It's not that I haven't been to America or to a Western country before. But I haven't lived here, and I can't seem to get used to it. I haven't got used to doors that open on their own when you stand in front of them, or looking at these supermarkets stuffed with goods. But when I'm here, I have to say that I don't necessarily feel, "Oh, look how much they have and how little we have." Because I think Americans themselves pay such a terrible price.

In what way?

In terms of emotional emptiness. Watching Michael Moore's film *Bowling for Columbine*, you suddenly get the feeling that here is a country with an economy that thrives on insecurity, on fear, on threats, on protecting what you have—your washing machines, your dishwashers, your vacuum cleaners—from the invasion of killer tomatoes or evil women in saris or whatever other kind of alien. It's a culture under siege. Every person who gets ahead gets ahead by stepping on his brother, or sister, or mother, or friend. It's such a sad, lonely, terrible price to pay for creature comforts.

I think people here could be much happier if they could let their shoulders drop and say, "I don't really need this. I don't really have to get ahead. I don't really have to win the baseball match. I don't really have to come first in class. I don't really have to be the highest earner in my little town." There are so many happinesses that come from just loving and companionship and even losing.

You write in your essay "Come September" that the Bush administration is "cynically manipulating people's grief" after September 11 "to fuel yet another war—this time against Iraq." You're speaking out about Iraq and also Palestine. Why?

Why not?

But you know that those are stories that are very difficult for most Americans to hear. There's not a lot of sympathy in the United States for the Palestinians, or for the Iraqis, for that matter.

But the thing is, if you're a writer, you're not polling votes. I'm not here to tell stories that people want to hear. I'm not entering some popularity contest. I just say what I have to say, and the consequences are sometimes wonderful and sometimes not. But I'm not here to say what people want to hear.

Let's talk a little bit about the mass media in the United States. You write that "thanks to America's 'free press,' sadly, most Americans know very little" about the US government's foreign policy.

Yes, it's a strangely insular place, America. When you live outside it, and you come here, it's almost shocking how insular it is. And how puzzled people are—and how curious, now I realize, about what other people think, because it's just been blocked out. Before I came here, I remember thinking that when I write about dams or nuclear bombs in India, I'm quite aware that the elite in India don't want to know about dams. They don't want to know about how many people have been displaced, what cruelties have been perpetrated for their own air conditioners and electricity. Because then the ultimate privilege of the elite is not just their deluxe lifestyles, but deluxe lifestyles with a clear conscience. And I felt that that was the case here too, that maybe people here don't want to know about Iraq, or Latin America, or Palestine, or East Timor, or Vietnam, or anything, so that they can live this happy little suburban life. But then I thought about it. Supposing you're a plumber in Milwaukee or an electrician in Denver. You just go to work, come home, you work really hard, and then you read your paper or watch CNN or Fox News and you go to bed. You don't know what the American government is up to. And ordinary people are maybe too tired to make the effort, to go out and really find out. So they live in this little bubble of lots of advertisements and no information.

Third World Resurgence, an excellent magazine out of Penang, Malaysia, had a recent article on the Bhopal disaster of 1984. More than half a million people were seriously injured and some three thousand people died on December 3, 1984, when a cloud of lethal gas was released into the air from Union Carbide's Bhopal facility in central India. More than twenty thousand deaths have since been linked to the gas.

The article features a leader among Bhopal survivors named Rasheeda Bee—you can tell from the name she's Muslim—who lost five members of her immediate family to cancer after the disaster, and she herself continues to suffer from diminished vision, headache, and panic. At the Earth Summit in Johannesburg a few weeks ago, Rasheeda tried to personally hand over a broom to the president of Dow Chemical, which has now taken over Union Carbide, and here's what she said: "The Indian Government has received clear instructions from its masters in Washington, DC. The [Indian] government has made it clear to us [that is, the victims] that if it comes to choosing between holding Dow [Chemical]/[Union] Carbide liable (or punishing Warren Anderson [who was the CEO of Union Carbide]) and deserting the Bhopal survivors, it will opt for the latter without batting an eyelid."

Even the absurd compensation that the Indian courts agreed upon for the victims of Bhopal has not been disbursed over the last eighteen years. And now the governments are trying to use that money to pay into constituencies where there were no victims of the Bhopal disaster. The victims were primarily Muslim, but now they're trying to pay that money to Hindu-dominant constituencies, to look after their vote banks.

You were speaking to some students in New Mexico recently, and you advised them to travel outside the United States, to put their ears against the wall and listen to the whispering. What did you have in mind in giving them that kind of advice?

That when you live in the United States, with the roar of the free market, the roar of this huge military power, the roar of being at the heart of empire, it's hard to hear the whispering of the rest of the world. And I think many US citizens want to. I don't think that all of them necessarily are coconspirators in this concept of empire. And those who are not need to listen to other stories in the world—other voices, other people.

Yes, you do say that it's very difficult to be a citizen of an empire. You also write about September 11. You think that the terrorists should be "brought to book." But then you ask the questions, "[I]s war the best way to track them down? Will burning the haystack find you the needle?"

Under the shelter of the US government's rhetoric about the war against terror, politicians the world over have decided that this technique is their best way of settling old scores. So whether it's the Russian government hunting down the Chechens, or Ariel Sharon in Palestine, or the Indian government carrying out its fascist agenda against Muslims, particularly in Kashmir, everybody's borrowing the rhetoric. They are all fitting their mouths around George Bush's bloody words.

After the terrorist attack on the Indian Parliament on December 13, 2001, the Indian government blamed Pakistan (with no evidence to back its claim) and moved all its soldiers to the border. War is now considered a legitimate reaction to terrorist strikes. Now through the hottest summers, through the bleakest winters, we have a million armed men on hair-trigger alert facing each other on the border between India and Pakistan. They've been on red alert for months together. India and Pakistan are threatening each other with nuclear annihilation. So, in effect, terrorists now have the power to ignite war. They almost have their finger on the nuclear button. They almost have the status of heads of state. And that has enhanced the effectiveness and romance of terrorism.

The US government's response to September 11 has actually privileged terrorism. It has given it a huge impetus, and made it look like terrorism is the only effective way to be heard. Over the years, every kind of nonviolent resistance movement has been crushed, ignored, kicked aside. But if you're a terrorist, you have a great chance of being negotiated with, of being on TV, of getting all the attention you couldn't have dreamt of earlier.

When Madeleine Albright was the US ambassador to the United Nations in 1994, she said of the United States, "We will behave multilaterally when we can and unilaterally when we must." I was wondering, in light of the announcement last week [on September 17] of the Bush doctrine about preemptive war, if that may not be used as legitimacy for, let's say, India to settle scores with Pakistan. Let's say the Bharatiya Janata Party government in New Delhi says, "Well, we have evidence that Pakistan may attack us, and we will launch a preemptive strike."

If they can borrow the rhetoric, they can borrow the logic. If George Bush can stamp his foot and insist on being allowed to play out his insane fantasies, then why shouldn't Prime Minister

A. B. Vajpayee or General Pervez Musharraf in Pakistan? In any case, India does behave like the United States of the Indian Subcontinent.

You know the old expression "Beauty is in the eye of the beholder." Maybe "terrorist" is the same thing. I'm thinking, for example, Yitzhak Shamir and Menachem Begin were regarded by the British as terrorists when they were controlling Palestine. And today they're national heroes of Israel. Nelson Mandela was considered for years to be a terrorist, too.

In 1987, when the United Nations wanted to pass a resolution on international terrorism, the only two countries to oppose that resolution were Israel and the United States, because at the time they didn't want to recognize the African National Congress and the Palestinian struggle for freedom and self-determination.

Since September 11, particularly in the United States, the pundits who appear with boring regularity on all the talk shows invoke the words of Winston Churchill. He's greatly admired for his courage, and he's kind of a model of rectitude to be emulated. In "Come September," you have a very unusual quote from Winston Churchill that often does not get heard anywhere. Can you paraphrase it?

He was talking about the Palestinian struggle, and he basically said, "I do not believe that the dog in the manger has the right to the manger, simply because he has lain there for so long. I do not believe that the Red Indian has been wronged in America, or the Black man has been wronged in Australia, simply because they have been displaced by a higher, stronger race."

And he said this in 1937, I believe.

Yes.

You conclude your essay, "War Is Peace," by wondering: "Have we forfeited our right to dream? Will we ever be able to reimagine beauty?"

That was written in a moment of despair. But we as human beings must never stop that quest. Never. Regardless of Bush or Churchill or Mussolini or Hitler, or whoever else. We can't ever abandon our personal quest for joy and beauty and gentleness. Of course we're allowed moments of despair. We would be inhuman if we weren't, but let it never be said that we gave up.

Vandana Shiva, who's a prominent activist and environmentalist in India, told me a story once about going to a village and trying to explain to the people there what globalization was doing to people in India. They didn't get it right away, but then somebody jumped up and said, "The East India Company has come back." So there is that memory of being colonized and being recolonized now under this rubric of corporate globalization. It's like the sahibs are back, but this time not with their pith helmets and swagger sticks, but with their laptops and flow charts.

We ought not to speak only about the economics of globalization, but about the psychology of globalization. It's like the psychology of a battered woman being faced with her husband again and being asked to trust him again. That's what is happening. We are being asked by the countries that invented nuclear weapons and chemical weapons and apartheid and modern slavery and racism—countries that have perfected the gentle art of genocide, that colonized other people for centuries—to trust them when they say that they believe in a level playing field and the equitable distribution of resources and in a better world. It seems comical that we should even consider that they really mean what they say.

In DAM/AGE there's an incredibly moving scene where the Supreme Court in New Delhi is surrounded by people who have come from the Narmada valley and elsewhere and are chanting your name and giving you support. There was just so much love and affection, and tears came to your eyes. As I recount it, I'm getting the chills myself. It was very beautiful.

I was very scared that day. Now that it's over it's okay to say what I'm saying. But while it was happening, while I was surrounded by police, and while I was in prison—even though I was in prison for a day—it was enough to know how helpless one can be. They can do anything to you when you are in prison.

I knew that people from the Narmada valley had come. They hadn't come for me personally. They had come because they knew that I was somebody who had said, with no caveats, "I'm on your side." I wasn't hedging my bets like most sophisticated intellectuals, and saying, "On the one hand, this, but on the other hand, that." I was saying, "I'm on your side." So they came to say, "We are on your side when you need us."

I was very touched by this, because it's not always the way people's movements work. People don't always come out spontaneously onto the streets. And one of the things about resistance movements is that it takes a great deal of mobilization to keep a movement together and to keep them going and to do things for one another. There are so many different kinds of people putting their shoulders to the wheel. It's not as though all of them have read *The God of Small Things*. And it's not as if I know how to grow soya beans. But somewhere there is a joining of minds and a vision of the world.

CHAPTER 3

Privatization and Polarization

You just finished writing an introduction to Noam Chomsky's For Reasons of State, *which is being reissued after being out of print for several years. What did you learn as you read his essays?*

The one fact that shocked me was that Chomsky had searched mainstream US media for twenty-two years for a single reference to American aggression in South Vietnam, and had found none. At the same time, the "free world" is in no doubt about the fact that the Russians invaded Afghanistan, using exactly the same model, the same formula—setting up a client regime and then inviting themselves in.

I'm still taken aback at the extent of indoctrination and propaganda in the United States. It is as if people there are being reared in a sort of altered reality, like broiler chickens or pigs in a pen. In India, the anarchy and brutality of daily life means there are more free spaces, simply because it's impossible to regulate. People are beyond the reach of the bar code. This freedom is being quickly snatched away.

Reading Chomsky gave me an idea of how unfree the free world is, really. How uninformed. How indoctrinated.

Why did you call your introduction "The Loneliness of Noam Chomsky"?

This interview was conducted in New Delhi on November 20 and 21, 2002.

There was a poignant moment in an old interview when he talked about being a fifteen- or sixteen-year-old boy in 1945 when the atomic bomb was dropped on Hiroshima. He said that there wasn't a single person with whom he could share his outrage. And that struck me as a most extreme form of loneliness. It was a loneliness which evidently nurtured a mind that was not willing to align itself with any ideology.

It's interesting for me, because I grew up in Kerala, where there was a Communist government at the time of the war in Vietnam. I grew up on the cusp between American propaganda and Soviet propaganda, which somehow canceled each other out.

Really the line is between the citizen and the state, regardless of what ideology that state subscribes to. Even now in India, or anywhere else, the minute you allow the state to take away your freedoms, it will. So whatever freedoms a society has exist because those freedoms have been insisted upon by its people, not because the state is inherently good or bad. And in India and all over the world, freedoms are being snatched away at a frightening pace. I think it's not just important but urgent for us to become extremely troublesome citizens, to refuse to allow the state to take away what it is grabbing with both hands just now.

In your essay "Come September" you write that in country after country, freedoms are being curtailed in the name of protecting freedom. In the United States, there's the USA PATRIOT Act, and you have something similar in India, called POTA, the Prevention of Terrorism Act. Do you see any similarities?

Terrorism has become the excuse for states to do just what they please in the name of protecting citizens against terrorism. Hundreds of people are being held in prisons under the antiterrorism law in India. Many of them are poor people, Dalits and Adivasis, who are protesting against "development projects" that deprive them of their lands and livelihoods. Poverty and protest are being conflated with terrorism. There was a fake "encounter" in New Delhi's Ansal Plaza just a couple weeks ago, on November 3. The police claimed that they had foiled a terrorist attack, and that the people they killed were Pakistani terrorists. But from eyewitness reports, it's pretty clear that that police story was concocted.

Similarly, on the thirteenth of December—soon after the September 11 attack in New York—there was an attack on the Indian Parliament. Five men were killed on the spot. Nobody knows who they really were. The government, as usual, claims they were Pakistanis. They've held four additional suspects in prison for almost a year now: a Kashmiri Muslim professor from Delhi University, two other Kashmiri Muslim men, and a woman who's Sikh but married to Shaukat Ali, one of the accused. During the trial, it seemed as if almost every piece of evidence had been manufactured by the police. As for the professor, Syed Abdul Rehman Geelani, there's no evidence whatsoever to support his arrest. All three men have been sentenced to death. It's outrageous.

In March 2000, just before Bill Clinton came here, there was a massacre of Sikhs in Chittisinghpura in the valley of Kashmir. The police claimed they killed terrorists who were responsible for the massacre. It now turns out that the people they killed were not terrorists, but just ordinary, innocent villagers. The chief minister of Kashmir actually admitted that the DNA samples that were sent to a lab for testing were fake. But nothing happens. You've killed these people, you've admitted to fudging the DNA samples, but nothing happens. Holes are blown into every bit of evidence, but nothing happens.

There's been the Tehelka scandal. The secretary of the BJP, Bangaru Laxman, and the secretary of the Samata Party, Jaya Jaitly, were caught on film accepting bribes for fake arms deals. Nothing happens. So there's this kind of marsh into which everything sinks. A citizen's rights are such a fragile thing now.

A few years ago there was a major massacre of Sikhs right here in the capital of India. Thousands of Sikhs were killed after the assassination of Indira Gandhi. And in Bombay after the Babri Masjid was destroyed in Ayodhya, several thousand Muslims were massacred.

Yes, and nothing happened. And in Gujarat now, Narendra Modi is spearheading an election campaign, and the Congress Party and the BJP are both openly talking about playing the Hindu card, or using the caste card versus the Hindu card. So we have to ask ourselves, What is the systemic flaw in this kind of democracy that makes politicians function by creating these vote banks divided along caste lines, or communal lines, or regional lines? As I wrote in my essay "Democracy: Who Is She When She Is at Home?" democracy is India's greatest strength, but the way in which electoral democracy is practiced is turning it into our greatest weakness.

We both attended a solidarity meeting on behalf of Professor Geelani, who teaches Arabic at Delhi University, and you are on the committee in his support. I'm sure you're besieged with requests to be on such-and-such a committee, to write a letter, to do this and that. How do you make those kinds of choices?

I use my instinct, because that's the only thing I can do. I understand clearly and deeply that no individual matters all that much. It doesn't matter all that much eventually what I do and what I don't do. It matters to me. I can help as much as I can help. But ultimately it isn't the way a battle must be fought—by the support of one individual or another. I don't believe in that kind of celebrity politics.

I just continue to do what I've always done, which is to write, to think about these things. I'm searching for an understanding. Not for my readers, for myself. It's a process of exploration. It has to further my understanding of the way things work. So in a way it's a selfish journey, too. It's a way of pushing myself further and deeper into looking at the society in which I live. If I were to be doing it not as an exploratory thing, but just as a politician might, with some fixed agenda, and then trying to convince people of my point of view, I think I'd become jaded. Curiosity takes me where it takes me. It leads me deep into the heart of the world.

After the publishing of The God of Small Things, *you could have had your pick of any publisher in New York. I'm sure they were clamoring for you. Yet you chose a small, independent press based in Cambridge, Massachusetts, South End Press, to publish* Power Politics *and, coming up,* War Talk. *Was that that kind of spontaneous, instinctive choice you made?*

It wasn't some big policy decision on my part. I didn't even think at the time, actually, that this is a political step. But I use my political instincts a lot. It's important for me to stay that way. People really imagine that most people are in search of fame or fortune or success. But I don't think that's true. I think there are lots of people who are more imaginative than that. When people describe me as famous and rich and successful, it makes me feel queasy. Each of those words falls on my soul like an insult. They seem tinny and boring and shiny and uninteresting to me. It makes me feel unsuccessful because I never set out to be those things. And they make me uneasy. To be famous, rich, and successful in this world is not an admirable thing. I'm suspicious of it all.

Failure attracts my curiosity as a writer. Loss, grief, brokenness, failure, the ability to find happiness in the saddest things—these are the things that interest me. I don't want to play out the role of someone who's just stepped out of *The Bold and the Beautiful*. At the same time, it is interesting to be able to meditate on wealth and fame and success, because I have them, and I can play with them, disrespect them, if you know what I mean. I don't suppose that if you haven't been there, you fully understand how empty it all is, in so many ways.

And yet, there are wonderful things about being a writer who is widely read. I can go to Korea, to Japan, to South Africa, to Latin America, and I know that I'll meet kindred souls. And they won't be hard for me to find. I won't have to spend ten years looking for them because my writing has preceded me. I'm a paid-up member of SIN—the Sweethearts International Network. It's a bond between people that arises from literature and politics. I can't think of a more wonderful thing. Writing gives you this gift. It plugs you directly into the world.

There used to be a saying in American journalism—it's not being followed today because of the corporatization of the media—that the function of journalists was to comfort the afflicted and afflict the comfortable. In a way, what you're saying seems to mirror that. That you feel that you want to make those people in power uneasy and uncomfortable.

I don't think that people in power become uneasy and uncomfortable. But you can annoy and provoke them. People who are powerful are not people who have subtle feelings like uneasiness. They got there because of a certain capacity for ruthlessness. I don't even consider their feelings when I write. I don't write for them.

That reminds me of something connected with Chomsky. I've attended many of his lectures. He's often introduced as someone who speaks truth to power. I asked him about that once. He said he doesn't do that. He's not interested in that.

Power knows the truth.

He wants to provide information to people who are powerless, not to those who are oppressing them.

Isn't there a flaw in the logic of that phrase—"speak truth to power"? It assumes that power doesn't know the truth. But power knows the truth just as well, if not better, than the powerless know the truth. Enron knows what it's doing. We don't have to tell it what it's doing. We have to tell other people what Enron is doing. Similarly, the people who are building the dams know what they're doing. The contractors know how much they're stealing. The bureaucrats know how much they're getting as bribes.

Power knows the truth. There isn't any doubt about that. It is really about telling the story. Good fiction is the truest thing that ever there was. Facts are not necessarily the only truths. Facts can be fiddled with by economists and bankers. There are other kinds of truth. It's about telling the story. As a writer, that's the best thing I can do. It's not just about digging up facts.

When I wrote *The God of Small Things*, it isn't just that I had a story and then told it. The way you tell a story, the form that narrative takes, is a kind of truth, too. When I wrote "The Greater Common Good," it isn't that no one knew these facts before. There were volumes and volumes of books on dams—pro-dam, anti-dam, balanced views, and so on. But really in the end, it's about how you tell that story to somebody who doesn't know it. To me, as a writer, that is something that I take great pleasure in. Telling the story in a way that ordinary people can understand, snatching our futures back from the experts and the academics and the economists and the people who really want to kidnap or capture things and carry them away to their lairs and protect them from the unauthorized gaze or the curiosity or understanding of passersby. That's how they build their professional stakes, by saying, "I am an expert on something that you can't possibly understand. My expertise is vital to your life, so let me make the decisions."

Who tells the stories is absolutely critical. Who is telling the stories in India today?

This is a very important question. When *The God of Small Things* came out, my mother said to me, "Why did you have to call the village Ayemenem? Why did you have to say the river was the Meenachil?" I said, "Because I want people to know that we have stories." It's not that India has no stories. Of course we have stories—beautiful and brilliant ones. But those stories, because of the languages in which they're written, are not privileged. So nobody knows them.

When *The God of Small Things* won the Booker Prize, there was a lot of hostility toward me from regional-language writers, people who write in Hindi, Malayalam, Tamil, and Marathi. It was a perfectly understandable hostility. The Indian writers who are well known and financially rewarded are those who write in English—the elite.

All of my political writing is translated into Indian languages, Gujarati, Malayalam, Tamil, Bengali, Hindi, and so on. Now I have a relationship with the regional press in Kerala, the Hindi press in the north, in Bengal. Now the English-language media is far more hostile to me than the regional media.

It goes on forever, the question of who tells the story. Even within regional-language writing, the Brahmins and the upper caste have traditionally told the stories. The Dalits have not told their stories. There's an endless pecking order.

Look at, say, the case of Vietnam now. To the world today, thanks to Hollywood and thanks to the US mass media, the war in Indochina was an American war. Indochina was the lush backdrop against which America tested its technology, examined its guilt, worried about its conscience, dealt or did not deal with its guilt. And the "gooks" were just the other guys who died. They were just stage props. It doesn't matter what the story was. It mattered who was telling it. And America was telling it.

In India, I occupy an interesting space. As a writer who lives in India, writes in English, and has grown up in a village in Kerala, I have spent the first half of my life battling traditions, Indian traditions, that wanted me to be a particular kind of Indian woman, which I have refused to be. And now I'm up against the monstrosity of the other side. The monstrosity of the modern world. People like me confront this contradiction. It's a very interesting place to be in, really. Where even politically, you're caught between the fascist regional forces, the BJP and VHP, for instance, versus the monstrous market forces, the Enrons and the Bechtels.

Speaking of Enron, the Houston-based energy giant multinational which was deeply involved in a dam project in Maharashtra, it has collapsed, laying off thousands of workers, most of whom have lost their pensions and retirement benefits. There's been a corporate crime wave in the United States, a huge amount of corruption. You might recall that it wasn't too long ago that the United States was lecturing a lot of the world about having transparency and clear and open procedures. It's rather ironic.

People often don't understand the engine that drives corruption. Particularly in India, they assume government equals corruption, private companies equal efficiency. But government officials are not genetically programmed to be corrupt. Corruption is linked to power. If it is the corporations that are powerful, then they will be corrupt.

I think there have been enough studies that show that corruption has actually increased in the era of privatization. Enron, for instance, openly boasted about how it paid some twenty million dollars to "educate" Indian politicians. It depends on how you define corruption. Is it just the bribe-taker? Or is the bribe-giver corrupt as well?

Today we see a formidable nexus between the powerful elites in the world. Imperialism by email. This time around, the white man doesn't have to go to poor countries and risk diarrhea and malaria or dying in the tropics. He just has his local government in place, which takes charge of "creating a good investment climate." And those who are protesting against privatization and development projects—making investments unsafe—are called terrorists.

You're a critic of corporate globalization. But what kind of arrangements would you like to see, in terms of governance, of relations between different countries?

I am a critic of corporate globalization because it has increased the distance between the people who take decisions and the people who have to suffer those decisions. Earlier, for a person in a village in Kerala, his or her life was being decided maybe in Trivandrum or, eventually, in Delhi. Now it could be in The Hague or in Washington, by people who know little or nothing of the consequences their decisions could have. And that distance between the decision-taker and the person who has to endure or suffer that decision is a very perilous road, full of the most unanticipated pitfalls.

It's not that everything is designed to be malevolent, of course. Most of it is, but the distance between what happens on paper, in policy documents, and what happens on the ground is increasing enormously. That distance has to be eliminated. Decentralization and the devolving of power to local groups is very important. The current process is fundamentally undemocratic.

You have written that "a writer's bad dream" is "the ritualistic slaughter of language." Can you talk about some examples of how language is constructed?

The language of dissent has been co-opted. WTO documents and World Bank resettlement policies are now written in very noble-sounding, socially just, politically democratic-sounding language. They have co-opted that language. They use language to mask their intent. But what they say they'll do and what they actually do are completely different. The resettlement policy for the Sardar Sarovar Dam sounds reasonably enlightened. But it isn't meant to be implemented. There isn't the land. It says communities should be resettled as communities. But just nine-teen villages from Gujarat have been scattered in 175 different locations.

The policy's only function is to ease the middle class's conscience. They all say, "Oh, how humane the world is now compared to what it used to be." They can't be bothered that there's no connection between what's happening on the ground and what the policy says. So the issue is not how nice the World Bank president is or how wonderfully drafted their documents are. The issue is, who are they to make these decisions?

There's a sequence in DAM/AGE in which World Bank President James Wolfensohn is visiting New Delhi, and he comes out to meet some demonstrators from the NBA. He utters a stream of platitudes about how he cares for the poor, how his focus is on alleviating their suffering and their poverty. In the film you say that you couldn't bear to hang around and wait for him to come out of his meeting, to hear that.

I was there when they blockaded the road. It was evening by the time Wolfensohn was forced to come out. He arrived in his pinstriped suit like a cartoon white man coming to address the peasants of India. I couldn't bear to hear or see this played out again. At the end of the twentieth century, to see the White Man back again, addressing the peasants of India and saying how concerned he was about them.

Only a few weeks later, I was in London, at the release of the World Commission on Dams report, and Wolfensohn was there. He talked about how he had met with the people of the valley. Missing from his account were the police and those steel separators, and the fact that he had been dragged out of the office and forced to meet them. He made it sound like a genuine grassroots meeting.

There are some exciting things happening culturally in India. In addition to DAM/AGE, *the documentary by Aradhana Seth, there's another one by Sanjay Kak called* Words on Water, *about resistance in the Narmada valley. Are you encouraged that those kinds of films are being made and seen?*

There are many independent filmmakers who are doing interesting work. But more important in India is that there is a vital critique of what is happening. For instance, in Madhya Pradesh there is a huge and growing resistance to the privatization of power. Privatization of the essential infrastructure, water, power, is strangling the agricultural community. Mass protests are building up. The move to corporatize agriculture, the whole business of genetically modified foods, pesticides, cash crops like cotton and soya bean, are crushing the Indian agricultural sector. The myth of the Green Revolution is coming apart.

In Punjab, the lands irrigated by the Bhakra Dam are becoming salinized and waterlogged. The soil is yielding less and less, and the farmers have to use more and more fertilizers. Punjabi farmers, once the most prosperous in India, are committing suicide because they're in debt.

The WTO has now forced India to import rice, wheat, sugar, milk, all these products which India has in abundance. The government's warehouses are overflowing with excess food grains while people starve. They're all being dumped. In Kerala, coffee, tea, and rubber plantations are closing down, laying off their labor or not paying them.

In India now there is a move toward Hindutva, and more and more communal politics. This hasn't happened overnight. People point to December 6, 1992, when the mosque in Ayodhya, the Babri Masjid, was destroyed by Hindu fundamentalists. But it must have its roots deeper than just ten years ago.

It has its roots in the independence movement. The RSS was set up in the 1920s. Today it is the cultural guild to which L. K. Advani and Vajpayee and all of these people owe allegiance. So the RSS has been working toward this for eighty years now.

There is a link between religious fascism and corporate globalization. When you impose corporate globalization onto an almost feudal society, it reinforces inequalities. The people who are becoming more and more prosperous are the ones who have had social advantages over many, many years. It's the kind of situation in which fascism breeds.

On the one hand, you have the government privatizing everything, selling off the public sector in chunks—telecommunications, water, power—to multinationals. On the other hand, they orchestrate this baying nationalism, nuclearism, communalism. I've talked about this in my essays "Power Politics" and "Come September."

Every day The Times of India *has a quote on the front page, and today's is from George Eliot: "An election is coming. Universal peace is declared, and the foxes have a sincere interest in prolonging the lives of the poultry." What do you think about elections as a mechanism for democracy? I ask that because people have had enormous influence and impact outside the electoral system, for example, Gandhi or Martin Luther King Jr. They never ran for elective office.*

I think it is dangerous to confuse the idea of democracy with elections. Just because you have elections doesn't mean you're a democratic country. They're a very vitally important part of a democracy. But there are other things that ought to function as checks and balances. If elections are the only thing that matter, then people are going to resort to anything to win that election.

You can only campaign in a particular constitutional framework. If the courts, the press, the parliament are not functioning as checks and balances, then this is not a democracy. And today in India, they are not functioning as checks and balances. If they were, Narendra Modi would be in jail today. He would not be allowed to campaign for office. Several candidates would be in jail today. Not to mention several senior people in the Congress Party who ought to have been in jail from 1984 onward for their roles in the massacre of Sikhs in Delhi after the assassination of Indira Gandhi.

The good thing about elections is that, however unaccountable politicians are, at least every five years they have to stand for election. But the bureaucracy and the judiciary are completely unaccountable. Nobody understands the terrifying role that the judiciary is playing in India today. The Supreme Court is taking the most unbelievable positions. Its decisions affect the lives of millions of people. Yet to criticize them is a criminal offense.

Recently, the chief justice of India, B. N. Kirpal, made an outrageous order on the day before he retired. Out of a case that had nothing to do with linking rivers, Kirpal ordered that all the rivers in India should be linked up in ten years' time. It was an arbitrary, uninformed order based on a whim—nothing more. He asked state governments to file affidavits. They never did. The government of India filed an affidavit stating that the project would take forty-one years and cost billions of dollars. This kind of decision is almost, if not more, dangerous than communal politics. Yet, because of the contempt of court law, nobody will question the court. Not the press. Everybody's scared of going to jail.

By sending me to jail, think of what they did: I had a one-year criminal trial, for which you have to have a criminal lawyer, which costs an unimaginable amount of money. How is any journalist going to afford a one-year criminal trial and then face the prospect of going to jail, of losing his or her job? What editor, which journalist is going to take that risk? So they've silenced the press. And now the courts have started to rule on vital issues like globalization, privatization, river-linking, the rewriting of history textbooks, whether a temple should be built in Ayodhya—every major decision is taken by the court. No one is allowed to criticize it. And this is called a democracy.

So you're saying that dissent is being criminalized in India.

I'm saying that a democracy has to function with a system of checks and balances. You cannot have an undemocratic institution functioning in a democracy, because then it works as a sort of manhole into which unaccountable power flows. All the decisions are then taken by that institution because that is the one institution that cannot be questioned. So there is a nexus between the judiciary and the executive. All the difficult decisions are being taken by the judiciary, and it looks as if the judiciary is admonishing the executive and saying, "You're very corrupt. We are forced to become an activist judiciary and to take these decisions."

If you speak to the middle class, they believe that the Supreme Court is the only institution that functions properly. There's a sort of hierarchical thinking that the buck must stop somewhere. They like the fact that the Supreme Court is so supremely unaccountable.

The contempt of court law is so draconian that if tomorrow I had documentary evidence to prove that a judge was corrupt and had taken money from somebody to make a particular decision, I couldn't produce that evidence in court because it would constitute contempt of court. It would be seen to be "lowering the dignity of the court," and in such a case, truth is not a defense.

Are there nongovernmental organizations—NGOs—in the country that are working on this issue? The issue of the autocracy of the court?

It's a very important political issue that we need to fight. But few have understood it yet.

This business of NGOs is a very interesting one in India. I'm no great fan of NGOs. Many of them are funded by various Western agencies. They end up functioning like the whistle on a pressure cooker. They divert and sublimate political rage and make sure that it does not build to a head. Eventually it disempowers people.

In the first interview we did, in early 2001, you described India as two separate convoys going in different directions. One into the digital future of the promised land of glitzy electronic things, and the rest of the country, the poor, the anonymous, going in the other direction. Since then, do you see those convoys coming closer together, or are they getting more and more distant from each other?

The way that the machine of neoliberal capitalism works, that distance has to increase. If what you have to plow back into the system is always your profit, obviously that distance is going to increase. Just mathematically, it's going to increase. Whoever has more makes more, and makes more, and makes more.

Tell me about the current situation in the Narmada valley. It seems that despite the heroic efforts and sacrifices that the NBA and its members and supporters have made, the dams are going through. Is that assessment correct?

Construction on the Maheshwar Dam has been stopped for now, but the Sardar Sarovar Dam is inching up. That part of the anti-dam movement has really come up against a wall. The question has to be asked: If nonviolent dissent is not viable, then what is?

If reasoned nonviolent dissent is not honored, then by default, you honor violence. You honor terrorism. Because you cannot just put this plastic bag over the head of the world and say, "Don't breathe." Across India, insurgents and militants have taken over great swaths of territory where they just won't allow the government in. It's not just Kashmir. It's happening all over: Andhra Pradesh, parts of Bihar, Madhya Pradesh, and almost the whole of the northeast, which doesn't consider itself a part of India.

Do you see the possibility of the NBA extending itself beyond its current lifespan into a more national movement of resistance? Could it be a model that people could emulate?

People in cities think that the movement has lost. In one sense, they're right, because the Sardar Sarovar Dam is going up. But if you go to the valley, you'll see the great victories of that movement, which are cultural, which are empowering. People know that they have rights. In the Narmada valley, the police cannot treat Adivasis, and in particular Adivasi women, the way they do elsewhere. These are great and important victories. The section of the NBA that was fighting against the Maheshwar Dam are the younger activists in the valley. They have now expanded their operations way beyond the valley and are fighting the privatization of power in the whole state of Madhya Pradesh. They are spearheading the anti-privatization movement.

Do you see any opening for resolving the conflict between India and Pakistan over Kashmir? The Indian prime minister has said, "Kashmir is ours. They," presumably the Pakistanis or the Kashmiris, "will never get it. That decision has been made." Tens of thousands of Kashmiris have died. It's a militarized state. There's martial law. There's a suspension of the constitution. You know better than I do about the human rights abuses that go on there.

Kashmir is the rabbit that the governments of both India and Pakistan pull out of their hats whenever they're in trouble. They don't want to resolve the conflict. For them, Kashmir is not a problem; it's a solution. Let's never make the mistake of thinking that India and Pakistan are searching for a solution and haven't managed to find one. They're not searching for a solution, because if they were, you would not hear intractable statements like this—absurd statements like this—being made.

After the nuclear tests that India and Pakistan conducted, the issue of Kashmir has been internationalized to some extent. That could be a good thing, though not if the United States acts as a unilateral superpower and takes it upon itself to impose a "solution." Before, you would not discuss human rights violations in Kashmir. There were only these militants who were shot in encounters, Pakistani terrorists and so on. That has changed.

Now with the elections, the dislodging of Farooq Abdullah, and Mufti Mohammad Sayeed coming in, I sense a slight break in the refusal to admit what is really happening in Kashmir. I hear people asking questions about the status of Kashmir. I hear more people saying that maybe Kashmiris should be consulted, instead of this being made to seem like an issue between India and Pakistan.

The first step toward a solution would be for India and Pakistan to open up the borders, to allow people to come and go. If you think of the world as a global village, a fight between India and Pakistan is like a fight between the poorest people in the poorest quarters—the Adivasis and the Dalits. And in the meantime, the zamindars are laying the oil pipelines and selling both parties weapons.

You're from the southwest of India, Kerala, and now you're living in the north. Language, music, food—there's a completely different vibration between the north and the south. Also it seems that the communal tensions in the south are much less than in the north. Am I misreading that?

Kerala has the highest number of RSS cells now. But so far, you're absolutely right. The BJP just haven't even managed to get a toehold in the electoral political scene, but they are very hard at work. The first time I ever saw an RSS march—with all these men in khaki shorts—was this year in Kerala, when I went to court. I was just shocked to see them marching in the gloom. It put a chill into my heart.

Talk a little bit about the print media.

The difference between Indian newspapers and newspapers that you'd see in America or England or Europe is the number of stories that there are about politics and politicians. Almost too many. Politicians keep us busy with their shenanigans, and eventually every single issue, whether it's a caste massacre in Bihar or communal violence in Gujarat or the issue of displacement by dams, is turned into a noisy debate about whether the chief minister should resign or not. The issue itself is never followed up. The murderers are never punished.

If you know anything about a particular issue, if you know the facts and the figures, you see how shockingly wrong newspapers always are. It's quite sad, the lack of discipline in terms of just getting it right, the lack of rigor. The encouraging thing is that there is a tradition of little magazines, community newspapers, pamphlets—an anarchic network of maverick publications, which makes the media hard to control. The big English national dailies don't reach the mass of the people in India. They don't matter as much as they imagine they do. But let's say there's a war against Pakistan or somebody, everybody just becomes jingoistic and nationalistic, just like what happens in the United States. It's no different.

BJP leader L. K. Advani is one of the most powerful members of the government. He took issue with Amartya Sen, the Nobel Prizewinner in economics, on the issue of economics and India.

He said that it was much more important for India to have weapons than to educate people.

Education and health was not the answer for India's development. It was defense.

Advani is the hard core of the center—though today I was delighted to read on the front page of the papers that Advani has been denounced by the Vishwa Hindu Parishad as a "pseudo-secularist." *Pseudo-secularist* was a term that Advani had coined to dismiss all those who were not communal fascists, and for him to have his own coinage used against him is delightful.

The Sangh Parivar—the Hindu right-wing family of parties, cultural guilds, the Hindutva lot—squabble with each other in public in order to make everybody feel they're at loggerheads. At the end of it all, Vajpayee keeps the moderates happy, Advani keeps the hard-liners happy, the VHP and the Bajrang Dal keep the rabid fringe happy. Everybody thinks they actually have differences, but the differences are just short of being serious. It's like a traveling, hydra-headed circus. It's like a Hindi movie. It has everything: sex, violence, pathos, humor, comedy, tragedy. Full value for the money. You go home satiated.

India Today, *a weekly magazine, has a fairly large circulation. It recently had a cover story entitled "India Is Now the Electronic Housekeeper of the World." General Electric, American Express, Citibank, AT&T, and other US corporations are shifting what they call their back-office operations to India. It's called the fastest-growing industry in India, and the workers are mostly young women. Many are hired to answer customer service questions for US customers. They might be on the other end of the line when I want someone to look up the balance on my credit card account or when Avis telemarkets a cheap vacation package to San Diego. They take on American names and American personas and tell jokes in American English. The people who are in favor of corporate globalization say this is a great thing. These girls would not ordinarily get jobs, and now they have an opportunity to earn some money. Is there anything wrong with that argument?*

The call center industry is based on lies and racism. The people who call in are being misled into believing that they are talking to some white American sitting in America. The people who work in those call centers are told that they're not good enough for the market, that US customers will complain if they find out that their service is being provided by an Indian. So Indians must take on false identities, pretend to be Americans, learn a "correct" accent. It leads to psychosis.

One way of looking at this is to say, "These people at least have jobs." You could say that about prostitution or child labor or anything—"At least they're being paid for it." Their premise is that either these workers don't have jobs or they have jobs in which they have to humiliate themselves. But is that the only choice? That's the question.

We hear all this talk about integrating the world economically, but there is an argument to be made for not integrating the world economically. Because what is corporate globalization? It isn't as if the entire world is intermeshed with each other. It's not like India and Thailand or India and Korea or India and Turkey are connected. It's more like America is the hub of this huge cultural and economic airline system. It's the nodal point. Everyone has to be connected through America, and to some extent Europe.

When powers at the hub of the global economy decide that you have to be X or Y, then if you're part of that network, you have to do it. You don't have the independence of being nonaligned in some way, politically or culturally or economically. If America goes down, then everybody goes down. If tomorrow the United States decides that it wants these call center jobs back, then overnight this billion-dollar industry will collapse in India. It's important for countries to develop a certain degree of economic self-sufficiency. Just in a theoretical sense, it's important for everybody not to have their arms wrapped around each other or their fingers wrapped around each others' throats at all times, in all kinds of ways.

There's a lot of talk about terrorism. In fact, it's become almost an obsession for the media in the United States. But it's a very narrow definition of terrorism.

Yes. It completely ignores the economic terrorism unleashed by neoliberalism, which devastates the lives of millions of people, depriving them of water, food, electricity. Denying them medicine. Denying them education. Terrorism is the logical extension of this business of the free market. Terrorism is the privatization of war. Terrorists are the free marketeers of war—people who believe that it isn't only the state that can wage war, but private parties as well.

If you look at the logic underlying an act of terrorism and the logic underlying a retaliatory war against terrorism, they are the same. Both terrorists and governments make ordinary people pay for the actions of their governments. Osama bin Laden is making people pay for the actions of the US state, whether it's in Saudi Arabia, Palestine, or Afghanistan. The US government is making the people of Iraq pay for the actions of Saddam Hussein. The people of Afghanistan pay for the crimes of the Taliban. The logic is the same.

Osama bin Laden and George Bush are both terrorists. They are both building international networks that perpetrate terror and devastate people's lives. Bush, with the Pentagon, the WTO, the IMF, and the World Bank. Bin Laden with Al-Qaeda. The difference is that nobody elected bin Laden. Bush was elected (in a manner of speaking), so US citizens are more responsible for his actions than Iraqis are for the actions of Saddam Hussein or Afghans are for the Taliban. And yet hundreds of thousands of Iraqis and Afghans have been killed, either by economic sanctions or cruise missiles, and we're told that these deaths are the result of "just wars." If there is such a thing as a just war, who is to decide what is just and what is not? Whose God is going to decide that?

The United States has only 3 or 4 percent of the world's population, yet it's consuming about a third of the world's natural resources, and to maintain that kind of disparity and imbalance requires force, the use of violence.

The US solution to the spiraling inequalities in the world is not to search for a more equal world, or a way of making things more egalitarian, but to espouse the doctrine of "full-spectrum dominance." The US government is now speaking about putting down unrest from space. It's a terrorist state, and it is laying out a legitimate blueprint for state-sponsored terrorism.

Do you find the persistence of romantic images of India in the West—that this is a country of sitar players and yogis and people who meditate, who are in a kind of ethereal zone? Are those clichés still pretty alive and active?

All clichés are structured around a grain of truth, but there are other clichés now, too. I think that the BJP's few years in power have given an ugly edge to India's image internationally. What happened in Gujarat—the pogrom against the Muslim community—has also become a part of the image of what India is: complex, difficult to understand, full of anachronisms and contradictions, and so on.

People from India are in the center of a lot of the intellectual debate about where the world is headed. I think the anarchy of Indian civil society is an important example in the world today, even though India has its back against the wall, and is being bullied and bludgeoned by the WTO and the IMF, and by our own corrupt politicians.

I was in Italy last month at a film festival, and there were documentary films being screened about the Narmada and about other human rights issues. The whole Italian press had gathered. Journalists were expecting me to talk about how terrible things are in India. I did talk about that. But I said, "We're not yet in such a bad way that we have a prime minister who owns six television channels and three newspapers and all the publishing houses and the retail outlets and the book shops. And at least when I'm taken to prison, I know that I'm taken to prison. I know that physically my body is being put in prison. It's not like my mind has been indoctrinated to the point that I think I'm free when I'm not."

In India, we are fighting to retain a wilderness that we have. Whereas in the West, it's gone. Every person that's walking down the street is a walking bar code. You can tell where their clothes are from, how much they cost, which designer made which shoe, which shop you bought each item from. Everything is civilized and tagged and valued and numbered and put in its place. Whereas in India, the wilderness still exists—the unindoctrinated wilderness of the mind, full of untold secrets and wild imaginings. It's threatened, but we're fighting to retain it. We don't have to reconjure it. It's there. It's with us. It's not got signposts all the way. There is that space that hasn't been completely mapped and taken over and tagged and trademarked. I think that's important. And it's important that in India, we understand that it's there and we value it.

Just from hearing you speak and the expression on your face, which I wish people could see, it's obvious that you care a lot about this country. You have a deep affection for it.

I'm not a patriot. I'm not somebody who says, "I love India," and waves a flag around in my head. It's my place. I'm used to it. When people talk about reclaiming the commons, I keep saying, "No, reclaim the wilderness." Not reclaim it, but claim it, hold on to it. It's for that reason that I cannot see myself living away from India. As a writer, it's where I mess around. Every day, I'm taken by surprise by something.

I don't know if I'm making myself clear. There is just a space for the unpredictable here, which is life as it should be. It's not always that the unpredictable is wonderful—most of the time it isn't. Most of the time it's brutal and it's terrible. Even when it comes to my work and myself, I'm ripped apart here. I'm called names. I'm insulted. But it's the stuff of life. The subjects I write about raise these huge passions. It's why I keep saying, "What's dissent without a few good insults?" You have to be able to take that. If they call you names, you have to just smile and know that you've touched a nerve.

The point is that we have to rescue democracy by being troublesome, by asking questions, by making a noise. That's what you have to do to retain your freedoms. Even if you lose. Even if the NBA loses the battle against the Sardar Sarovar, it has demonstrated the absolute horrors of what it means to displace people, what it means to build a big dam. It's asked these questions. It hasn't gone quietly. That's the important thing. It's important not to just look at it in terms of winning and losing.

If you look at it another way, look at what we're managing to achieve. We're putting so much pressure that the other side is having to strip. It's having to show itself naked in all its brutality. It's having to drop its masks, its disguises, and reveal its raw and crude and brutal nature. And that's a victory. Not just in terms of who's winning and who's losing, because I'm the kind of person who will always be on the losing side by definition. I have to be, because I'm on this side of the line. I'll never be on that side of the line.

Many journalists have come to you: the BBC, Deutsche Welle. What is interesting for you in these interviews? They must have the same questions, like, "When are you going to write another novel?"

I'm the kind of person who sharpens my thinking in public. It could be in an interview or at a lecture. I like talking to strangers. I like talking to people who have read my work. It's a process of thinking aloud. It's not just journalists that ask you the same question. In our lives, whether you're famous or not famous, there's so much repetition, and it's not a terrible thing. If you look at every person you're talking to as a human being, and you're having a conversation with them, then it's never boring. It's only if you're not interested in that person and you're only interested in yourself that it becomes boring. Then you start reciting what amounts to press handouts, which would be terrible.

I'm not necessarily the kind of writer who holes up some-where and then emerges. I did that with my novel. I don't talk when I'm writing fiction. It's a very private act. But in my polit-ical work, I think aloud. I like to pit my mind against another person's, or think together with people. It's not necessarily just with journalists, or interviewers with whom I work. It's an in-teresting process.

There's a great historic figure in American history, the African Amer-ican abolitionist Frederick Douglass. He once said that "[p]ower con-cedes nothing without a demand. It never did and it never will."

In India, very often, people—not just the government, but people—say, "Oh look, we're so much better off than, say, peo-ple in Afghanistan or people in Nepal or people in Pakistan." Somehow they seem to suggest that this has to do with the fact that our government is not as violent as the governments in these other countries. But I think it's because the people are more anarchic, in the sense that it is because we are a troublesome people, a troublesome constituency. And that is why it's difficult to imagine India under army rule. It's unthinkable that Indian society would defer to the army like it does in Pakistan. Even if resistance movements like the movement in the Narmada valley don't succeed in their ultimate goal of stopping a particular dam or "development" project, they do create a spirit among exploit-ed, oppressed people: "You can't do this to us. And if you do, we're going to be extremely troublesome about it."

There were a lot of people who were very annoyed with me when I criticized the Supreme Court and I refused to apologize. But you have to ask these public questions. The minute you start giving ground, you're on a slippery slope.

If you put your ear to the ground in this part of the world today, what do you hear?

Communal talk. Talk about religious identity, ethnic iden-tity, tribal identity. Economically, as globalization is pushed down our throats, people are fractured into tribal, communal groups. The world is getting more and more fractured. Nationalism, nuclearism, communalism, fascism, these things are springing up.

There's always been tension between the majority community—the Hindus in India—and the large Muslim minority. But you are clearly seeing an increase in that tension.

There was a terrible episode of bloodshed and massacre and mayhem during the Partition. About a million people were massacred. The wounds of that were never allowed to heal by the Congress Party, which harnessed this hatred and used it to play electoral games. Our kind of electoral democracy seems to demand the breaking up of the electorate into vote banks. But today all the things that the Congress Party did at night, the BJP and its Sangh Parivar does in the daytime. They do it with pride, as policy. Now they're in power, they're in government, they have penetrated every state organ. Whether it's rewriting the history books, or placing their people in the bureaucracy, in the police, in the army. Of course, when the Congress Party was in power, it was their people. But their people were not self-professedly communal people. They did it as a sly, undercover game.

In the past, historians or politicians or bureaucrats would not openly say that India is a Hindu country. But now nobody is shy about saying this. The RSS now has thousands of branches all over the country. They have funds, they have means, they have resources to indoctrinate young minds. Once you inject this poison into the bloodstream, it's very hard to work it out of the system. So now the fact is, whether the BJP wins the next elections or not, their agenda is on the table. The country has been militarized and communalized and nuclearized. The Congress has no means to deal with it. It hasn't been able to counter that in any moral or political way.

Let's say you want to write about a particular topic that interests you. First of all, how do you make that selection, and then how do you go about researching it?

You should never ask me these method questions, because there's never any method! It's not as though I cold-bloodedly go out and select some topic for academic or career reasons. In the case of the nuclear tests, the nuclear tests happened while I was in the United States. My first reaction was one of rage at the hypocrisy there: "The Blacks can't manage the bomb." Then I came back here and saw the shrill jingoism. So I wrote "The End of Imagination." When you start getting into the debate about national security, every country can justify having nuclear weapons. I think it's very important not to enter the debate on their terms, on the terms that the army and the politicians and the bureaucracy would like to set. Because every country can have a pragmatic realpolitik justification for why it needs nuclear weapons.

In the case of the Narmada, it was more something that I really had for years wanted to understand. In February 1999, the Supreme Court lifted its stay on the building of the Sardar Sarovar Dam. Suddenly it looked as if this battle, which many of us on the outside of this movement had thought was being won, had been dealt a body blow. I started reading. I went to the valley, I met the activists, and felt that the movement needed to tell its story in a way which is accessible to an ordinary reader. It needed a novelist's skill. It's a complex issue, and much of the time the establishment depends on the fact that people don't understand. I wanted to build a narrative that could puncture that—to deal with all their arguments, to deal with their facts and figures, to counter them in a way ordinary people could understand.

One thing leads to another. If you read all the political essays, each one dovetails into the next. Going to the Narmada valley, you see that the fight against the Sardar Sarovar, which is a state-built dam, is different from the fight against the Maheshwar Dam, which was the first privatized project in India. Then you start asking these questions about the privatization of infrastructure and it leads you to the whole question of privatization and what is going on there. So that led to my essay "Power Politics."

It is interesting to see how the establishment deals with dissent. It gives you a fair idea of who the establishment really is. You see who crawls out of the woodwork to take you on. Very often, it's an unexpected person. It's not the people who are completely on the other side of the spectrum, who are completely opposed to your point of view. It will be cowardly people who position themselves as being "balanced" critics. They really can't deal with the real questions, because they're instinctively undemocratic. There is nothing they condemn more passionately than passion. But I insist on the right to be emotional, to be sentimental, to be passionate. If displacement, dispossession, killing, and injustice on the scale that takes place in India does not enrage us, what will?

When people try to dismiss those who ask the big public questions as being emotional, it is a strategy to avoid debate. Why should we be scared of being angry? Why should we be scared of our feelings, if they're based on facts? The whole framework of reason versus passion is ridiculous, because often passion is based on reason. Passion is not always unreasonable. Anger is based on reason. They're not two different things. I feel it's very important to defend that. To defend the space for feelings, for emotions, for passion. I'm often accused of the crime of having feelings. But I'm not pretending to be a "neutral" academic. I'm a writer. I have a point of view. I have feelings about the things I write about—and I'm going to express them.

That reminds me of a famous Urdu couplet by Muhammad Iqbal: "Love leaped into Nimrod's fire without hesitation. / Meanwhile, reason is on the rooftop, just contemplating the scene." There is that kind of juxtaposition of the intellect versus feeling.

I think the opposite. I think that my passion comes from my intellect. So much of the way I love comes from the way I think. Thinking makes great loving. I don't acknowledge this artificial boundary between the intellect and the heart. They're not as separate as literature and poetry makes them out to be. Their fusion is what makes artists and writers. I believe in succumbing to the beauty of feelings, and I believe in the rigor of the intellect, too. I don't believe in overripe passion. But I believe that there isn't anything as wonderful as a fierce intellectual passion.

Do you ever experience writer's block, where you have real difficulty in writing? Do you have any techniques to get out of it? Do you exercise or walk around the block or eat oranges?

No. I haven't gone through that. Not yet. I don't look at writing as a profession, a career. If I can't write, I won't write. I'll do something else. It's important to understand that one is not that significant. It doesn't matter. If you can do something, great; if you can't do it, it's okay.

Often I tell myself, "Don't do it. Don't write." Because I don't want to enter an arena that I know will consume my soul. I don't want to take on Narendra Modi or write about the riots in Gujarat. But it's very hard to keep quiet. This hammering sets up in my head.

My nonfiction is wrenched out of me. It's written when I don't want to write. So when people say, "You're very brave" or "You're very courageous," I feel a bit embarrassed. Because it isn't bravery or courage. I have to do it. Often I don't want to see or understand. But I can't not, because the story clamors to be told and then I'm just the go-between that sits down and tells it, in some way.

What advice would you give to people, in terms of thinking outside the box, outside of what's called conventional wisdom, for example?

I'm very bad at giving advice!

For yourself, then, how do you do it? And how did you develop it, because it's something that's acquired. It's not necessarily innate, like a sense of smell.

I wonder. I didn't grow up within a conventional kind of family and I wasn't in a city. I was this child who was wandering all over the place, spending hours on the river alone, fishing. My childhood's greatest gift was a lack of indoctrination. So it's not that I'm somebody who's remarkable because I've learned to think outside the box. The fact is that the box was never imposed on me. I never went to a formal school until I was about ten. There was a delightful absence of a box.

We were in a way very cosmopolitan and in a way completely local and rural. It's an odd combination. I always had trouble if anyone asked me the most normal questions, like, "Where are you from, what's your name, what's your mother tongue, what does your father do?" I had no answers for any of these questions, because I just didn't know my father and it was difficult to explain the complexities of my childhood. But if you asked me completely unconventional questions, then I could answer them, because I would think about them. These normal things were not easy for me to reply to.

As you've grown older, have you gotten an opportunity to know your father?

I've met him. Yes. At least I know what he looks like.

I was at Delhi University a few days ago, and a student asked me, "What would you do in a public sector that is inefficient and has an over-bloated bureaucracy and is losing money?" What's wrong with privatizing that?

People in India especially, but in the third world generally, are being made to believe that this is the only choice. You have a choice between a corrupt public sector and an efficient private sector. If those are the only two options, anyone would say, "I'll have the efficient private sector." In fact, many of the public sector units that are being privatized were actually profit-making. For instance, Bharat Heavy Electricals, which manufactures turbines and heavy electrical machinery, was one of the foremost manufacturers in the world. As soon as the government decided to privatize it about ten years ago, they deliberately allowed everything to go to seed, and then they said, "Look, isn't it terrible?"

It's propaganda, this opposition of the sleek, efficient private sector and the corrupt, terrible government. Of course the public power sector has been incredibly corrupt and inefficient. The transmission and distribution losses have been tremendous. But what does the government do? It signs up with Enron. What is happening with Enron today? The government is paying Enron not to produce electricity, because it's so expensive.

So Enron, even though it's bankrupt in the United States and disgraced, is still sucking money out of the Indian economy?

There's a big litigation process on, but, yes, that's the situation.

Bill Gates of Microsoft, one of the sahibs of the new world economic order, was shopping in Delhi last week. He met with top government officials and CEOs. You saw something very interesting on TV about how Indians view Gates.

I was watching some music channel—not MTV, but some other music channel—this morning. On the screen it said, "What does Bill Gates really want?" Then they had interviews with maybe twenty young students. Every single one of them said he's here to blow open the market for Windows and he's just trying to get publicity by giving money for AIDS. Nobody was under any illusions about what his visit was about.

Does that encourage you, that people have that understanding?

Three or four months ago, I went to a seminar on the power sector, and I thought to myself, "What are you doing here? How can you be sitting in this seminar on the privatization of power?" If someone had told me four years ago that I would be attending meetings about electricity, I would have laughed. But it was uplifting to listen to the kind of minds that are at work here. People can just take the whole thing apart and critique it. The first critique of the Power Purchase Agreement with Enron came from a small NGO in Pune, called Prayas. Everything they said has come true. That is a great thing about India. There is a very strong intellectual ability to take something apart, in a way that I really appreciate and admire.

To what extent do you think that the British used "divide and rule" as a strategy to maintain control of India—a vast country? The British had very few soldiers and administrators here.

The British certainly used divide-and-rule tactics, but the British empire survived because it co-opted the Indian elite. It's the same technique that empire uses now to propagate its neoliberal reign.

Have you read the work of Martin Luther King Jr.? He was influenced by Gandhi. People in the United States generally know about his "I Have a Dream" speech from the 1963 March on Washington, but not a lot of Americans know about the speech he gave in New York in 1967 at Riverside Church. He became increasingly radical later in his life, and in New York he said, "True compassion is more than flinging a coin to a beggar. It comes to see that an edifice which produces beggars needs restructuring."

That is the terrible dilemma of living in India, isn't it? Every moment of every day, you're faced with the brutal inequalities of the society you live in. So it is impossible to forget, even for a moment. Just to enjoy the ordinary daily things—the clothes you wear, the fun you have, the music you listen to, the roof over your head, the meal in the evening—involves knowing that other people don't have these privileges.

We have been taught that peace is the opposite of war. But is it? In India, peace is a daily battle for food and shelter and dignity.

Martin Luther King Jr. wrote in his "Letter from Birmingham Jail" that true peace is not merely "the absence of tension" but "the presence of justice."

Or at least the journey toward justice, toward some vision of egalitarianism. Which is what I think is fundamentally the problem with the whole ethic of neoliberal neocapitalism. You make it all right to grab. You say that it's all right to get ahead by hitting the next person on the head. It's all right to accumulate capital and profits at someone else's expense. It destroys the fabric of concern and fellow-feeling. There is a finite amount of capital in the world, and if you accumulate, you're grabbing from somebody. That's not right.

Another of the sahibs who recently has been in Delhi is Paul O'Neill, the US treasury secretary. He was talking on November 22 to an audience of corporate leaders, and he was very critical of India, a country, he said, where "corruption and bribery are widespread, frightening away honest businessmen and investors."

If it's frightening away investors like Enron and Bechtel, it can only be a good thing.

It's interesting that he should be lecturing Indians about corruption and bribery, because the United States has just gone through what Business Week calls the most unprecedented "corporate crime wave" in its history. Not just Enron, but WorldCom, Xerox, Tyco, Arthur Andersen—a huge number of corporations have been guilty of insider trading and all kinds of shenanigans.

When have America's own shortcomings prevented it from lecturing to other people? That's par for the course.

Howard Zinn, the great American historian, said there was the Bronze Age, the Iron Age, and today we live in the Age of Irony.

Irony is a kind word for the crimes of the American empire.

In your essay entitled "Come September," you are very critical of US policy in support of Israel and its repression of the Palestinians. You must know that this is a hot-button issue in the United States. It's difficult to talk about Israel critically without immediately being labeled in the most unflattering terms. Why did you choose to talk about this?

I was talking about the eleventh of September, and I thought I should remind people that the eleventh of September 1922 was when imperial Britain marked out a mandate on Palestine, after the Balfour Declaration. Eighty years on, the Palestinians are still under siege. How can one come to the United States and not mention Israel's illegal occupation of Palestinian territory? The US government is funding it and supporting it politically and morally. It's a crime.

Diaspora communities are notorious for having very inflammatory views. If you look at the most right-wing, unreasonable, vituperative Hindus, many live in the United States. Every time you get a letter to the editor saying, "I think there should be nuclear war and Pakistan should be destroyed," it will be somebody who lives in Champaign-Urbana or some other US town. I've never been to Israel, but I've been told that in Israel the media reflects a broader spectrum of opinion than you see in the United States.

What do you think of the report that just came out looking at the Indian diaspora community in the United States? Apparently, some segments of it are sending a lot of money to support Hindu fundamentalist organizations.

The report seems quite credible. It's quite important that this kind of dogged work is being done. It's really wonderful. These groups hide behind the fact that they do charity work, though their charity is all about the Hinduization of tribal people. But in India these things will not be investigated.

What was your take on the US presidential election in the year 2000, especially in light of the US tendency to be very critical of how elections are conducted in other countries?

I have to say that I didn't follow it very closely, because if you don't live in America, whether it's Bush or Clinton or Gore, it doesn't seem to make that much difference. I personally feel that if the September 11 attacks had happened when Clinton was in power, it could have been worse for the world in a way, because he at least doesn't sound as stupid as Bush. Bush is vicious but he's comical. He's easy meat. Whereas Clinton is far cleverer and more calculating. He's more of a show man. I don't think there's much to choose between them.

You have used the word bully to describe the United States and its policies. I think maybe some Americans might have difficulty identifying their state as a bully because of a lack of information about what's going on outside.

People from poorer places and poorer countries have to call upon their compassion not to be angry with ordinary people in America. I certainly do. Every time I write something, that anger does come out, and then I pull it back, because I tell myself, "They don't know. These are people who don't know what is being done in their name." Yet, I keep wondering if that's because it suits them not to know. I have to remind myself about the extent of the brainwashing that goes on there. But I think that if most people knew what was being done in their names, they would be mortified. The question is: How do we let them know?

Ben Bagdikian and others have written extensively about how the corporate media operates in the United States and, by extension, in the rest of the world because of its enormous reach. Do you think that the people who work for these corporations know the reality, know the facts about what's going on and are repressing it? Or are they truly ignorant?

I'm sure the senior people know. The junior people are sent on a beat and told to cover something, and they cover it. So I don't think everybody knows the key secret and is suppressing it. Journalists have the illusion of independence. But certainly the people who make the decisions know.

Where are the spaces for dissidents in the Indian context? What about television?

There's no space on TV whatsoever. Not even to show a documentary film, like, say, Sanjay Kak's film on the Narmada. We don't even begin to think that it will be shown on TV.

Why not? Why isn't there a station or a network?

Why not? You can't even have a private screening of a documentary film without a censor certificate. When Anand Patwardhan made his documentary about the nuclear issue, the censor board told him, "You can't show politicians in your film." You can't show politicians in your film! What does that mean? You can't have politicians making political speeches in your film! It's really Kafkaesque. Yet they can't police everything. It's too difficult.

In a country like the United States where books like Chomsky's *9–11* are starting to reach wider audiences, aren't people going to feel a bit pissed off that they had no idea about what was going on, and what was being done in their name? If the corporate media continues to be as outrageous in its suppression of facts as it is, it might just lift off like a scab. It might become something that's totally irrelevant, that people just don't believe. Because, ultimately, people are interested in their own safety.

The policies the US government is following are dangerous for its citizens. It's true that you can bomb or buy out anybody that you want to, but you can't control the rage that's building in the world. You just can't. And that rage will express itself in some way or the other. Condemning violence is not going to be enough. How can you condemn violence when a section of your economy is based on selling weapons and making bombs and piling up chemical and biological weapons? When the soul of your culture worships violence? On what grounds are you going to condemn terrorism unless you change your attitude toward violence?

With very few exceptions, the September 11 attacks are presented as actions by people who simply hate America. It's separated from any political background. That has confused a lot of people.

It was a successful strategy, this isolation of the events of September 11 from history, insisting that terrorism is an evil impulse with no context. The minute you try and put it into a context, you are accused of excusing it or justifying it. It's like telling a scientist who is researching drugs for malaria that he or she is in cahoots with the female Anopheles mosquito.

If you're trying to understand something, it doesn't mean you're justifying it. The fact is, if you can justify all the wars that you have fought, all the murders that you've committed, all the countries that you've bombed, all the ecologies that you've destroyed, if you can justify that, then Osama bin Laden can certainly use the same logic to justify September 11. You can't have a political context for one kind of terrorism and no political context for another.

So if you were to talk to an average American, what would be something that you would say, in terms of trying to understand why there is animosity toward the United States, why there is rage and anger?

I was in America in September 2002, as you know. I was very reluctant to come. I thought there just wasn't any point in saying these things, because I don't believe in "speaking truth to power." I don't believe that there is any way in which you can persuade that kind of power to act differently unless it's in its own self-interest. There isn't any point. But my editor, Anthony Arnove, persuaded me to come, and I'm so glad that I did, because it was very, very nice for me to see how human and open the people I met were. People were clearly trying to understand what was going on in the world.

It was an important trip for me. I had exactly the opposite experience from what I expected. I had people coming up to me on the street saying, "Thank you for saying what you said," and, "We can't say it because we're so scared, but thank you." It was wonderful for me that it happened. It made me believe that the reason that so much energy and money is poured into manipulating the media is because the establishment fears public opinion. They know that ordinary people are not as ruthless, as cold, as calculating, as powerful people.

Ordinary people do have a conscience. Ordinary people don't necessarily always act in their own selfish interests. If the bubble were to burst, and people were to know all of the horrendous things that have been carried out in their name, I think it would go badly for the American establishment. And I think it has begun. I think all America's family secrets are spilling out backstage on the green room floor. I really think so.

Yes, it's true that the corporate media just blanks out everything, but on the Internet, some of the most outraged, incandescently angry pieces are written by Americans. A film like *Bowling for Columbine* has been shown everywhere and it connects the dots in ways which ordinary people can understand. This is important. I think it's beginning to unravel, actually. I think the propaganda machine is going to come apart.

What about the role of intellectuals in the propaganda machine? In the United States, intellectuals are supposed to be neutral. They're supposed to accumulate facts and present them without presuming to be on one side or the other. They're encouraged to use obscure jargon. For example, there are no ideas—everything is a "notion." No one talks, it's all "discourse." It's what we call pomo, postmodernism. Do you have something like that in India?

We have pomo in India, too. Definitely. A lot of it has to do with the sad business of creating a little expertise, so that you come off sounding special, as if the world couldn't do without you. A little hunk of expertise that you can carry off to your lair and guard against the unauthorized curiosity of passersby. My enterprise is the opposite: to never complicate what is simple, to never simplify what is complicated. But I think it's very important to be able to communicate to ordinary people what is happening in the world. There's a whole industry working hard at trying to prevent people from understanding what is being done to them.

Chomsky calls them a mandarin class of specialists.

Experts take away the ability to make decisions from people. In courts, language has evolved in such a way that ordinary people simply can't understand. You have this phalanx of lawyers and judges who are deciding vitally important issues, but people can't understand what is being said, what the procedure really is, what's going on.

I noticed that in the film DAM/AGE. *It was difficult to follow some of the pronouncements from the Supreme Court.*

"Vicious stultification and vulgar debunking cannot be allowed to pollute the stream of justice" [laughs]. What is the other one? "Contumacious violation . . ." I've forgotten. I used to know it by heart.

Do you see any role for specialized knowledge?

I see a role for specialized knowledge, but I think that it's important for there to be an arena where it is shared, where it is communicated. It's not that somebody shouldn't have specialized knowledge. The ability to dig a trench and lay a cable is a kind of specialized knowledge. Farmers have specialized knowledge, too. The question is: What sort of knowledge is privileged in our societies? I don't think that a CEO is more valuable to society and ought to be paid $10 million a year, while farmers and laborers starve.

The range of what is valued has become so extreme that one lot of people have captured it and left three-quarters of the world to live in unthinkable poverty, because their work is not valued. What would happen if the sweepers of the city went on strike or the sewage system didn't work? A CEO wouldn't be able to deal with his own shit.

Macaulay, a Raj official in the nineteenth century, imperiously declared that "a single shelf of a good European library [is] worth the whole native literature of India and Arabia." In recent years there's been an enormous surge of writing produced not only by Indian writers such as yourself but also writers of Indian origin who live outside of India, like V. S. Naipaul. Why is that happening now?

It's not that enormous a surge, actually. I remember when my novel was first published, the *New Yorker* organized to shoot one big photograph of Indo-Anglian writers. There were maybe ten or fifteen of us. They'd organized this huge bus to take us to lunch, and the bus was empty. Everyone's talking about this surge, but you can count the people who are known on your fingertips. It's being made out to be something more than it is, I think.

Like a fad?

There are people writing, but it's not some renaissance or anything that's happening. If it is a fad for the Western world, then that's their business. I don't care.

Some people might say that writing in English automatically means you're writing for a yuppie audience, because English in India particularly is a language of privilege.

That's true. But at the same time, any language in India is very limited. If you write in Malayalam, only someone from Kerala can read it. If you write in Hindi, only those from a few states in the north can read it. So language is a very complicated issue in India. It's interesting that *The God of Small Things* has been published in forty languages, so in a way it's about language, but not as in English or German or French or Hindi. It's something more than that. It's language as communication, more or less.

My political writing is published in many, many Indian languages. The Hindi translation of *The God of Small Things* is almost ready. So it's no longer just for yuppies. And anyway it's not just yuppies who speak English in India. There are more people who speak English in India than in England. It's a huge number.

One of the pleasures for me about having written *The God of Small Things* is that many of the people who are reading it would not normally read an English novel. So a sub-inspector from Muzaffarnagar or some person from some village somewhere will come to me and say, "I read it with a dictionary. I understood it." So I love the range of readers—from John Updike to a policeman in Muzaffarnagar.

Your articles and essays appear in The Nation *magazine, and you're publishing now with South End Press.* Power Politics *is your first book with them, and* War Talk *is the next one. Are you getting a lot of response from outside India? Are people writing to you?*

I do receive a lot of letters, but it's difficult for me to deal with the volume of responses and requests that I get. I'm under pressure to turn myself into an institution, to have an office and secretaries and people dealing with my mail and my accounts. I'm just not like that. I can't be like that. So I choose the inefficient model, which is not to deal with it. I do what I can. Obviously I have a literary agent in America and in England. They help me. But in my own space, I just don't have that. It's hard, but it's a choice that I make, that I just continue to be an individual who gets a lot of mail and can't handle it.

Himanshu Thakkar is someone whom you admire. You mention him in the introduction to The Cost of Living. *I happened to meet him, and he told me, "You know, it's remarkable. The women are*

*the leaders in the country. The women are advancing the movements
for social justice." Why is that?*

I don't know, but it's absolutely correct. In India, the legacy
of the freedom struggle has been a great respect for nonviolent
resistance. The pros and cons of violent and nonviolent resistance
can be debated, but I don't think there can be any doubt that violent resistance harms women physically and psychologically in
deep and complex ways. Having said that, Indian society is still
deeply disrespectful of women. The daily violence, injustice, and
indignity heaped on women is hard to believe sometimes.

*But this takes place against a backdrop of an institutionalized mi-
sogyny that is deeply culturally embedded. One example was a report
in the* Times *of India a couple of days ago that there's a crisis in
Haryana because there are not enough marriageable girls. Why aren't
there enough marriageable girls? Because of female feticide. The families have to buy brides for their sons from outside the state and their
community. It's interesting that the* Times *said that "[d]esperate boys
are willing to marry girls from any caste." That's another one of these
incredible contradictions.*

That is India. We don't even blink when someone brings up a
contradiction. What is interesting is that a lot of the women who
are involved in resistance movements and who are activists are also
redefining what "modern" means. They are really at war against
their community's traditions, on the one hand, and against the
kind of modernity that is being imposed by the global economy,
on the other. They decide what they want from their own tradition
and what they will take from modernity. It's a high-wire act. Very
tiring but exhilarating.

*Another thing everyone probably has to deal with here is the persis-
tence of color, the emphasis on being fair skinned. I was reading about
Kareena Kapoor, a rising young Bollywood starlet (who is opening,
incidentally, a Pizza Hut in Gurgaon), and she was described as
"cream colored." It's a very favorable designation.*

I'm so glad that you brought this up, because most people, foreigners, don't even notice that there's a color difference between white Indians and Black Indians. But it's something that really drives me crazy here. India is one of the most racist modern societies. The kind of things people will say about being Black skinned are stunning.

There was a television program a few years ago about this. In the audience there was a Sudanese man, an albino man, and a Punjabi woman who runs a marriage bureau. I've never seen anything more ridiculous. The Sudanese man talked about how terrible it was for him to live here, and how girls would cross to the other side of the road. How people would pull his hair on the bus and call him *hubshi*, which is roughly equivalent to the N-word. Then the albino said, "I don't know whether I would be considered fair or dark." So he asked the woman who runs the marriage bureau whether she could get him a bride. She looked at him and said, "I can get you a polio victim."

This was all being done without irony. At the end of it, the man who was presenting the show said, "It looks like all of us are very color conscious. In actual fact, why do we spend so much time thinking about the packaging? Black people are also nice from underneath."

If you look at the newspapers, you see advertisements for some cream called Afghan Snow or Fair and Lovely. And all these white women in Bollywood films! Ninety percent of the women in India are Black. But, according to Bollywood, if you're not white, you're not beautiful. The rising international popularity of Bollywood films worries me. Most of them reinforce some terrible, some very disempowering values.

Poor people, the Dalits and the Adivasis, are mostly Black. There's an apartheid system at work here, for anyone who cares to notice.

Let's go to another Bombay Bollywood star, from an older generation, Nargis. She complained bitterly about Satyajit Ray, the great

Indian filmmaker, saying that his films only show poverty. Then she was asked, "Well, what would you rather see in Indian cinema?" And she said "dams."

"You're not showing India in a proper light." That's the great middle-class complaint: "Why can't you show McDonald's and Pizza King?" Because here, you see, people have learned not to see the poverty. They have these filters, these contact lenses, that filter it out. They don't understand why "outsiders" get so exercised about it. They take it as a kind of affront.

I'm interested in how that operates. I've seen it myself, and I see it in myself when I'm here. How do you look away from someone who's terribly poor and indigent?

It's a survival technique. Meaning, how else are you to survive? You have to find a way of continuing with your life. So you just filter it out.

CHAPTER 4

Globalization of Dissent

In March 2002, a pogrom was carried out against the Muslim population of Gujarat. You've written an essay on this entitled "Democracy: Who Is She When She Is at Home." What happened in Gujarat?

In February 2002, the BJP was gearing up for elections in Uttar Pradesh. They had trundled out their favorite campaign issue, the building of the Ram temple in Ayodhya. Communal tension was at a fever pitch. People were traveling to Ayodhya by train to participate in the building of the temple. At the time, Gujarat was the only major state in India to have a BJP government. It had for some time been the laboratory in which Hindu fascism had been conducting an elaborate experiment. In late February, a train carrying belligerent VHP and Bajrang Dal activists was stopped by a mob outside the Godhra station. A whole compartment of the train was set on fire and fifty-eight people were burnt alive.

Nobody really knew who was responsible for the carnage. Within hours, a meticulously planned pogrom was unleashed against the Muslim community. About two thousand Muslims were killed. One hundred and fifty thousand were driven from their homes. Women were publicly gang-raped. Parents were bludgeoned to death in front of their children. The leaders of the mob had computer-generated lists marking out Muslim-owned shops, homes, and businesses, which were burned to the ground.

This interview was conducted in Los Angeles, California, on May 26, 2003.

Muslim places of worship were desecrated. The mob was equipped with trucks loaded with thousands of gas cylinders that had been hoarded weeks in advance. The police did not merely protect the mob, but provided covering fire. Within months, Gujarat's chief minister, Narendra Modi, announced proudly that he wanted to have early elections. He believed that the pogrom would win him Hindu hearts.

Modi was right, wasn't he?

Modi's reelection is something that has shaken many of us to the core of our beings. It's one thing to have a dictator who commits genocide. It's another thing to have an elected government with officials who have been accused of actively abetting mass murder being reelected. Because then all of us must bear the shame of that. All of us must bear some responsibility for that.

But thinking deeply about it, I don't see that it's all that different from the American public electing president after president who has killed and massacred and bombed people all over the world. A child asked me quite recently, "Is Bush better or is Modi better?" I said, "Why are you asking?" He said, "Because Modi killed his own people, and Bush is killing other people." That's how clear children can be. Eventually, after thinking about it, I said, "Well, the people they killed are all people." We have to think like that.

What happened in Gujarat has raised very serious questions. When you speak to somebody and tell them that two thousand Muslims were massacred on the streets of Gujarat, and women were raped, and pregnant women had their stomachs slit open, normal people, or people who are outside that situation, recoil in horror. But people inside that situation say things like, "They deserved it." And how do you deal with that?

It isn't a coincidence that the massacre of Muslims in Gujarat happened after September 11. Gujarat is also one place where the toxic waste of the World Trade Center is being dumped right now. This waste is being dumped in Gujarat, and then taken off to Ludhiana and places like that to be recycled. I think it's quite a metaphor.

The demonization of Muslims has also been given legitimacy by the world's superpower, by the emperor himself. We are at a stage where democracy—this corrupted, scandalous version of democracy—is the problem. So much of what politicians do is with an eye on elections. Wars are fought as election campaigns. In India, Muslims are killed as part of election campaigns. In 1984, after the massacre of Sikhs in Delhi, the Congress Party won, hands down. We must ask ourselves very serious questions about this particular brand of democracy.

What was the response of the political class in India and the media to Modi being reelected?

The media in India can roughly be divided into the national English media and the local regional-language newspapers. Typically, their understandings of similar events are completely different. The local Gujarati press was vehemently anti-Muslim. It manipulated events and supported what was happening. But the English press was very outspoken and condemnatory of what Modi was doing in Gujarat.

It's important to understand that the killing in Gujarat had a long run-up. The climate was created soon after the BJP came to power and India conducted nuclear tests. This whole business of unfettered Hindu nationalism, where else was it going to lead?

The national press supported that idea from the beginning. It supported the Kargil War uncritically. The English-language press in India supports the project of corporate globalization fully. It has no time for dispossession and drought and farmers' debts, the ravages that the corporate globalization project is wreaking on the poor of India. So to suddenly turn around and condemn the riots is a typical middle-class response. Let's support everything that leads to the conditions in which the massacre takes place, but when the killing starts, you recoil in middle-class horror, and say, "Oh, that's not very nice. Can't we be more civilized?"

Once Modi won the elections, the English-language press began to whip itself and say, "We got it wrong. Maybe the secularists are taking too much of an anti-Hindu position," and rubbish like that. They began to negotiate with the fascists, basically. The Chamber of Indian Industry apologized to Modi for having said things about the fact that genocide was bad for business. They promised to reinvest in Gujarat. So as soon as he won this election, everybody was busy negotiating and retracting. I've lost track of the number of references I've seen in the media to "Modi magic."

What was the response of the so-called intellectual class, academics and writers, to Gujarat and Modi's reelection?

I think everybody felt whipped and beaten, because Modi was gloating. Everybody felt as if they had taken a pounding, which they had, to an extent. I think it threw the opposition—I don't mean the Congress Party when I say the opposition, but the critics of this kind of politics—into disarray, because they felt that, and they were made to feel that, they had no place in modern India. These voices of sanity and reason felt that they had no place.

Academics have this problem. If you are an economist, you are only an economist. If you are a sociologist, you are only a sociologist. If you are a historian, you're only a historian. And now, to understand what's going on, you must cross disciplines, and you must see the connections between the dispossession and the despair created by corporate globalization flowing into the bitterness of Partition, flowing into the rhetoric of cultural nationalism. All these things come together to create this situation.

Gujarat is also, ironically, the home state of Mahatma Gandhi. In 1930, there was a very interesting event there. He led a Salt March to the coastal town of Dandi. Why don't you recount that, so people have another kind of historical perspective?

Whatever critique one may or may not have of him, Gandhi's understanding of politics and public imagination is unsurpassed, I would say, by any politician in world history. He knew how to strike at the heart of empire. The Salt March—the Dandi March—when Indians marched to the sea to make salt, was a strike against the salt tax. It wasn't just a symbolic weekend march, but struck at the heart of the economic policies of the colonial regime. What has happened in the evolution of nonviolent resistance is that it's become more and more symbolic, and less and less real. When a symbol unmoors itself from what it symbolizes, it loses meaning. It becomes ineffective.

Fifteen million people marched against the war in Iraq on February 15, 2003, in perhaps the biggest display of public morality ever seen. It was fantastic. But it was symbolic. Governments of today have learned to deal with that. They know how to wait out a demonstration or a march. They know the day after tomorrow, opinions can change or be manipulated into changing. Unless civil disobedience becomes real, not symbolic, there is very little hope for change.

That's a very important lesson that we need to learn from the civil disobedience and the nonviolent resistance of the Indian independence struggle. It was fine political theater, but it was never, ever merely symbolic. It was always a real strike against the economics of imperialism. What was *swadeshi* about? It was saying, "Don't buy British products." It was saying, "Make your own yarn. Make your own salt. We have to take apart the economic machinery of empire now, and strike at it." These marches and songs and meetings of today—they are beautiful, but they are often mostly for us. If all our energies go into organizing these things, then we don't do any real damage to the establishment, to the empire.

There's a lot of talk in the United States now about empire. A new book by British historian Niall Ferguson, Empire, *celebrates the many positive aspects of imperialism, particularly of British rule. The jewel in the crown of Britain, of course, was colonial India.*

It's rather staggering that people like Ferguson are touting the benefits of imperialism. By the middle of the eighteenth century, just about the time that the British took it over, India accounted for nearly 25 percent of the world's global trade. When the British left in 1947, this figure had dwindled to around 4 to 5 percent. Much scholarly research has demonstrated that during British rule, India's economy underwent a process of peasantization, where urban areas were ruralized, essentially.

Recently, traveling to the West, it's the first time it's even occurred to me that people can actually justify imperialism. Let me say that categorically—politically, socially, economically—there is no justification for colonialism. Next these people will be justifying genocide or slavery. Weren't they the foundations of the American empire?

Do you think that the people of South Africa, or anywhere on the continent of Africa, or India, or Pakistan are longing to be kicked around all over again? Is Ferguson aware of how many million people died in India in the late nineteenth century because of the drought and the famine while food and raw materials were being exported to England? How dare they even talk like this? It's grotesque that anybody can sit down and write a reasoned book on something like this. It is nothing short of grotesque.

Thomas Friedman, the Pulitzer Prize–winning columnist for the New York Times, *has written that "America is in an imperial role here, now. Our security and standing in the world ride on our getting Iraq right."*

Well, it isn't doing it right, is it? But the point is that the justification for going to war against Iraq has been forgotten. The weapons of mass destruction have not been found. You were told in the United States that Iraq was going to annihilate you, just as Cuba was, and Nicaragua was, and El Salvador was, and all the tiny little countries of the world were. After the war, you were told, America was going to be secure. But today, after the war, the terrorist alerts keep being set to purple, or whatever the highest register is. And now you're saying, "Al-Qaeda is in Iran, or maybe it's in Syria, or maybe it's in North Korea."

The point is that any kind of justification, any kind of nonsense works because there isn't any real media left in the United States. It's just a kind of propaganda machine that spews out whatever suits the occasion, and banks on people's short memory span.

When you spoke at the World Social Forum in Porto Alegre, Brazil, in late January 2003, you were certain that the United States was going to attack Iraq. In fact, you said, "It's more than clear that Bush is determined to go to war against Iraq, regardless of the facts—and regardless of international public opinion."

I don't think you needed to be a genius to be certain. There is a strategy at work which has nothing to do with the propaganda that's being put out. And when you start to see the pattern, then you have a sense of what is going to happen. After the attack on Afghanistan, you started to see the preparations for the next war against Iraq. And now they are laying the basis for even more wars.

I find it shocking that people should think that world public opinion should have changed because the United States "won" the war. Did anybody think it wasn't going to? Here is a country that is so ruthless in what it is prepared to do that it's going to win every war that it fights, except if its own people do something about it. There isn't any country that can fight a conventional war against US forces and win.

Talk about how war is viewed as a product to be marketed and sold to the consumers, in this case the American public.

Referring to the timing of the Iraq war, a Bush administration spokesperson said, "From a marketing point of view, you don't introduce new products in August." They were asking themselves, what's the best season to introduce this new product? When should you start the ad campaign? When should you actually launch it? Today, the crossover between Hollywood and the US military is getting more and more promiscuous.

War is also an economic necessity now. A significant section of the US economy depends on the sale of weapons. There has to be a turnover. You can't have cruise missiles lying around on the factory floor. The economics of Europe and the United States depend on the sale and manufacture of weapons. This is a huge imperative to go to war. Apart from this, the United States needs millions of barrels of oil a day to keep its bloated economy chugging along. It needs Iraq. It needs Venezuela.

What accounts for the brazenness of the Bush administration? For example, Paul Wolfowitz, the deputy secretary of defense, was talking about Syria, saying it was "behaving badly," like the headmaster wagging his finger at the bad student. How is this attitude seen outside the United States?

I think in two ways. On the one hand, it's seen as a kind of uncouth stupidity. On the other hand, it's seen as just the insulting language of power. You speak like that because you can.

In an interview you did in Socialist Worker, *you said, "The greatest threat to the world today is not Saddam Hussein, it's George Bush (joined at the hip to his new foreign secretary, Tony Blair)." Talk about Tony Blair. Why has he attached himself to American power with such fervor and vigor?*

That's a much more intriguing question than why the Bush regime is so brazen. The combination of stupidity, brutality, and power is an answer to the first question. But why is Blair behaving the way he is? I've been thinking about it, and my understanding is that what has happened is that the American empire has metamorphosed from the British empire. The British empire has morphed into the American empire. Tony Blair wants to be part of empire because that's where he thinks he belongs. That's where his past, his country's past, has been, and it's a way of staying in the imperial game.

I was reading an article in the *New York Times* the other day that was appropriately called something like "Feeding Frenzy in

Iraq." It said that countries "representing their corporate interests" are bidding for subcontracts from Bechtel and Halliburton. Among the countries that are petitioning Bechtel and Halliburton, Bush administration officials said that Britain has the best case, because it "shed blood in Iraq." I wondered what they meant by that, because the little British blood that was shed was basically shed by Americans. And since they hadn't specified whose blood was shed, I presume they mean that the British shed Iraqi blood in Iraq. So their status as co-murderers means that they ought to be given privileged access to these subcontracts.

The article went on to say that Lady Symons, who is the deputy leader of the House of Lords, was traveling in the United States with four British captains of industry. They were making the case that they should be given preference not only because they were co-murderers but because Britain's had a long and continuous relationship with Iraq since imperial days, right up to the time of the sanctions, which means that they were trading with Iraq, were doing business in Iraq, through Saddam Hussein's worst periods.

The idea that you're actually trying to petition for privilege because you were once the imperial master of Iraq is unthinkable for those of us who come from former colonies, because we think of imperialism as rape. So the way the logic seems to work is, first you rape, then you kill, and then you petition to rape the corpse. It's like necrophilia. On what grounds are these arguments even being made? And made without irony?

What factor does racism play in this construction of imperial power?

Racism plays the same part today as it did in colonial times. There isn't any difference. I mean, the only people who are going to argue for the good side to imperialism are white people, people who were once masters, or Uncle Toms. I don't think you're going to find that argument being made by people in India, or people in South Africa, people in former colonies. The only ones who want colonialism back in its new avatar of neoliberalism are the former white masters and their old cohorts—the "native elites"—their point men then and now.

The whole rhetoric of "We need to bring democracy to Iraq" is absurd when you think of the fact that the United States supported Saddam Hussein and made sure that he ruled with an iron fist for all those years. Then they used the sanctions to break the back of civil society. Then they made Iraq disarm. Then they attacked Iraq. And now they've taken over all its assets.

The people who supported the military attack on Iraq may concede today, "Well, those reasons that we gave perhaps are not valid. We can't find the plutonium and uranium and biological and chemical weapons. Let's say we concede those points. But, after all, Miss Roy, we've got rid of a terrible dictator. Aren't the Iraqi people better off now?"

If that were the case, then why are they busy supporting dictators now all over Central Asia? Why are they supporting the Saudi regime?

We're told that "Saddam Hussein is a monster who must be stopped now. And only the United States can stop him." It's an effective technique, this use of the urgent morality of the present to obscure the diabolical sins of the past and the malevolent plans for the future. This "present urgency" can always be used to justify your past sins and your future sins. It's a nonargument.

Islam is being targeted and demonized in much of the media and also among what I can only describe as mullahs and ayatollahs here in the United States, people like Franklin Graham, son of Billy Graham, who called Islam "a very evil and wicked religion." Jerry Falwell said Muhammad was a "terrorist." Jerry Vines, who is a very prominent preacher, described Muhammad as a "demon-obsessed pedophile."

This seems to integrate with a lot of the rhetoric coming from the Hindu nationalists in India, about Islam. Vajpayee said recently, "Wherever Muslims are, they do not want to live peacefully."

The mullahs of the Islamic world and the mullahs of the Hindu world and the mullahs of the Christian world are all on the same side. And we are against them all. I can tell you that, insult for insult, you will find the mullahs in Pakistan or in Afghanistan or in Iran saying the same things about Christianity. And you will find the mullahs in India, and the RSS people in the Hindu right wing, saying the same things about each other. I see Praveen Togadia of the VHP and Paul Wolfowitz and John Ashcroft and Osama bin Laden and George Bush as being on the same side. These are artificial differences that we waste our time on, trying to figure out who is insulting who. They are all on the same side. And we are against them all.

You've traveled to the United States on several occasions. You give talks, and you meet and talk with lots of people. Why do you think Americans have been so susceptible to the Bush propaganda, specifically about Iraq being such an imminent threat to the national security of the United States, and that Iraq was responsible for September 11, and that Iraq is connected to Al-Qaeda, when there is simply no empirical evidence to support any of those assumptions?

I think on one level, the fact is that the American media is just like a corporate boardroom bulletin. But on a deeper level, why are Americans such a frightened people? After all, many of us routinely live with terrorism. If Iraq or El Salvador or Cuba is going to destroy America, then what is the point of all these weapons, these $400 billion spent every year on weapons, if you are that vulnerable in the end? It doesn't add up.

It's $400 billion a year, not including the Iraq war, which is a supplemental expenditure.

So what is it that makes a country with all these bombs and missiles and weapons the most frightened country and the most frightened people on earth? Why is it that people in a country like India, which has nothing in comparison, are so much less scared? Why do we live easier lives, more relaxed lives?

People are so isolated, and so alone, and so suspicious, and so competitive with each other, and so sure that they are about to be conned by their neighbor, or by their mother, or by their sister, or their grandmother. What's the use of having 50 percent of the world's wealth, or whatever it is that you have, if you're going to live this pathetic, terrified life?

Michael Moore's documentary Bowling for Columbine *explores this to some degree.*

What is wonderful about *Bowling for Columbine* is that it's accessible to ordinary people. It broke through the skin of mainstream media.

The language of the left must become more accessible, must reach more people. We must acknowledge that if we don't reach people, it's our failure. Every success of Fox News is a failure for us. Every success of major corporate propaganda is our failure. It's not enough to moan about it. We have to do something about it. Reach ordinary people, break the stranglehold of mainstream propaganda. It's not enough to be intellectually pristine and self-righteous.

There is a growing independent media movement in the United States, and it's connected with movements and organizations such as Sarai. net in New Delhi and Independent Media Centers all over the world. There are a lot of young people getting involved in the media who are frustrated with the corporate pablum that they receive, and they're doing something about it. You're in touch with some of these activists in India.

The fact that hundreds of thousands of people in the United States were out on the streets, marching against the war, was partly because of that independent media. Unfortunately, it's not enough to walk out on the street on a weekend. One of the things that needs to be done is for the alternative media to reach a stage where the corporate media becomes irrelevant. That has to be the goal. Not that you attack it, but that you make it irrelevant, that you contextualize it.

How do you develop the ability to discern fact from fiction in approaching news from mainstream outlets?

I think the only way to do it is to follow the money. Who owns which newspaper? Who owns the television network? What are their interests? Assume that corporate media has an agenda. And so the least you can do is to cross-check a particular story with other sources of information that are independent. If you can do that, you can see the discrepancies. Compare, for example, the way the US media and the British media cover the same war, the same event. How does this differ from how Al Jazeera covers it? It's not as if these other media don't have an agenda. But if you look at the two, at least your head is not being messed with completely.

In the United States, there are a number of very well-funded right-wing think tanks. And these think tanks provide many of the voices that are heard and seen in the media. For example, one of the most prominent is the American Enterprise Institute. Someone there— the holder of the Freedom Chair, incidentally—Michael Ledeen, said this, reported on the National Review *online: "Every ten years or so, the United States needs to pick up some small, crappy little country and throw it against the wall, just to show the world we mean business."*

What can one say to that?

How are voices like this given such prominence in the media, while voices like Noam Chomsky or Howard Zinn or Edward Said or Angela Davis and others are completely marginalized?

But that's the project, isn't it? That's the Project for the New American Century. Why are we asking these questions or feeling surprised? We know that. And the brazenness of it is perhaps not such a bad thing. I'm for the brazenness, because at least it clarifies what is going on. And you know, you have to believe that eventually all empires founder, and this one will.

What about women's role in the globalization project? What factor does gender play?

That's not an easy question to answer. What if you were to reverse it and say, "What factor does gender play, vis-à-vis men?" Women are as complex as men, and different women benefit differently and suffer differently. So when it comes down to, say, the privatization of water, obviously, in an Indian context, it affects women much more than men, because they are the ones who have to walk not one kilometer, but fifteen kilometers now to fetch water. And that could be millions of women's whole lives, just going to scratch water out of some little place. To get just one pot of water, you could have to walk miles.

But it's not a question that I can answer that easily, because there are so many aspects to what we mean by globalization. The first half or more of my life was spent fighting the cruelties of tradition, dreaming of escaping from this little village that I grew up in, hoping that I wouldn't have to marry one of those men and produce children for them. And then I came up against the vulgarity of what modernity offers, and I had to refuse that, too, and walk a high wire, if you like, between the two. One is constantly, constantly making political choices.

And I am one of the lucky ones. Others don't have that choice, or don't see it that way, because sometimes what you are running from is so cruel that you can only run. This is a particularly complex subject, so let's just say that the project of corporate globalization increases the distance between those who make decisions and those who have to suffer them. Let's say neoliberal capitalism is a flawed machine. Inevitably, it leads to this huge disparity between the rich and the poor. And within the poor, it pushes women to the bottom.

Beyond the immediate excitement of being with people from many, many countries, what value is there in gatherings like the World Social Forum? Earlier you suggested that maybe we need to move beyond the marches and the typical demonstrations.

There's a tremendous value in the World Social Forum, and it has been central to making us feel that there is another world. It's not just possible. It is there. But I think it's important that we don't sap all our energies in organizing this event. It's an act of celebration of solidarity, but it's for us. It's not a strike against them. If you want to send out one million emails and enjoy the World Social Forum, you can, but let's reserve our energies for the real fight.

And that real fight is waiting to happen now. We need to clearly demarcate the battle lines. We cannot take on empire in its entirety. We have to dismantle its working parts and take them on one by one. We can't use the undirected spray of machine gun fire. We need the cold precision of an assassin's bullet. I don't mean this literally. I am talking about nonviolent resistance. We need to pick our targets, and hit them, one by one. It's not possible to take on empire in some huge, epic sense. Because we simply don't have the kind of power or reach or equipment to do that. We need to have an agenda, and we need to direct it.

At a press conference in New York, the day before your Riverside Church speech, you said, "We have to harm them." In what way can we harm them? Do we stop buying their cars? Do we stop traveling on their planes?

First of all, we have to understand that we cannot be pure. You can't say, "Arundhati, if you are against empire, then why are you flying to America?" Because we can't do it in any virginal, pristine way. All of us are muddy. All of us are soiled by empire and included in it in some way. We can only do our best. But certainly I believe that, for instance, a great starting point would be to target a few companies that have been given these reconstruction contracts in Iraq, and shut them down, just to show ourselves that we can do it, if nothing else.

If Bechtel or Halliburton was trying to establish some business in India, you would think that Indians should boycott them.

Absolutely—but also target their offices around the world, their other privatization projects around the world, target the CEOs, the members of the board, the shareholders, the partners, and let them know we will not allow them to profit off the occupation of Iraq. We need to disrupt business as usual.

The US civil rights movement was ignited in 1955 by a bus boycott in the city of Montgomery, Alabama.

That's the thing. We need to be very specific now about what we have to do. Because we know the score. Enough of being right. We need to win.

You felt that the massive demonstrations on February 15 made a very powerful moral statement.

I think so. I think there was a huge difference between the display of public morality on the streets of the world and the vacuous, cynical arguments in the UN Security Council. We know all that talk about morality by old imperialists was rubbish. The minute war was announced, these supposed opponents of the war rushed to say, "I hope you win it." But I also think that the demonstrations and the peace movement really stripped down empire, which was very important. It stripped off the mask. It made it very clear what was going on. And if you look at general public perception of what the US government is about, it's very different today. Not enough people knew what the US government was up to all these years. People who studied it knew. Foreign policy scholars knew. Ex-CIA people knew. But now it's street talk.

The National Security Strategy of the United States of America, which formally lays out the doctrine of preemption, actually has the statement in it that the events of September 11 presented the United States with "vast, new opportunities."

It did. Which is why I keep saying Bush and bin Laden are comrades in arms. But contained within those "opportunities" are the seeds of destruction. The fact is that here is an empire that, unlike other empires, has weapons that could destroy the world several times over and has people at the helm of power who will not hesitate to use them.

What was the position of the Indian government on the attack on Iraq?

It was pretty inexcusable. There was a very subdued response to it in India. Because you see, the right-wing Indian government is trying very hard to align itself with the Israel–US axis.

What do you mean by that?

Ariel Sharon is coming to India to visit quite soon. And the rhetoric against Muslims in the United States locks in with the fascist rhetoric against Muslims in India. Meanwhile India and Pakistan are behaving like the *begums* of Sheik Bush, competing for his attention.

Explain what "begum" means.

A begum is part of the sheik's harem.

How much of the traditional Orientalism that Edward Said has written about plays a factor in shaping and forming public opinion about the East, or "them," or "those people over there"?

I think outright racism would be a more accurate explanation. We are all expendable, easily expendable. Orientalism is a more gentle art. Crude racism powers all this.

You spoke in New York at the Riverside Church on May 13, 2003. How did you prepare for that, knowing that that church was where Martin Luther King gave his April 4, 1967, speech opposing the Vietnam War?

It was important to me to come to the United States and speak in that church. Apart from what I said in the talk, which is available as a text, there was a lot unsaid which was very political. A Black woman from India speaking about America to an American audience in an American church. It's always historically been the other way around. It's always been white people coming to Black countries to tell us about ourselves. And if anybody from there comes here, it's only to tell you about us and what a bad time we're having. But here is something else happening. Here citizens of an empire want to know what other people think of what that empire is doing. Globalization of dissent begins like that. That process is very, very important.

You've used the phrase "the checkbook and the cruise missile." What do you mean by this?

Once you understand the process of corporate globalization, you have to see that what happened in Argentina, the devastation of Argentina by the IMF, is part of the same machine that is destroying Iraq. Both are efforts to break open and to control markets. And so Argentina is destroyed by the checkbook, and Iraq is destroyed by the cruise missile. If the checkbook won't work, the cruise missile will. Hell hath no fury like a market scorned.

W. B. Yeats lamented in one of his most famous poems that "the best lack all conviction, while the worst / Are full of passionate intensity." I think when it comes to you, it's the exact opposite. You have that passionate intensity, and the total conviction. Thank you very much.

You're welcome, David. I am always happy to be flattered [laughs].

CHAPTER 5

Seize the Time!

We're going to have a conversation, perhaps punctuated with some readings by Arundhati Roy. I must confess I'm a little bit nervous to be doing this.

He's lying. It's just an act.

I'm nervous because typically we meet and do interviews in the back seats of cars. Our first interview was, in fact, from Amherst to Logan Airport in Boston. It was nerve-racking to be trying to control the tape recorder, as well as my notes flying all over the place, and trying to keep a coherent interview going. But, be that as it may, here we are. It's wonderful to be here.

I'd like to start with a quote from a recent interview I did with Arundhati Roy that's published in the July–August issue of International Socialist Review. *And the quote was about what "the real fight" is. Roy said, it's "that we are up against an economic system that is suffocating the majority of people in this world. What are we going to do about it? How are we going to address it?" So I thought that would be a really easy way to get into the evening. What are we going to do about it, and how are we going to address it?*

That's not fair [laughs]. I've just been in America for three days now, and I obviously have felt the electricity in the air about the

This interview was conducted during an event at Town Hall in Seattle, Washington, August 17, 2004.

coming election. And just in May we had a very important election in India. I think one of the dangers that we face is that it all becomes about personalities, and we forget that the system is in place and it doesn't matter all that much who is piloting the machine. So as I was saying last night at the ASA (American Sociological Association) in San Francisco, this whole fierce debate about the Democrats and the Republicans and whether Bush or Kerry is better is like, in fact, being asked to choose a detergent. Whether you choose Tide or Ivory Snow, they're both owned by Procter & Gamble.

And so, first of all, we have to understand that elections are just an apparent choice now. In India, we were faced with outright fascism with the BJP and sort of covert communalism that the Congress Party had indulged in for fifty years, preparing the ground in many ways for the right wing. It was the Congress Party that actually opened India's markets to corporate globalization. But the one difference was that in their election campaign, at least they had to lie. At least they had to say that they were against their old policies.

But here they don't even do you the dignity of that. The Democrats are not even pretending that they're against the war or against the occupation. And that, I think, is very important, because the antiwar movement in America has been so phenomenal a service, not just to Americans, but to all of us in the world. And you can't allow them to hijack your beliefs and put your weight behind somebody who is openly saying that he believes in the occupation, that he would have attacked Iraq even if he had known there were no weapons of mass destruction, that he will actually get UN cover for the occupation, that he will try and get Indian and Pakistani soldiers to go and die in Iraq instead, and that the Germans and the French and the Russians might be able to share in the spoils of the occupation. Is that better or worse for somebody who lives in the subject nations of empire?

The fact is that we all know that what is happening is that there is a system of economic disparity that is being entrenched in the world today. It isn't an accident that 580 billionaires in the world have greater income than—I think the figure is 170 of the poorest countries. I don't quite remember the exact figure. But the fact is that the disparities in the world are huge. And the disparities are not between rich countries and poor countries but between rich people and poor people. So what do we do about it?

We understand a few things. One is that the system of electoral democracy as it stands today is premised on a religious acceptance of the nation-state but the system of corporate globalization is not. The system of corporate globalization is premised on the fact that liquid capital can move through poor countries at an enormous scale, dictating the agendas, dictating economic policy in those countries by insinuating itself into those economies. And that capital requires the coercive powers of the nation-state to contain the revolt in the servants' quarters. But it ensures that individual countries cannot stand up to the project of corporate globalization, which is why you have even people like Lula of Brazil or Mandela of South Africa who were giants in the opposition but reduced to dwarfs on the global stage, blackmailed by the threat of capital flight.

So theoretically the only way to confront this is with what all of us are involved with, which is the globalization of dissent, which is the joining of hands of people who do not believe in empire. We have to join hands across countries and across continents in very specific ways and stop this. Because it isn't inevitable, globalization. It is signed by specific contracts with specific signatures and specific governments and specific companies. And we have to bring that to its knees.

Imperialism, years ago, was only the province of certain Marxist scholars. It was a dirty word that couldn't be spoken in polite company. But today you have people like Michael Ignatieff, who seems to have unlimited access to the New York Times Magazine, *writing cover stories extolling the virtues of what he calls "imperialism lite." And you have someone like Salman Rushdie saying that "America did, in Afghanistan, what had to be done and did it well." I wonder now, given three years since the attack on Afghanistan, with the return of the warlords, the huge surge in opium trafficking, what your views are?*

Afghanistan has just been thrown back to the warlords the way it was abandoned after the American government funded the mujahideen in order to get the Russians out. And today, Hamid Karzai, the CIA man who worked for Unocal, can't even entrust Afghans with his own security. That has to be private mercenaries. Just as everything else has been privatized, now security and torture and prison administration and all of this is being privatized. So what can you say to Michael Ignatieff?

I've grown up in India, and I've lived all my life there. I've never spent any large amounts of time in the West. So you come here and you listen to that talk, you think, Even our fascists are not saying that. I've often been asked to come and debate imperialism as the lesser evil, and I think it's like asking me about the pros and cons of child abuse. Is it a subject that I should debate?

Every little bylane that we walk down in India, are people saying, "Bring them back. We miss it so badly"? So it's a kind of new racism. And it isn't even all that new, so we can't even give them points for originality on this. These debates have taken place in the colonial time in almost exactly the same words: civilizing the savages and the whole missionary thing and all of that. So that isn't even something I think is worth the dignity of a debate. It is just an aspect of power. It is what power always will say. And we can't even allow it to deflect our attention for six seconds.

It was in that first back-seat interview that you recalled growing up as a kid in Kerala during the 1960s and wondering whether you would be considered a "gook." And today the language is "raghead" and "towelhead" and "Haji" and "Ali Baba."

Yes, because Kerala was very much like Vietnam. We, too, had rice fields and rivers and Communists. We were just a few thousand miles west of Vietnam. So I do remember wondering whether we would be "gooks" blown out of the bushes while you had some Hollywood score playing.

Nothing has changed all that much, except that it's gone back to the workshop and come out with its edges rounded. This year at the World Social Forum in Mumbai, the talk I gave was called "Do Turkeys Enjoy Thanksgiving?" And there is a small passage in it which I'll read to you, which talks about the New Imperialism.

> Like Old Imperialism, New Imperialism too relies for its success on a network of agents—corrupt local elites who service empire. We all know the sordid story of Enron in India. The then-Maharashtra government signed a power purchase agreement that gave Enron profits that amounted to 60 percent of India's entire rural development budget. A single American company was guaranteed a profit equivalent to funds for infrastructural development for about 500 million people!
>
> Unlike in the old days, the New Imperialist doesn't need to trudge around the tropics risking malaria or diarrhea or early death. New Imperialism can be conducted on email. The vulgar, hands-on racism of Old Imperialism is outdated. The cornerstone of New Imperialism is New Racism.
>
> The tradition of "turkey pardoning" in the United States is a wonderful allegory for New Racism. Every year since 1947, the National Turkey Federation has presented the US president with a turkey for Thanksgiving. Every year, in a show of ceremonial magnanimity, the president spares that particular bird (and eats another one). After receiving the presidential pardon, the Chosen One is sent to Frying Pan Park in Virginia to live out its natural life. The rest of the fifty million turkeys raised for Thanksgiving are slaughtered and eaten on Thanksgiving Day. ConAgra Foods, the company that has won the Presidential Turkey contract, says it trains the lucky birds to be sociable, to interact with dignitaries, schoolchildren, and the press. (Soon they'll even speak English!)

That's how New Racism in the corporate era works. A few carefully bred turkeys—the local elites of various countries, a community of wealthy immigrants, investment bankers, the occasional Colin Powell or Condoleezza Rice, some singers, some writers (like myself)—are given absolution and a pass to Frying Pan Park. The remaining millions lose their jobs, are evicted from their homes, have their water and electricity connections cut, and die of AIDS. Basically they're for the pot. But the Fortunate Fowls in Frying Pan Park are doing fine. Some of them even work for the IMF and the WTO—so who can accuse those organizations of being anti-turkey? Some serve as board members on the Turkey Choosing Committee—so who can say that turkeys are against Thanksgiving? They participate in it! Who can say the poor are anti-corporate globalization? There's a stampede to get into Frying Pan Park. So what if most perish on the way?

As part of the project of New Racism we also have New Genocide. New Genocide in this new era of economic interdependence can be facilitated by economic sanctions. New Genocide means creating conditions that lead to mass death without actually going out and killing people. Denis Halliday, who was the UN humanitarian coordinator in Iraq between 1997 and 1998 (after which he resigned in disgust), used the term *genocide* to describe the sanctions in Iraq. In Iraq the sanctions outdid Saddam Hussein's best efforts by claiming more than half a million children's lives.

In the new era, apartheid as formal policy is generally considered antiquated and unnecessary. International instruments of trade and finance oversee a complex system of multilateral trade laws and financial agreements that keep the poor in their Bantustans anyway. Its whole purpose is to institutionalize inequity. Why else would it be that the United States taxes a garment made by a Bangladeshi manufacturer twenty times more than it taxes a garment made in the United Kingdom? Why else would it be that countries that grow 90 percent of the world's cocoa bean produce only 5 percent of the world's chocolate? Why else would it be that countries that grow cocoa bean, like the Ivory Coast and Ghana, are taxed out of the market if they try and turn it into chocolate? Why else would it be that rich countries that spend over a billion dollars a day on subsidies to farmers demand that poor countries like India withdraw all agricultural subsidies, including subsidized electricity? Why else would it be that after having been plundered by colonizing regimes for more than half a century, former colonies are steeped in debt to those same regimes and repay them some $382 billion a year?

Colonies went out of fashion several decades ago, but with the US occupation and colonization of Iraq, you're calling for something rather dramatic in terms of what the US should do.

Not dramatic, just reasonable. They should pull out and pay reparations.

But "the maddened king," as you call W. Bush, says "the world is a safer place." Do you feel safer in India now that Saddam Hussein is no longer in power in Iraq?

I really miss those amazing Technicolor terror alerts in India—the polka-dotted and salmon pink and orange and lavender and whatever. In India, especially—I'm not talking about the elite, but among normal people—there is a distinction between the government and the people, between the *sarkar*, as we call it, and the public. But here, this whole regime of synthetically manufactured fear has bonded people to the government. And that bond is not because of public health care or looking after the old or education or social services, but fear. I think it would be a disaster for the American government if all of you started feeling safe.

If you look at, say, India, from 1989 to today—of course the Indian corporate press is no different from the American corporate press. In a twisted sense, the only lucky thing is that most people can't read it, so the lies and the indoctrination don't penetrate very deep. But if you did read it, would you possibly believe that in the last fourteen years, eighty thousand people have been killed in Kashmir? Every day there are terrorist attacks. In states like Andhra Pradesh, two hundred extremists are killed every year. Every day there are militant strikes. But none of us goes around feeling terrified. We all know that everybody has to just continue living as they do. People would laugh at the government if they started this Technicolor terror alert thing, because everyone has so many other problems.

So I think not to be frightened here is a political act.

Talking about the media, you say that Americans live in a "bubble of lots of advertisements and no information." How do you break through the bubble?

I think we need to think about what is it that the mass media are doing to us. People who live outside America sometimes find it hard to actually believe the levels of indoctrination that do take place through it. And because somehow, in a more anarchic society, which is the society that I live in, you can't indoctrinate it. One day you have the Kumbh Mela, with millions of people, and a *Naga sadhu* trying to pull the district collector's car with his penis. And you can't tell him that corporate globalization is the answer to your problems. Drink more Coke. So sometimes it's hard for us to understand the reach and penetration of television and newspapers here.

But I think one of the mistakes a lot of us activists make is railing against it to a point where we don't know what to do with it. And I think that there are two things. One is that you do have very strong alternative media as well. David Barsamian of Alternative Radio is sitting here. You have *Democracy Now!* You have the Internet. There is so much going on, so many places to look for other information. But also I think there is a kind of ad-busting to be done, which is, you read the mainstream media, but what you gather from it is not what they want to tell you. You have to learn to decode it, to understand it for the boardroom bulletin that it is. And therefore, you use its power against itself. And I think that's very important to do, because many of us make the mistake of thinking that the corporate media supports the neoliberal project. It doesn't. It *is* the neoliberal project. That's what it is.

You just see it so blatantly now. In America, just think of yourselves in 2001, what was going on in this country, and think of what is going on now. What a huge victory so many of you have won in terms of being this flag-waving, frightening place. I remember in 2003, when I spoke in Porto Alegre, I didn't even, frankly, believe what I was saying at that time. It was just wishful thinking. There in Brazil, I said activists and musicians and writers, so many people have worked together to strip empire of its sheen. And we've exposed it, and now it stands too ugly to behold itself in the mirror. That much I believed. And the next sentence was, soon it will not be able to rally its own people. And look what's happened. It's happening here. And it's because of you. So between that time and now, what used to be America's secret history is now street talk. And that's because of you. And it's such a brilliant job. And you just mustn't lose focus. You must stop thinking that now, if Kerry comes to power, we can all go back home and be happy.

The global demonstrations against the Iraq war on February 15, 2003, turned out at least ten million, by some accounts up to fifteen million people. You've called that one of the greatest affirmations of the human spirit and morality. But then the war started and people went home.

This is something we have to ask ourselves about, because the first part of this question is that you did have this incredible display of public morality. In no European country was the support for a unilateral war more than 11 percent. Hundreds of thousands marched on the streets of America. And still these supposedly democratic countries went to war. So the question is—A, is democracy still democratic? B, are governments accountable to the people who elected them? And, C, are people responsible in democratic countries for the actions of their governments? It's a very serious crisis that is facing democracies today. And if you get caught in this Ivory Snow versus Tide debate, if you get caught in having to choose between a detergent with oxy boosters or gentle cleansers, we're finished.

The point is, how do you keep power on a short leash? How do you make it accountable? And the fact is that we can't also only feel good about what we do. What we have done has been fantastic, but we must accept that it's not enough. And one of the problems is that symbolic resistance has unmoored itself from real civil disobedience. And that is very dangerous, because governments have learned how to wait these things out. And they think we're like children with rattles in a crib. Just let them get on with their weekend demonstration, and we'll just carry on with what we have to do. Public opinion is so fickle, and so on. The symbolic aspect of resistance is very important. The theater is very important. But not at the cost of real civil disobedience. So we have to find ways of implementing what we're saying seriously.

And you look at what's happening today. I feel that the Iraqi resistance is fighting on the front lines of empire. It's alright. We know that it's a motley group of former Ba'athists and fed-up collaborationists and Communists and all kinds of people. But no resistance movement is pristine. And if we are going to only invest our purity in pristine movements, we may as well forget it. The point is, this is our resistance, and we have to support it.

And you have to understand that the American soldiers who are dying in Iraq are conscripts of a poverty draft—you all know that—from the poorest parts of America being sent to war. In fact, they as well as the Iraqis are victims of the same horrendous system that asks for their lives in return for a victory that will never be theirs.

The book that David and I did together is called *The Checkbook and the Cruise Missile*. And the fact is that sometimes the cruise missile is highlighted, and you're thinking about the torture and the invasion and the army and the people dying and so on. But meanwhile, the contracts are being signed, the pipelines are being laid, everything is being put in place for the time when they can withdraw the cruise missile. But the system of appropriation is already in place. And you have these companies like Bechtel and Halliburton who did business with Saddam Hussein, who were on the Iraq Liberation Board, or whatever it was called, who are now profiting in the billions from the destruction and the reconstruction of Iraq. And those same companies were in Cochabamba, Bolivia, in water privatization. Those same companies are in India, along with Enron. Enron and Bechtel, for instance, were involved in the first private power project in India, where the profits were 60 percent of India's entire rural development budget.

The point I'm trying to make is, here is Iraq on the front lines of this war on empire, but each of these companies that are involved in this place have economic outposts across the world. So it gives us a foothold. It gives us a way of using our disparity but making it all bear down on individual corporations and companies. And if we can't shut them down, if we can't prevent them from doing what they're doing, then how can we call ourselves a resistance? We have to do it. We have to find a way of doing it.

And the thing is, it's not going to happen without us paying a price. It's not going to happen in our overtime or on weekends or anything like that. People in poor countries are being battered by the system. It's not only that empire arrives in their lives, as it has in Iraq. It also arrives in the form of exorbitant electricity bills that they can't pay, of water cut off, being dismissed from their jobs, and uprooted from their lands.

I was in South Africa in June. Just four days before I left, in a Black township called Phoenix, the police and the municipal police arrived to disconnect illegal electricity connections, because electricity has been privatized there and the poor have just been disconnected—millions of them. So they just reconnect illegally. Police went and removed all the cables. And an old lady went out and said, "Look, it's all right. Remove the cables. But just wait here. I want the press to come, and I want to explain to them why we need to steal electricity." So they started pushing her around. And a young boy, who was her son, a eighteen-year-old boy, came out and said, "Look, that's my mother you're pushing around." And they just put a gun to his head and shot him.

Empire is always seen by the repressive machinery of the states that it's in—the government, the police, the army, the bureaucracy. If you look at a country like India, we are old hands at the game. You have the Armed Forces (Special Powers) Act, which allows a noncommissioned army officer to kill anybody on suspicion of creating public disturbance. All over the northeast, all over Kashmir, you have the Gangster Act (The UP Gangsters and Anti-Social Activities (Prevention) Act), you have the Special Areas Security Act, you have the Terrorist and Disruptive Areas Act (which has lapsed but people are still being tried under it). And then you have POTA (the Prevention of Terrorism Act), where thousands of people are just being picked up and held without trial. And their crime is poverty. It isn't that they're terrorists. They're being called "terrorists," but their crime is poverty. So terrorism and poverty are being conflated. And states are becoming very sophisticated in their repression.

How do we counter that? This battle is not going to be won without us paying a price. That's one thing we have to understand. It's not going to be a cute war.

POTA, the Prevention of Terrorism Act—which some have called the "Production of Terrorism Act"—has its counterpart in the United States in the USA PATRIOT Act, which has greatly enhanced the ability of the state to surveil and imprison its citizens.

I think fundamentally the thing about these acts that we have to understand is that they are not meant for the terrorists, because the terrorists—or suspected terrorists—are just shot or taken, in the case of America to Guantánamo Bay. Those acts are meant to terrorize *you*. Basically all of us stand accused. It prepares the ground for the government to make all of us culprits and then pick off whichever one of us it wants to.

And, of course, we know that once we give up these freedoms, will we ever get them back? In India, at least when the Congress Party was campaigning, one of the main issues was that it was going to withdraw the Prevention of Terrorism Act. It probably will, but not before it puts into legislation other kinds of legislation that approximate it. So it won't be POTA. It will be MOTA or whatever. But here, are they even saying that they will repeal it? It's an insult to you that they don't even think they have to say it. Is it "populist" to say that we are going to deal in sterner ways with terror, and we are going to make America stronger and safer—with more oxy-boosters? I know a lot of people say that, "Oh, you know, Kerry is saying this, but when he comes to power, he will be different." But nobody moves to the left after they come to power. They move only to the right.

One of your essays is called "When the Saints Go Marching Out: The Strange Fate of Martin, Mohandas, and Mandela." "Mohandas" is the name of Mahatma Gandhi. Talk about Gandhi. He was able to devise strategies that exploited cracks in the empire.

Gandhi was one of the brightest, most cunning, and imaginative politicians of the modern age. He did what great writers do. Great writers expand the human imagination. Gandhi expanded the political imagination. But, of course, we mustn't ever think that the Indian freedom struggle was a revolutionary struggle. It wasn't. Because the Indian elite stepped very easily into the shoes of the British imperialists. Nor was it only a nonviolent struggle. That's the other myth—that it was an entirely nonviolent struggle. It wasn't. But what Gandhi did was democratic because of the ways in which he devised strategy. It included a lot of people. He found ways of including masses of people. For instance, in the Dandi March in 1930—when Gandhi marched to the coast twenty-one days, I think, to make salt in order to break the British salt tax laws, which prevented Indians from making salt—it was symbolic. But also, then millions of Indians began to make salt, and it struck at the economic underpinning of empire. So that was his brilliance.

But I think we really need to reimagine nonviolent resistance, because there isn't any debate taking place that is more important in the world today than the strategies of resistance. And there can never be one strategy. People are never going to agree about one strategy. It can't be that while we watch the American war machine occupy Iraq, torture its prisoners, appropriate its resources, we are waiting for this pristine secular, democratic, nonviolent, feminist resistance to come along. We can't prescribe to the Iraqis how to conduct their resistance, but we have to shore up our end of it by forcing America and its allies to leave Iraq now.

I think a lot of people here have on their minds the November 2 election and what to do, who to vote for. Tariq Ali, who is very critical of Kerry, recently said, "If the American population were to vote Bush out of office, I think the impact globally would be tremendous. . . . [O]ur option at the moment is limited. Do we defeat a warmonger government or not? Do we try our best to do it?" What do you think of Ali's perspective?

Look, it's a very complicated and difficult debate, in which I think there are two things you can do: you can act expediently, if you like, but you must speak on principle. I cannot sit here with any kind of honesty and say to you that I support Kerry. I cannot do that.

I'll give you a small example. In India, you may or may not be aware of the levels of violence and jingoism and fascism that we've faced over the last five years. In Gujarat, rampaging mobs murdered, raped, gang-raped, burnt alive two thousand Muslims on the streets and drove 150,000 out of their homes. And you have Rajasthan, you have Maharashtra, you have Madhya Pradesh. You have this plague of Hindu fascism spreading. And you had a central government which was supported by the BJP. A lot of the people that I work with and know work in the state of Madhya Pradesh, in central India, where there was a Congress state government for ten years. This government had overseen the building of many dams in the Narmada valley. It had overseen the privatization of electricity, of water, the driving out from their homes and lands of hundreds of thousands of people, the disconnection of single-point electricity connections, because they signed these huge contracts for privatization with the Asian Development Bank.

The activists in these areas knew that a lot of the reason that Congress was also so boldly doing these things was they were saying, "What option do you have? Do you want to get the BJP? Are you going to campaign for the BJP? Are you going to open yourself up not just to being physically beaten but maybe even killed?" But I want to tell you that they didn't campaign for the Congress. They didn't. They just said, "We do not believe in this, and we are going to continue to do our work outside." It was just a horrendous situation, because the BJP was pretending to be anti-reform, saying, "We'll stop this, we'll change that." They did come to power, the BJP, and within ten days they were on the dam site saying, "We are going to build the dam." So people are waiting for their houses to get submerged. This was the dilemma.

The point is, then, you have to say, "Look. Can you actually campaign for a man who is saying that 'I'm going to send more troops to Iraq?' How?" So I think it's very important for us to remain principled.

Let me tell you that during the Indian elections people used to keep asking me, "Aren't you campaigning for the Congress? Aren't you campaigning for the Congress?" Because, of course, I had spent the last five years denouncing the BJP. I said, "How can I campaign for the Congress that also oversaw the carnage of Sikhs in Delhi in 1984, that opened the markets to neoliberalism in the early 1990s?" And every time you're put under this pressure. I said, "I feel sometimes when I'm asked this question like I imagine that a gay person must feel when they're watching straight sex: I'm sort of interested but not involved." I think it's very important for us to understand that we are people of principle and we are soldiers who are fighting a different battle, and we cannot be co-opted into this.

So you've got to refuse the terms of this debate. Otherwise you're co-opted. I'm not going to say who you should vote for. I'm not going to sit here and tell you to vote for this one or vote for that one, because all of us here are people of influence and power, and we can't allow our power to be co-opted by those people. We cannot.

We talked about independent media a little earlier. I should mention Elliott Bay Book Company and this hall and South End Press, one of the best independent presses in the country, are examples of that. And here in Seattle, the Indy Media Center, a tremendously historically important development and innovation. So wherever possible we need to nurture independent media and we need to sustain it. So please do whatever you can to support these institutions. While we're trying to penetrate the corporate media, we're also trying to build parallel structures. And your support is absolutely critical, particularly when we're talking about independent bookstores in an age of borderization and Barnes & Nobleization of the countryside.

I just want to say something, back to the subject of the American election. You have to force the Democrats to say that they are against the war, otherwise you're not going to support them. They can't tell you what to do. They're the public servants. You have to tell them what to do.

Do you have any ideas about reaching beyond the choir? One of the frequent charges that's leveled against the left or progressives is that we talk among ourselves. We have a good time, and everyone nods their head, and then has a beer and goes home, and nothing happens. There is some truth to that. How do we get to a larger audience?

First of all, I don't get that feeling where I come from, because what we are saying is what a majority of India's poor are saying. So there is no question of preaching to the choir there. But I don't know how it is here.

I think, on another level, it is true that there is a sort of suspicion of success, of popularity among left intellectuals. You like to have this language that is sort of impenetrable. Not quite as bad as the postmodernists but getting there.

I think it's very important to say that Fox News's success is our failure. One of the things that I really try to do is to snatch our futures back from the world of experts, to say, "I'm sorry, but it's not that hard to understand and it's not that hard to explain." To do that, to tell the story, to join the dots. I must say that when the confrontation happened in Seattle at the WTO convention, for many of us in the subject nations of empire, it was a delightful thing to know that even people in imperialist countries shared our battles. It was really the beginnings of the globalization of dissent.

Corporate globalization wasn't something that was palpable earlier. Nobody really knew what it meant. The enemy wasn't corporeal. But it is now, because of the efforts of so many people. Now you go into any bookshop in America and look at the books. Seven, eight, nine years ago, would they have been there? No. And that's what we've done. And must continue to do.

Take documentary filmmaking. I'm not only talking about the high end of it, or *Fahrenheit 9/11*. Technology has enabled documentary film to become such a powerful tool both to the right and to the left. It's become such an important political tool in places such as India that governments are really frightened and are wondering how to censor it, how to stop these filmmakers who used to need grants from the Ford Foundation and some state film corporation but now can just go and do it on their own with a little camera. And those films are so subversive and so gripping. You go to a little village in India with a projector, and thousands of people will come.

So these are new tools that are being honed. I think I wrote an essay about it and spoke about "the buffalo and the bees." The mainstream corporate media is like the buffalo, and the alternate media is like this swarm of bees around the buffalo. And it's like contextualizing the buffalo. The buffalo sort of sets the agenda, but the bees are doing a pretty good job right now. And we have to just continue that in some way.

Michael Moore has been very successful in terms of reaching a much larger audience. In fact, he has two books on the bestseller list right now. His Fahrenheit 9/11 *has been seen by millions of people. What can we learn from those kinds of interventions?*

The obvious, I think—that those kinds of interventions have a space now and have to be exploited, because it blows open spaces. It changes what people expect from cinema, makes it all so much more exciting. I think there are other films, like *Control Room*.

A couple of years ago, you were at the United World College in Las Vegas, a small town in northern New Mexico. You were talking to the students there, and I took these notes. "It's difficult to be citizens of an empire, because it's hard to listen. Put your ear to the wall. Listen to the whisper." If you put your ear to the wall now, what would you hear?

I don't feel qualified to answer that properly, because I've just been here for a few days and have been speaking in places like this, where it's not exactly like I'm on the street listening to things. But I must say that soon after September 11, I wrote an essay called "The Algebra of Infinite Justice." And when I wrote it, I did think to myself, here is me writing this essay that's probably going to annoy this huge and powerful country, and that's the end of me. But then, as a writer, if I can't write what I think, that would be the end of me anyway. So let me just do it.

And instead I find that it's just so wonderful to arrive here and to know that you all are heroes. It gives so much strength to people. And I'm always called, of course, for strategic reasons, "anti-American." And I'm so far from being anti-American—isn't that funny? Because I have such a deep respect for what you do. I can assure you that if India and Pakistan were at war, it would be hard for me to find people to come out—not for me, for any of us—in the numbers in which you have come out and protested against what your government is doing. So, power to you. That's just fantastic. And it is something which encourages people everywhere. It blurs these national borders—you're this, I'm that. You don't even talk like this—you're an American, and I'm an Indian, and so-and-so is a Moroccan. We are finding a different kind of language in which to talk to each other, which is important.

I've said this just now, but I'll say it again. This idea that America's secret history is street talk is what I hear. That is all out in the open now. And the fact is that empires always overreach themselves and then crumble. Power has a short shelf life.

Kathy Kelly is an extraordinary woman. She's one of the founders of Voices in the Wilderness. She just served a jail four month sentence for civil disobedience at the School of the Americas training camp in Fort Benning, Georgia. Again, talking about courage, she says it's the ability to control fear, and we catch courage from one another. I know you've spent a lot of time with some very extraordinary women in the Narmada valley. What kind of courage were you able to catch?

One of the great things about the nonviolent political resistance in India, its legacy, is that it really has women at the heart of it. It really allows women into the heart of it. When movements become violent, not only does the state react with huge coercive power, but that violence by people on your own side is very soon turned on women. So because we have this legacy in places like the Narmada valley, women also realize that they are far bigger victims than the men are. Say, a hundred thousand people are being displaced by a dam and they're not being given land, because there is no land. The men are given some cash as compensation. The men buy motorcycles or get drunk, and then it's finished. And the women are left in a terrible situation. So they are fighting this battle much more fiercely. And everywhere you go, you see that they're really at the forefront.

I think, of all the women's resistance, the most remarkable today is RAWA, the Revolutionary Association of the Women of Afghanistan. What a tremendous battle they have waged and continue to wage. And what a principled battle. They were faced with the Taliban and the Northern Alliance, and the Americans in between. And we were made to feel that America was fighting a feminist war in Afghanistan. But look at their situation now. They didn't say, "Yes, yes, we'll support you and come in." At no point did they take an expedient position. I think we have to learn from that.

You conclude one of your essays with a paraphrase from Shelley's poem "Masque of Anarchy": "We be many and they be few." Talk about that.

That is what is happening. It is in the nature of capitalism, isn't it, that the more profit you make, the more you plow back into the machine, the more profit you make? And so now you have a situation in which, like I said, five hundred billionaires have more money than numerous whole countries put together. And that rift is widening everywhere.

I believe that wars must be waged from positions of strength. So the poor must fight from their position of strength, which is on the streets and the mountains and the valleys of the world—not in boardrooms and parliaments and courts, where they're just manipulated and abandoned. The strength we have is actually the opposite of being a little club of people who make each other happy and drink beer and go back home. I completely reject that, actually. I think we are on the side of the millions—and that is our strength. And we must recognize it and work with it.

There is an alternative to terrorism. What is it?

Justice.

How do we get there?

The point is that terrorism has been isolated and made to look like some kind of thing that has no past and has no future, and is just some aberration of maniacs. It isn't. Of course, sometimes it is. But if you look at it, the logic that underlies terrorism and the logic that underlies the war on terror is the same: both hold ordinary people responsible for the actions of governments. And the fact is that Osama bin Laden or Al-Qaeda, in their attacks on September 11, took the lives of many ordinary American people. And in the attack in Afghanistan and on Iraq, hundreds of thousands of Iraqis and Afghans paid for the actions of the Taliban or for the actions of Saddam Hussein. The difference is that the Afghans didn't elect the Taliban. The Iraqis didn't elect Saddam Hussein. So how do we justify these kinds of wars?

I really think that terrorism is the privatization of war. They are the free marketeers of war. They are the ones who say that they don't believe that legitimate violence is only the monopoly of the state. So we can't condemn terrorism unless we condemn the war on terror. And no government that does not show itself to be open to change by nonviolent dissent can actually condemn terrorism. Because if every avenue of nonviolent dissent is closed or mocked or bought off or broken, then by default you privilege violence. When all your respect and admiration and research and media coverage and the whole economy is based on war and violence, when violence is deified, on what grounds are you going to condemn terrorism? Whatever people lack in wealth and power they make up with stealth and strategy. So we can't just every time we're asked to say something, say, "Oh, terrorism is a terrible thing," without talking about repression, without talking about justice, without talking about occupation, without talking about privatization, without talking about the fact that this country has its army strung across the globe.

And then, of course, even language has been co-opted. If you say "democracy," actually it means neoliberalism. If you say "reforms," it actually means repression. Everything has been turned into something else. So we even have to reclaim language now.

I know you want to read from another essay.

Last year I spoke at Riverside Church in New York. The talk was called "Instant-Mix Imperial Democracy: Buy One, Get One Free." This is just the end of it, which I'll read to you.

We might as well accept the fact that there is no conventional military force that can successfully challenge the American war machine. Terrorist strikes only give the US government an opportunity that it is eagerly awaiting to further tighten its stranglehold. Within days of an attack you can bet that PATRIOT II would be passed. To argue against US military aggression by saying that it will increase the possibilities of terrorist strikes is futile. It's like threatening Brer Rabbit that you'll throw him into the bramble bush. Anybody who has read the document called "The Project for the New American Century" can attest to that. The government's suppression of the congressional Joint Inquiry into Intelligence Community Activities before and after the terrorist attacks of September 11, 2001, which found that there was intelligence warning of the strikes that was ignored, also attests to the fact that, for all their posturing, the terrorists and the Bush regime might as well be working as a team. They both hold people responsible for the actions of their governments. They both believe in the doctrine of collective guilt and collective punishment. Their actions benefit each other greatly.

The US government has already displayed in no uncertain terms the range and extent of its capability for paranoid aggression. In human psychology, paranoid aggression is usually an indicator of nervous insecurity. It could be argued that it's no different in the case of the psychology of nations. Empire is paranoid because it has a soft underbelly.

Its homeland may be defended by border patrols and nuclear weapons, but its economy is strung out across the globe. Its economic outposts are exposed and vulnerable.

Yet it would be naive to imagine that we can directly confront empire. Our strategy must be to isolate empire's working parts and disable them one by one. No target is too small. No victory too insignificant. We could reverse the idea of the economic sanctions imposed on poor countries by empire and its allies. We could impose a regime of Peoples' Sanctions on every corporate house that has been awarded a contract in postwar Iraq, just as activists in this country and around the world targeted institutions of apartheid. Each one of them should be named, exposed, and boycotted. Forced out of business. That could be our response to the Shock and Awe campaign. It would be a great beginning.

Another urgent challenge is to expose the corporate media for the boardroom bulletin that it really is. We need to create a universe of alternative information. We need to support independent media like *Democracy Now!*, Alternative Radio, South End Press.

The battle to reclaim democracy is going to be a difficult one. Our freedoms were not granted to us by any governments. They were wrested from them by us. And once we surrender them, the battle to retrieve them is called a revolution. It is a battle that must range across continents and countries. It must not acknowledge national boundaries, but if it is to succeed, it has to begin here. In America. The only institution more powerful than the US government is American civil society. The rest of us are subjects of slave nations. We are by no means powerless, but you have the power of proximity. You have access to the Imperial Palace and the Emperor's chambers. Empire's conquests are being carried out in your name, and you have the right to refuse. You could refuse to fight. Refuse to move those missiles from the warehouse to the dock. Refuse to wave that flag. Refuse the victory parade.

You have a rich tradition of resistance. You need only read Howard Zinn's *A People's History of the United States* to remind yourself of this.

Hundreds of thousands of you have survived the relentless propaganda you have been subjected to, and are actively fighting your own government. In the ultrapatriotic climate that prevails in the United States, that's as brave as any Iraqi or Afghan or Palestinian fighting for his or her homeland.

If you join the battle, not in your hundreds of thousands but in your millions, you will be greeted joyously by the rest of the world. And you will see how beautiful it is to be gentle instead of brutal, safe instead of scared. Befriended instead of isolated. Loved instead of hated.

I hate to disagree with your president. Yours is by no means a great nation. But you could be a great people.

History is giving you the chance. Seize the time.

CHAPTER 6

The Checkbook
and the Cruise Missile

You've participated in and you've reported on one of the most extraordinary, largely woman-driven movements, the Narmada Bachao Andolan, the movement to save the Narmada valley. Based on your experience and what you saw in the valley, what are the ingredients for a successful social movement?

First of all, if you don't mind, I just want to clarify one thing—which is that often the world that is in search of icons likes to confuse me as some kind of leader of that mass movement, and I'm not that. So I just want to clarify that to you. I'm a writer, as you all know. But I think the movement in the Narmada valley is a very, very interesting phenomenon now. In India, the Supreme Court gave a very, very retrogressive judgment two years ago that completely justified the building of big dams all over again and has opened the door to international finance coming back. So a lot of people look at that movement not as a successful movement but the opposite of that. And that isn't true. First of all, because there are many, many dams being built on that river, and some of them have been stopped by the Narmada Bachao Andolan, but the most contentious dam was called the Sardar Sarovar, and that dam is being constructed at speed now, as are other dams. And the violation of human rights in that scenario

This interview was conducted at Berkeley High School in Berkeley, California, on August 18, 2004.

is not something that the media highlights anymore, because it's bored. And it's not that people are getting slaughtered or people are getting killed. They're just getting relentlessly dispossessed and impoverished.

But I think a huge lesson in that movement, that I've learned certainly, is that the definitions of what we mean by success and what we mean by failure have to be changed. If you look at areas in India where there hasn't been the history of resistance, you can see how the police or the army can just go in, terrorize people, pick up women, rape them, torture them. They can do what they like.

They can't go into the Narmada valley and do that to anyone. So I think we have to understand that real victory is how you set yourself against power and how you insist on your rights, even if you're losing. If that sense of fight is in you, it's a huge victory, even if you seem to be losing to the outside world.

And there are such huge battles remaining to be fought. India is such a feudal country. Women in India are very deeply involved in resistance for two reasons. One, because the whole process of corporate globalization makes poorer women the first victims, so they stand to lose so much more. For example, when people are being displaced or dispossessed by a dam, they lose their lands and sometimes some of them are compensated with money. That money goes to the men. The men may buy a motorcycle or drink it away in despair. It leaves the women very vulnerable. So the women are at the core of the resistance. And also I think one of the reasons is because India has a huge tradition of nonviolent resistance, which does embrace women and allows them to be at the heart of it, even though I must say that we should remember that the Indian independence movement wasn't entirely nonviolent. It's a myth that it was entirely nonviolent.

What are the main obstacles in building a movement?

In my view, there are roughly two kinds of resistance movements happening in the world today. One is movements like the landless people's movement in Brazil or the Narmada movement or the Zapatistas or the Anti-Privatization Forum, people who are fighting their own states for radical change. And then you have movements like liberation struggles in Palestine, in Kashmir, in the northeast of India, in Tibet. These are struggles for self-determination along lines that were arbitrarily drawn by the imperialist powers in the last century. And those struggles face much harsher repression. So in a way they've also been pushed into retrogressive positions, sometimes speaking the same language as the states they hope to overthrow.

And then you have Iraq, which is, I think, another phase—recolonization. Because the capitalist machine now, in order to control natural resources, cannot do it that easily by the remote control of corporate globalization, so it goes in with military aggression and takes over natural resources in geopolitically strategic places. We all are waiting for Iraq to stage a pristine, feminist, democratic, secular resistance, while they are being brutalized by this most powerful country, with the most powerful weapons in the world. And if we are going to wait for a pristine resistance movement to invest our purity in, we're never going to find it.

So I think that before we begin to preach to the Iraqi resistance about how exactly they should conduct their war, we should shore up our end of the resistance by insisting that the US and its allies withdraw from Iraq and pay reparations. I just want to say that there is a very simple list of demands, which are not just demands but are a question of principle: that they withdraw from Iraq, that they pay reparations—not just reparations for the war but for the sanctions, that they annul these contracts that allow Iraq's resources to be taken over by American companies, and basically get out now.

Talk more about Iraq and the intersection of imperialism and racism.

Much has been made of the fact that corporate globalization is a new and different way of doing things. I don't think it's that new and that different. I think, basically, Old Imperialism went back into the workshop and got its jagged ends sandpapered down and came back sort of new, improved, weatherproofed.

In May, in India, there was an election. The Bharatiya Janata Party, a right-wing Hindu formation, was ousted and replaced by the Congress Party. Talk about that, and also the upcoming elections here in the United States. You've had an opportunity to hear Senator Kerry and the current occupant of the Oval Office.

It is somewhat dangerous to equate the Indian elections with the American elections, because obviously what happened in the Indian elections doesn't affect the world in quite the same way as the American elections. But let me say that we lived through five years of hell in India. We lived through a regime which was as close to fascist as you can get. We lived through times when a government-assisted pogrom took place in the state of Gujarat, where two thousand Muslims were killed, gang-raped, burned alive, and 150,000 were driven from their homes. In a time when all of us actually lived in fear of what would happen to any of us who were speaking out—and a realization that the economic despair that was setting in was such a wonderful breeding ground for this kind of fascism.

And when the elections came, none of us—when I say "us," I'm talking about people involved in the politics of opposition, and I don't mean party political opposition but genuine opposition—could bear the idea of actually openly campaigning for the Congress Party, because they really sowed the seeds for the right wing to walk through, whether it was the nuclear tests, or communalism, or neoliberalism. The Congress was there planting the seeds for the BJP to reap the harvest.

No election pundit, no national press, no exit polls really predicted that the Congress would win, because the urban elite and the national press in India are now so disconnected with what is happening in rural areas that they just didn't have a handle on the levels of despair that existed outside the glittering parts of the metropolitan cities. And so the Congress came to power as the biggest party. The left won historically its largest share of the vote ever. And it was very clearly a vote against fascism and neoliberal reform.

I was watching the media coverage of this election. And it was amazing that while the corporate press showed the spectacle of Indian democracy on the move—poor farmers and the journeys on elephant back, and the veiled women and their beautiful jewelry, and everybody with thick glasses and sticks hobbling to the election booths—as soon as the vote showed that the BJP had lost, there was panic because they thought maybe the Congress would actually implement its election promises.

So the poor, the millions who had come out to vote, were dismissed like badly paid extras on a film set. And suddenly all the television sets had split screens: half of it was outside Sonia Gandhi's office while she was cobbling together the coalition, and the other half was located twenty-four hours a day outside the Bombay Stock Exchange. The SENSEX plummeted. The next day, the media, whose own publicly listed stocks were plummeting, reported the news as if Pakistan had launched intercontinental ballistic missiles on Delhi. And even before the government was formed, the Congress was railroaded into—I can't say "railroaded," because I'm sure they did it quite willingly, but they promised that they wouldn't really radically change the privatization reforms. They assured the big business houses. So once the elections were over, the poor were just expected to bugger off home, and policy would be decided despite them.

Here you have quite a different scenario, I think, where the opposition party doesn't even do you the service of pretending to be an opposition. So I was talking at the American Sociological Association the other day, and I said, in watching this American election, it's actually quite frightening to see how it's been reduced to a personality contest between these two men. The biggest difference seems to me to be that Kerry says he likes Charlize Theron, and I don't know which actress Bush likes.

You have to understand that demonizing Bush has a downside, which is demonizing him at the expense of not understanding the way this machine works.

As somebody who lives in the subject nations, as somebody who is not living here, what is John Kerry saying? If the antiwar movement is going to openly campaign for him, then is it in support of his soft imperialist policies? Kerry is saying that he wants forty thousand more troops, that he agrees with Bush 100 percent on Israel, that he'll keep 98 percent of the tax cuts, and that the policy in Iraq is going to be that the UN is going to be cover for the American occupation, and that Indian and Pakistani soldiers are going to go there to do the killing and dying, and maybe the French and the Germans and the Russians will share in the spoils of Iraq's resources. So is it better for us to have a stupid emperor or a smarter emperor? I don't know. But the question is: Are we looking to challenge the system or not?

In India, as soon as the Congress comes to power, people who have been quite radical under the BJP, demanding the end to censorship and making very powerful statements against fascism, are suddenly saying, "No, no, censorship is actually not such a bad thing, because the Hindu fundamentalists should not be allowed to say the things they're saying." In a way, it co-opts resistance. So we have to understand that at this point in the world this democracy and voting in elections is not the true exercise of public power. Public power can only be exercised by a dissenting public.

And if you look at the way the world is being structured today economically and politically, you see how these kinds of electoral democracies are structured on an almost religious acceptance of the nation-state. But corporate globalization and its free movement of speculative, liquid capital is premised on exactly the opposite. So corporate globalization needs the nation-state and its coercive powers to put down the revolt in the servants' quarters. But no individual nation can stand up to corporate globalization. So the only people who can do it are resistance movements that join hands across national barriers.

Just to give you an example of this dilemma about elections—because I realize it's a dilemma. I'm not here to tell you what to do or to preach to you, or anything like that. But to just share our dilemma, many of the people that I'm very close to are involved in the struggle in the struggle in the Narmada valley, which is in the state of Madhya Pradesh. For ten years Madhya Pradesh was ruled by a Congress government. That Congress government was deeply enmeshed in the whole project of privatization, taking huge loans from the World Bank, from the Asian Development Bank, disconnecting the poorest people's electricity, giving huge subsidies to Coca-Cola and so on for their electricity, and building dams, which involved the complete dispossession of thousands of people in unbelievable ways. And then the election comes along. Madhya Pradesh is close by Gujarat, Maharashtra, Rajasthan. These are states where the Hindu right is very strong. Now all these killings are happening. Activists are in fear for their lives. They know that if they continue to campaign for the Congress, and the BJP comes in, they risk bodily harm. But how are they to campaign for this government that has done everything wrong in terms of economic policy and in terms of playing the soft Hindu right game? None of them campaigned for the Congress.

The BJP won. Within days it reannounced the same economic policies as the Congress. So this is the dialectic of elections. It doesn't matter what they are saying. Eventually it's a question of believing in oppositional politics and believing that the only way out is to keep power on a short leash, to force them to be accountable.

In terms of challenging the system, what role does culture play in resistance?

I think that we have to look out for what is being done to us. Among the major things that has been done is the slaughter of language. So now when you say "democracy," it means neoliberal capitalism. When you say "reforms," it means repression. When you say "empowerment" and "deepening democracy," I get scared.

So what is it that we are going to do now? The whole thing, "But you all are just against things. You're against globalization, you're against this, and you're against that. But what are you for?" This is not true. We are actually the people who really believe in globalization. We believe in the globalization of nuclear treaties. We believe in signing the Kyoto protocol. We believe in the banning of chemical and biological weapons. We believe in the International Court of Justice. So where is the question of us being against everything?

But the fact is that we also have to understand that, as people we can only keep power on a short leash if we actually are against incumbent power, if we are questioning it, if we are refusing its lies, if we are refusing the stories and the histories of the victors. So in terms of culture, just a few years ago, when I first wrote an essay on privatization and what it means, it ended with saying that what is happening to the world is just outside the realm of public understanding, and it is the duty and the delight of the writers and the actors and the singers and the filmmakers and the activists to bring this into the realm of public understanding so that we can see our corporeal enemy.

Every time I write something, I have to brace myself, in India anyway, for three weeks to a month of insults. But writers and artists and filmmakers and singers have done it. We know empire stands completely exposed, and we know who we are fighting. So that is a huge victory. And we can't ever undermine that.

The important thing is now that we mustn't allow symbolic resistance to replace real civil disobedience. The theatrical part of resistance is very important, but it becomes meaningless if it's the only part. I know millions of people marched against the war on the fifteenth of February. And when the war didn't stop, they just said, "It didn't help. So now what's the point of doing anything?" We can't stop a war with a weekend march. To stop the empire from moving forward in the way it does, soldiers have to refuse to fight, people have to refuse to load weapons. The alternative media has to be listened to. We have to expose the mainstream press for the boardroom bulletin that it is, and then start ignoring it or laughing at it or reading between the lines so that you actually use their power against them. That's what all of us do.

Pacifica and Alternative Radio and *Democracy Now!* are doing such a huge service, not just to this country but to the world.

I'll just read you just this one page. It was the end of this talk called "Confronting Empire."

> What can we do?
>
> We can hone our memory, we can learn from our history. We can continue to build public opinion until it becomes a deafening roar.
>
> We can turn the war on Iraq into a fishbowl of the US government's excesses.
>
> We can expose George Bush and Tony Blair—and their allies—for the cowardly baby killers, water poisoners, and pusillanimous long-distance bombers that they are.
>
> We can reinvent civil disobedience in a million different ways. In other words, we can come up with a million ways of becoming a collective pain in the ass.
>
> When George Bush says "You're either with us, or you are with the terrorists," we can say "No, thank you." We can let him know that the people of the world do not need to choose between a malevolent Mickey Mouse and the mad mullahs.
>
> Our strategy should be not only to confront empire but to lay siege to it. To deprive it of oxygen. To shame it. To mock it. With our art, our music, our literature, our stubbornness, our joy, our brilliance, our sheer relentlessness—and our ability to tell our own stories. Stories that are different from the ones we're being brainwashed to believe.
>
> The corporate revolution will collapse if we refuse to buy what they are selling—their ideas, their version of history, their wars, their weapons, their notion of inevitability.
>
> Remember this: We be many and they be few. They need us more than we need them.

There is an alternative to terrorism. And that alternative is called justice. And the fact is that no amount of nuclear weapons, no amount of daisy cutters, no amount of full-spectrum dominance is going to be able to control this, because as much as there are people who wish ascendancy and who wish to be the most powerful people on earth, their urge will be matched with greater intensity by people who only want to live with dignity. So that battle will be joined. That battle will be waged. Whether it's a beautiful battle or whether it's a bloody battle depends on us. But it will be joined.

If on November 2 there is regime change in the US, and Kerry replaces Bush—

That's not regime change.

—exchanging Ivory Snow for Tide, what might people do the next day?

Don't let up, don't miss a beat. Just keep demanding what you've been demanding. Don't be co-opted. Don't say, "Let's give this guy a little time, a few months, a couple of years." Because people are dying. The world is changing every day while the cruise missiles are raining down on people. Also, contracts are being signed, and pipelines are being laid, and water and petrol and copper and nickel and gold and diamonds are being stolen from poor countries. So there isn't time. The poor don't have time. The rich have time, but the poor don't have time.

You talk about the cruise missile but also three secretive organizations that essentially rule the world: the WTO, the IMF, and the World Bank. Argentina is a kind of textbook example of how the checkbook operates.

I don't think there is a country on God's earth which isn't in the crosshairs of the IMF checkbook or the American cruise missile. So if the checkbook doesn't work, then the cruise missile will. Because it's in the nature of the beast, it's in the nature of this whole capitalistic machine that you have to extract more and more in order to make more and more profit. So that's why in a way the argument may never be won, because there will be those who throw in their lot with power. There are those who have a comfortable relationship with power, and those who have an adversarial relationship with power. There are those who want dominance at the cost of justice, and there are those who want justice. So that's why there has to be a struggle. And we're not going to win that struggle without paying a price. It's going to be a hard fight.

Naomi Klein has said you come up with "these killer one-liners." Indeed, you're masterful in terms of your craft and your artistic and poetic command of language. The God of Small Things, *the novel that won the Booker Prize, which has now sold seven million copies and been translated into forty languages, is an example of that. I think it would it would be nice to close this evening with a reading from* The God of Small Things *from the goddess of large things, Arundhati Roy.*

I would love to read for a few minutes, but I just want to say that eventually what we are all fighting for is not some new ideology, ironclad, to replace an old one, but a different way of looking at the world. And for that, literature and music and painting are so important.

I'm going to read to you a part in *The God of Small Things* where everybody has a problem with classification, which is a problem that I frequently have.

> From the dining-room window where she stood, with the wind in her hair, Rahel could see the rain drum down on the rusted tin roof of what used to be their grandmother's pickle factory.
>
> Paradise Pickles & Preserves.
>
> It lay between the house and the river.
>
> They used to make pickles, squashes, jams, curry powders and canned pineapples. And banana jam (illegally) after the FPO (Food Products Organization) banned it because according to their specifications it was neither jam nor jelly.

Too thin for jelly and too thick for jam. An ambiguous, unclassifiable consistency, they said.

As per their books.

Looking back now, to Rahel it seemed as though this difficulty that their family had with classification ran much deeper than the jam-jelly question.

Perhaps Ammu, Estha, and she were the worst transgressors. But it wasn't just them. It was the others too. They all broke the rules. They all crossed into forbidden territory. They all tampered with the laws that lay down who should be loved and how. And how much. The laws that make grandmothers grandmothers, uncles uncles, mothers mothers, cousins cousins, jam jam, and jelly jelly.

It was a time when uncles became fathers, mothers lovers, and cousins died and had funerals.

It was a time when the unthinkable became thinkable and the impossible really happened.

Even before Sophie Mol's funeral, the police found Velutha.

His arms had goosebumps where the handcuffs touched his skin. Cold handcuffs with a sourmetal smell. Like steel bus rails and the smell of the bus conductor's hands from holding them.

After it was all over, Baby Kochamma said, "As ye sow, so shall ye reap." As though she had had nothing to do with the Sowing and the Reaping. She returned on her small feet to her cross-stitch embroidery. Her little toes never touched the floor. It was her idea that Estha be Returned.

Margaret Kochamma's grief and bitterness at her daughter's death coiled inside her like an angry spring. She said nothing, but slapped Estha whenever she could in the days she was there before she returned to England.

Rahel watched Ammu pack Estha's little trunk.

"Maybe they're right," Ammu's whisper said. "Maybe a boy does need a Baba." Rahel saw that her eyes were a redly dead.

They consulted a Twin Expert in Hyderabad. She wrote back to say that it was not advisable to separate monozygotic twins, but that two-egg twins were no different from ordinary siblings and that while they would certainly suffer the natural distress that children from broken homes underwent, it would be nothing more than that.

Nothing out of the ordinary.

And so Estha was Returned in a train with his tin trunk and his beige and pointy shoes rolled into his khaki holdall. First class, overnight on the Madras Mail to Madras and then with a friend of their father's from Madras to Kolkata.

He had a tiffin carrier with tomato sandwiches. And an Eagle flask with an eagle. He had terrible pictures in his head.

Rain. Rushing, inky water. And a smell. Sicksweet. Like old roses on a breeze.

But worst of all, he carried inside him the memory of a young man with an old man's mouth. The memory of a swollen face and a smashed, upside-down smile. Of a spreading pool of clear liquid with a bare bulb reflected in it. Of a bloodshot eye that had opened, wandered, and then fixed its gaze on him. Estha. And what had Estha done? He had looked into that beloved face and said: Yes.

Yes, it was him. . . .

In a purely practical sense it would probably be correct to say that it all began when Sophie Mol came to Ayemenem. Perhaps it's true that things can change in a day. That a few dozen hours can affect the outcome of whole lifetimes. And that when they do, those few dozen hours, like the salvaged remains of a burned house—the charred clock, the singed photograph, the scorched furniture—must be resurrected from the ruins and examined. Preserved. Accounted for.

Little events, ordinary things, smashed and reconstituted. Imbued with new meaning. Suddenly they become the bleached bones of a story.

Still, to say that it all began when Sophie Mol came to Ayemenem is only one way of looking at it.

Equally, it could be argued that it actually began thousands of years ago. Long before the Marxists came. Before the British took Malabar, before the Dutch Ascendency, before Vasco da Gama arrived, before the Zamorin's conquest of Calicut. Before three purple-robed Syrian bishops murdered by the Portuguese were found floating in the sea, with coiled sea serpents riding on their chests and oysters knotted in their tangled beards. It could be argued that it began long before Christianity arrived in a boat and seeped into Kerala like tea from a teabag.

That it really began in the days when the Love Laws were made. The laws that lay down who should be loved, and how. And how much.

CHAPTER 7

Brave New India: Uprisings

All nations have ideas about themselves that are repeated without much scrutiny or examination: the United States, "a beacon of freedom and liberty"; India, "the world's largest democracy" and dedicated to secularism.

India has done a better job than the United States in recent years. The myth about the United States being a beacon of liberty has been more or less discredited among people who are even vaguely informed. India, on the other hand, has managed to pull off almost a miraculous public relations coup. It really is the flavor of the decade. It's the sort of dream destination for world capital. All this done in the name of "India is not Afghanistan," "India is not Pakistan," "India is a secular democracy," and so on.

India has among the highest number of custodial deaths in the world. It's a country where perhaps one-fourth of its territory is out of control of the government. But where the light is shone is where the Sensex stock market is jumping and investments are coming in. And where the lights are switched off are the states where farmers are committing suicide and Kashmir, where tens of thousands have been killed, whether it's Chhattisgarh, whether it's parts of Andhra Pradesh. And while there are killings going on, say, in Chhattisgarh, the media's attention is on a festival in Tamil Nādu or a cricket match between India and Australia in Adelaide.

This interview was conducted in New Delhi, India, on December 29, 2007.

We are at the cusp where the definition of terrorism is being expanded. Under the Bharatiya Janata Party—the radical Hindu government previously in power—much of the emphasis was on Islamic terrorism. But now Islamic terrorism is not enough to net people the government wants. Now, with the massive displacement from huge development projects and special economic zones, the people protesting those have to be called terrorists, too. They can't be Islamic terrorists, so now we have the Maoists.

The militancy in Kashmir and the expansion of the Maoist cadres are both realities, but ones that both sides benefit from exaggerating. When Prime Minister Manmohan Singh says Maoism is the greatest internal security threat, it allows various state governments to pass all kinds of laws that could name anybody a terrorist. If they came into my house tomorrow, just the books I have would make me qualify as a terrorist. In Chhattisgarh, if I had these books and if I weren't Arundhati Roy, I could be put into jail. The very well-known doctor Binayak Sen has just been arrested on charges of being a Maoist. He's being made an example of to discourage people from having any association with people resisting this absolutely lawless takeover of land. Thousands and thousands of acres are being handed over to corporates. So now we're sort of on the cusp of expanding the definition of terrorist so that people who disagree with this mode of development can be imprisoned—and are being imprisoned.

Until recently, even after the 1990s, when the neoliberal model was imported into India, we were still talking about the privatization of water and electricity, the devastation of the rivers. But when you look at privatization of water and electricity, companies had to find their markets here, even if it was for the Indian elite, while making water and electricity too expensive for everyone else. But with the opening up of the mineral sector and the discovery of huge deposits of bauxite and iron ore in Odisha and Chhattisgarh, for example, we are watching these places change. Now you don't have to find a local market. You just take the whole mountain of bauxite, store it in the desert in Australia, and trade bauxite on the futures market.

So the corporates are here, and their guns are trained on these minerals. If you look at a map of India, you will see that where there are forests, there are Adivasis, tribal people. And under the forests are minerals. So the most ecologically and socially vulnerable parts of India that are now in the crosshairs. The Tatas, who until just a few years ago were trying to be the sort of "good uncle" corporation, have now decided to aggressively enter the world market. They signed a memorandum of understanding with the Chhattisgarh government for the mining of iron ore. And within days, not by coincidence, we saw the announcement of what's known as the Salwa Judum, a people's militia, which purportedly is a spontaneous movement that sprang up to fight the menace of the Maoists. Salwa Judum is armed by the government. Something like four hundred villages have been evacuated and moved into police camps. Chhattisgarh is in a situation of sort of civil war, which is exactly what happened in Colombia. And while our eyes are on this supposed civil war, obviously the mining, the minerals, everything can be just taken away.

Odisha has bauxite mountains, which are beautiful and densely forested, with flat tops, like air fields. They are porous mountains, which store water for the fields in the plains. And whole mountains have just been taken away by private corporations, destroying the forests, displacing the tribals, and devastating the land.

It's hard to know what to say or how to think about it anymore. We are all well versed in Noam Chomsky's thesis of the manufacture of consent, but here we're living in the era of the manufacture of dissent. For example, the way the bauxite business works is that the corporates pay the Odisha government a tiny royalty, and they are making billions. And with those billions they mop up all the intellectuals and environmentalists. Alcan has given a million-dollar environmental award to one of the leading environmental activists in India. There's Vedanta

University in Odisha. The Tatas have the Jamsetji and the Dorabji Tata Trusts, which they use to fund activists, to stage cultural events, and so on.

So these people are funding the dissent as well as the devastation. The dissent is on a leash. It's a manufactured situation in which everyone is playing out a kind of theater.

Clearly, the state must be enabling these kinds of situations to continue.

This is the genius of the Indian state. It's an extremely sophisticated state. It has a lot to teach the Americans about occupation. It has a lot to teach the world about how you manage dissent. You just wear people down and wait things out. When they want to mow people down, when they want to kill and imprison, they do that, too. Who doesn't believe that India is a spiritual country where everybody thinks that if it's not okay in this life, it will be okay in the next one? Yet it is one of the most devastatingly cruel societies. Which other culture could dream up the caste system? Even the Taliban can't come up with the way Indian civilization has created Dalits.

Explain who Dalits are.

Dalits are the so-called untouchables of India.

They're on the bottom of the economic, social ladder.

They're on the bottom of *everything*. They are routinely bludgeoned, butchered, killed. I don't know whether it made it to the American press, but, for example, Dalits, because they have been at the bottom of Hindu society, often have converted and become Muslims, Christians, or Sikhs. But they continue to be treated as untouchables even in those religions. It's so pervasive.

There was recently a man called Bant Singh, who is a Sikh Dalit. Even in India people would jump at the idea of there being such a thing as a Sikh Dalit. But, actually, 30 percent of Sikhs are Dalits and about 90 percent of them are landless. Because they are landless, obviously they work as labor on other people's farms. Their women are very vulnerable. Upper castes all over India think that they have the right to pick up a Dalit woman and have sex with her or rape her. Bant Singh's young daughter was raped by the upper-caste people in his village. Bant Singh was a member of the Communist Party of India (Marxist-Leninist), known as Naxal-ites, and he filed a case in court. They warned him. They said, "If you don't drop the case, we will kill you." He didn't drop the case, so they caught him, and they cut off his arms and his legs.

He was in hospital in Delhi. I went to see him there. It was a lesson to me about how being a political person saved him. He said, "Do you think I don't have arms and legs? I do. Because all my comrades are my arms and legs."

He's a singer, so he sang a song which is about a young girl's father getting her dowry ready for her just before her marriage, her trousseau. And she says to him, "I don't want this sari and these jewels. What will I do with them? Just give me a gun." Unfortu-nately, I think because of what happened with the Narmada move-ment—the fact that people fought for fifteen years using nonvio-lent methods and were just flicked aside like chaff—you hear more and more people saying, "I don't want the bangles, I don't want Gandhi. Just give me a gun."

You once described Narmada Bachao Andolan as the greatest nonvi-olent movement since independence.

I did. But I think people, including myself, are very disillu-sioned by what happened. And I personally feel that we really need to do a sort of postmortem. The state did what's in its nature—and it has won that battle. The Supreme Court in 2001 was a devastat-ing blow, but in my opinion that should have been the time when people began to question institutions. Instead, people have gone on and on and on, trying to find some embers of hope in the court, and have not broken the faith. I have broken the faith. I don't look to the court for any kind of real help, which is not to say that every single court judgment that comes out is terrible, but there is a systemic problem with the Supreme Court of India, its views, its ideologies. This is a huge subject separate—and one of the most important things that needs to be discussed.

But the Narmada movement now refuses to question itself. I think that's a problem. It was a wonderful and a magnificent effort, but it wasn't faultless. Unless we try and think through what happened, and what went wrong, we can't move on. In fact, as I said, many people have felt that there is a futility in these kind of fasts and *dharnas*, sit-ins, and sitting on the pavement singing songs. In fact, to some extent, the government loves that. Now Sonia Gandhi is talking about satyāgraha. We have satyāgraha fairs in Connaught Place where they sell herbal shampoos. When the government starts promoting satyāgraha, it's time for us to think about it.

I think it's time to question radically many things, including what this joyful freedom movement of 1947 was about, who it benefited, and if it was really a middle-class revolution that, as usual, fired its guns off the shoulders of the poor, which I think it was. The Indian elites stepped very easily into the shoes of our white sahibs.

Talk about Narendra Modi and Gujarat. In December 2007, he and his party are reelected. It was Modi in 2002 who presided over a pogrom resulting in the death of two thousand people, primarily Muslims, in Gujarat. What accounts for his ability to be reelected despite this record of promoting communal violence?

No, it's not *despite*, it's *because*. Muslims were massacred on the streets, women were gang-raped, 150,000 Muslims were driven from their homes and now live in ghetto conditions, economically and socially ostracized in Gujarat. This was all an election campaign. So I think we really need to question, structurally, what is this democracy? It's pointless to demonize Modi, because there are going to be people like Modi who understand that there is an organic link between democracy and majoritarianism—and between majoritarianism and fascism.

As I keep saying, there is fire in the ducts. What is a politician spawned by this complex society going to do? He's going to try to forge a majority for himself using the lowest common denominator, which will then be a sort of faithful vote bank. That's what Modi did. Modi is a brilliant politician, and he has the corporates eating out of his hand. So the connection between the fascists and the big corporations we saw in Nazi Germany is once again at play. Tata, Reliance, all these people say Gujarat is the dream destination for capital.

Having a fascist dictator is one thing, but having a fascist democrat elected to power, fattened on the approbation of millions of people, is a different thing. Because we have now millions of little Modis running around in Gujarat. Recently, just before the elections, *Tehelka* news magazine did a sting operation. On a major prime-time channel, people spoke very openly about how they had raped and then pulped Muslim women, and hacked people to death, and then Modi had given them refuge or sent them out of Gujarat to protect them.

This was all well documented.

These guys say it themselves. All the documentation exists in great detail from human rights groups such as the People's Union for Democratic Rights and Communalism Combat. But when the evidence was aired on television, everybody's reaction was, "What terrible timing. Now Modi is going to win the elections." Because these people are boasting about this kind of massacre. It's going to win him votes. So that's what I meant by saying it's not despite, it's because of.

Having said that, it is important to note that Modi in many constituencies just won by three hundred, five hundred, or one thousand votes. It was close.

Still, if you look at how democracy has begun to function in India, I really find it chilling. Consider what happened to a member of the legislative assembly, Ehsan Jafari, a poet, who lived in Ahmedabad in a housing society called Gulbarga. When the mobs began to gather during the Gujarat massacre, a group of Muslims sought protection from Jafari, thinking he's an MLA and he's not going to get killed. A mob of some twenty thousand people gathered and started baying for his blood. This man made more than a hundred phone calls that day—from Modi, to the home minister, Advani, to the police, to Sonia Gandhi—saying, "Please help." The police even came to his home, and went away. Ehsan Jafari was pulled out of his house, and in front of everyone, in broad daylight, was hacked into pieces. Something like twelve women were gang-raped and killed, and others were burned alive. And the policeman who was there was promoted. The man who was organizing this now became the police commissioner of Gujarat. The lawyers who were representing the Muslims had been the lawyers for the accused. Some of the survivors knew who the killers were. The police refused to write their names in the First Information Reports, stating that it was general mob violence.

The Supreme Court made some very virtuous sounds at that time, saying Modi was like a "modern-day Nero," fiddling while Gujarat burned. And then they just clammed up. Nothing happened. And then you have these men come out and boast on prime-time TV of having raped and killed and looted, saying things like, "We know that these Muslims are terrified of being burned. They would need to be buried. That's why we decided to burn them." And nothing happened.

So everything just goes on, every single institution has been penetrated by these people and functions, as long as you are open for investments, as long as all the Tatas and Reliance and all the rich people are happy. We're looking at something that no dictator could do. This level of penetration of all these various institutions drives you completely crazy. You sit there, and you just don't know what to think. And even the political parties like, say, the Communist Party of India, that opposes Modi, then goes and does a Nandigram.

Nandigram is in West Bengal, a state that is ruled by the Communist Party. You went to Nandigram. Can you explain what happened?

Nandigram is a district that consists of many, many villages. The Communist Party of India (Marxist), which is in coalition with the center right now, has been in power in West Bengal for thirty years—unchallenged. I grew up in Kerala, which also has had a Communist government, but it's been in and out of power. When I went to Bengal, I realized the first question one has to ask is: How, in this tumultuous place, can a party remain in power for thirty years unchallenged? There is something terribly wrong there.

It's difficult, but I'll try and explain it simply, because this has led to a lot of confusion. Except in Bengal and to some extent in Kerala, the CPI(M) does not have any cadres anywhere else in India, so it was consciously trying to sort of associate itself with various people's movements that have existed in India for many years and the World Social Forum in India.

The forum was held in Mumbai in 2005.

But very many people who were associated with the CPI(M) were involved in the forums that were held in Porto Alegre, Brazil.

And then a year and a half or two years ago, the Indian government announced this whole policy of Special Economic Zones, or SEZs, an acronym that has spawned many sarcastic variants, such as Slavery Enabled Zones. These SEZs are huge economic enclaves. India used to be a feudal society, with huge feudal zamindars.

Big landowners.

And then there was a failed process of land reform in various states. The state where the most successful land reforms happened, oddly enough, was Kashmir. Kashmiris are still enjoying the benefits of that. But there were some land reforms in places like Bengal and elsewhere. But now this whole business of SEZs is essentially reversing that process by taking away land to give it to big corporations like Reliance and Tata.

The CPI(M) went from vociferously opposing SEZs to suddenly turning around to create one of the biggest SEZs in West Bengal, which is to be this chemical hub in the district of Nandigram. Nandigram is right near Haldia port, and an Indonesian corporation called the Salim Group was its sort of front.

Trouble started in West Bengal first with the Tatas in a place called Singur, where the government gave the Tatas something close to one thousand hectares of land to make small cars. You can imagine the Communist government wanting to make small cars, the people's car. You know who else made the people's car. . . . So there was a huge resistance. There was open fire. People were killed in Singur.

But then notices went out for land acquisition for this chemical hub in Nandigram—something like eighteen thousand hectares. Thousands and thousands of people were going to be affected. And Nandigram just rose up in revolt. It was interesting, because Nandigram used to be a CPI(M) stronghold. I think this was a case of a party being so unused to any kind of opposition that it just misread the situation and thought it could do exactly what it wanted. It resulted in basically the party having what the people in Nandigram call the cadre police, which is party people dressed in police uniforms going in and committing acts of violence and even murder.

The first uprising was in March. It's a whole mess with all kinds of politics, but it was a fantastic resistance. People dug up the roads, refused the police entry, and said, "You can't come in, and you can't have our land."

I'll just tell you what happened when I was there. The government keeps saying that because the people barricaded Nandigram, "They're not allowing us in to do development work. We can't give polio drops." There is not a single health center in all those villages. The nearest hospital is in Nandigram town, which is very, very far for people to go. All these years, people lacked electricity. And suddenly you're talking about polio drops. Really this is about regaining complete control.

The second time I went, which was just last week, the people I met the first time sent messages saying, "Please don't come to us. Please don't acknowledge us, because we'll just be eliminated." Anyone who pops their head up, it's off with their heads. Just a few days ago, I was present at the exhumation of a body in a field, a man whose legs were smashed and who had two bullets in his back. His wife had identified the body. The neighbor said to me that the man was a member of the Bhoomi Uchhed Pratirodh Committee, which is the resistance organization, and had been told several times that he must join the CPI(M). Otherwise he would be killed. And when he didn't, they made an example of him.

The CPI(M) government keeps saying, "Oh, it was the Maoists. It wasn't the local people. It was outsiders." How dare a Communist party say this is the work of "outsiders." What do they mean by outsiders? Beyond the district or outside Bengal? If they believe in that kind of rhetoric, what gives them the right to comment about Gujarat or fascism or the BJP or anything?

I really salute the resistance in Nandigram. I think it is so important for everyone else in India that they force the government to say they will not build the hub.

Kashmir is an area of conflict, but it's largely unreported, particularly in the United States. The little information that is available is usually that conflict is about Islamic extremists and terrorists. Now, since September 11, they're labeled as Taliban and Al-Qaeda. You have been going to Kashmir. What have you learned?

Kashmir is one of those places where every time I hear people say, "Oh, it's more complicated than that," I get a rash. All you need to do is to get out of the airport to see the reality of the occupation. To fight a full-blown war in Iraq, the US military had 135,000 troops. In Kashmir, you have something like 700,000 security personnel of different kinds—the army, the police, the paramilitary, the counterinsurgency. Certainly the situation has been made complicated by spies and double agents and informers and money being poured in by intelligence agencies from India and Pakistan. But the bottom line is that it is the Indian government that is seeking to subvert the people's will.

Why is India so frightened of a referendum in Kashmir? What is it that so frightens the Indian government that they do not wish to assess what the people really want? And how can you talk about holding democratic, free, and fair elections in a place where a person isn't even allowed to breathe without an AK-47 being stuck up his nostril?

The situation in Kashmir has been complicated by the instrument of accession, genuine or not.

The transfer from the princely state of Jammu and Kashmir to the Indian union in 1947.

Right. What is it that the people want now? If we are going to be talking about democracy as being the foundation, the keystone of democracy being the will of the people, everybody seems to feel that they can speak on behalf of the will of the people, but nobody wants to ascertain what is the will of the people.

I don't think that we're going to have an idealistic solution to the problem of Kashmir. India is never going to give up anything. Right now, it's stronger than it ever was. So how that fight, how that battle is joined, still remains to be seen. But it's clear that after having almost lost a whole generation of young people, the Kashmiris are nowhere close to saying, "We give up." Of course, there is an elite that's been co-opted and is being made to feel like its stakes in peace are huge. But I think India is as far away from a solution to Kashmir as the United States is from a solution to Iraq or Afghanistan.

The Jammu Kashmir Coalition of Civil Society has published numerous reports about human rights violations, disappearances, torture, molestation and rapes of women, and extrajudicial executions. What kind of attention has this attracted in civil society in the rest of India?

Almost none.

Because?

Because this whole rhetoric of Muslim terrorism is very deep. You see trucks going past that on the back say, "*Doodh mango to kheer deingay, Kashmir mango to cheer deingay.*" It means, "Ask for milk and we'll give you cream." Meaning: ask for Kashmir and we'll disembowel you. Every part of the state machinery, including the press, fully believes the propaganda.

At least Kashmiris have the hope, even if it's never realized, of freedom inside them. At least they have the dignity that they are doing battle. Kashmir is in some ways an old-world, classical battle for freedom, like Algeria. But what do you do for the people in Chhattisgarh or the Muslims in Gujarat? Where are they going to go?

I experienced one of the most beautiful moments of my life recently in Kerala. I heard that four thousand Dalit and Adivasi families had captured a corporate rubber estate, about two hours away from where my mother lives. So I went there. It was amazing to me to see, in the place that I had grown up, a kind of nation rise up before me of people who are just disappeared by our society. It was the opposite of Nandigram, where the corporates are grabbing people's land. Here the people are grabbing corporate land. Each of them has a little blue plastic sheet that they've made into a hut under a rubber tree. They've been there for something like three hundred days. There are twenty thousand people, women and children, and each of them says that they have a five-liter can of petrol in their house. "If the police come, we are just going to immolate ourselves, because we have nowhere else to go."

They said, "Look, this corporation has thirty-three estates. It has some fifty-five thousand to sixty thousand hectares of land. I have nowhere to sleep. I'm taking it." And I thought to myself, I write. I've got all these figures and footnotes and statistics. Am I turning into a clerk? Is this the way I want to fight? Because eventually who is one trying to convince? The people who read these things are never going to give up what they have. They have to be forced to.

That is the battle that's coming here in India. The government is spawning these private militias. In Chhattisgarh, you have the Salwa Judum. In Gujarat, you have the Bajrang Dal. In West Bengal, you have the CPI(M) cadre police. In Odisha, the corporates have their own thugs. And never mind that they are not even talking about what's happening in the northeast of India, an ongoing situation since 1947, which is worse than Kashmir.

For myself, I think it's very important for us to continue to question ourselves and what we do and our role. Today in India, it's very easy for everybody to keep saying the Maoists are terrible, the government is also terrible, all violence is bad. One is the other side of the coin from the other, these platitudes. Unless I'm prepared to take up arms, I'm not in a position to tell others to take up arms. Unless I'm in a position where I'm at the other end of this battering ram, I'm also not going to sit around saying, "Let's go on a hunger strike" and "Let's go and sing songs outside the Ministry of Water Resources." I'm through with all that.

At the World Tribunal on Iraq in Istanbul in June 2005, you made some comments about resistance and the right of resistance that raised a few eyebrows. Have your views on that changed since then?

My views on that have not changed since then. Maybe they've evolved. I think that it's very important for us to understand that people are being decimated every day. I was one of the people who said that the globalization of dissent was the way to fight the globalization of corporate capital. But that was the era of the World Social Forum. I think things have changed since then. The World Social Forum has been taken over. What has happened is a kind of corporatization of dissent. And the globalization of dissent then ends up creating hierarchies, where you pick and choose your genocide—or you pick and choose the worst thing that's happening.

Is what's happening in Nandigram worse than what happened in the Congo? Of course it's not. Everything gets slotted in to some schema, and people get disempowered locally.

Everyone is looking for recommendations from the superstars of resistance. Even someone like me. I'm always being asked to say something about things I don't know enough about. I feel that it's very important not to disempower people who are fighting—and not to tell them how to fight. For example, in India it's come to a stage where the only thing that people can do is to really do what the people in Nandigram did: dig the roads up and say, "You can't come in." Because the minute they go in, the minute they start taking over, they co-opt, they pick off the leaders, they buy off someone. There is a certain amount of brutality now that even resistance has to have, because the co-optation is amazing, the NGO-ization is amazing.

I'll tell you a very interesting story. I put a lot of the royalties from my work into a trust. A few of us, friends, activists, run it. The only money that comes into the trust is the money from my writing and so on. It's not about trying to raise money, just trying to give it out in solidarity with people. It's called Zindabad, which means "long live." We received a letter recently from the Tata Institute of Social Sciences, which disburses funds to various activists and movements from the Tata trusts. The letter says, "Dear Zindabad Trust, The tribals of Madhya Pradesh are grateful to the Tatas for having supported their struggles for rights and livelihood. And now, in order to expand their base, they want to have a seminar in the India International Centre to which judges and bureaucrats and activists and Adivasis will be invited." And there is a budget in which, obviously, the bureaucrats' and judges' travel allowances are huge and the Adivasis' and activists' are very small. And there is a list of the activists and Adivasis, all of whom are funded by the Tatas. They are asking us to fund that seminar. It's like opening a frog on a dissecting table. You see how the world works. And I said, let's write to them and say we basically can't afford to fund the seminar, but why not call the survivors of the people that were shot in Kalinganagar and Singur for Tata projects to put their views across and disseminate them?

In the last couple of years, India has an expanding military relationship with the United States and Israel. What are the implications of that?

After being part of the nonaligned movement, India is now part of the completely aligned movement. The government of India never tires of saying that Israel and the United States are its natural allies. So the nuclear deal, joint military exercises, the US–India Knowledge Exchange are all ways of tying itself intricately to America by people who have no idea about the history of America's nonwhite allies.

Before the coup in Chile, the Americans had a whole posse of young Chilean students taken to the University of Chicago to study under Milton Friedman and learn free-market economic orthodoxy. In India, they don't even have to trouble themselves to do this. The Indian elite are just wagging their tails and lining up. The most successful secessionist movement in India has been the secession of India's elite into this transnational class. Almost every bureaucrat, every politician, every senior member of the judiciary, of industry, of the business class, of academia, has a very close relative, as in a son or a daughter or a brother, in the United States. We are organically tied and linked.

Manmohan Singh, the Indian prime minister, has never won an election in his life, and has no imagination outside that of the IMF and the World Bank. He doesn't sound to me like he's ever read a primary textbook on history. He's probably the only prime minister in the history of the world of a former colony that has gone to Oxford University and thanked colonialism for democracy and the British for every institution of state repression that India has today—the colonial police, the bureaucracy, everything. So it is a country that's run on the lines of a colonial state, equally extractive, except that the colonizers are the upper caste.

This is something Frantz Fanon wrote about in The Wretched of the Earth, *that the old colonial masters would be replaced by their native equivalents.*

Absolutely. It's just like a comic book over here.

I remember your saying "it is a dangerous time to be a tall poppy." One such tall poppy was Hrant Dink, an Armenian Turkish journalist who was murdered by a Turkish nationalist in the streets of Istanbul in January 2007. You've been asked to speak on the occasion of the anniversary of his killing. I know you're bombarded with requests from all over the world. What factors go into your decision? Why go to Istanbul?

I think Turkey is fascinating. It's so similar to India in terms of its aggressive secular elite, its religious fundamentalism, its ugly nationalism. I think it's far less subtle in some ways. It needs to take some lessons from the Brahmins.

How do you survive as a writer in a society like this? This topic fascinates me.

Recently in India, when the whole Nandigram issue erupted, one of the clever things that the CPI(M) did was to conjure up a protest against Taslima Nasrin, whose book *Dwikhondito* had been published four years before. It was on bestseller lists, but no one had anything to say about it at the time.

The Bangladeshi novelist.

She was sort of thrown out of Bangladesh and moved to Kolkata. The first people to ask for a ban were the CPI(M). Then the high court lifted the ban. The book was published. Nothing happened. And then just at the time when massive protests erupted against the CPI(M) for the first time in thirty years—because of Nandigram, where the bulk of the peasants to be displaced were Muslims—suddenly they are saying, "Taslima Nasrin insults Islam" and "Get her out of here."

So how do you function in societies like Turkey and India as a writer? How do you continue to say the things you say? How do you try your best not to get killed? How do you understand that the countries that speak loudest and longest and have the most complex legislation about free speech, such as the United States, don't have free speech but have managed to hypnotize people into thinking that they do. All these things interest me.

Obviously, the denial of the Armenian genocide is so blatant. Why does Turkey deny it? Is it an admission that it's such a horrendous thing that you need to deny it? Is denial the best form of acceptance? That you can't bear to think that there was such a thing in your past?

Maybe it has some analogy with the Indian government's stand vis-à-vis Kashmir.

I don't think it is an analogy, because the government is quite proud of what it does in Kashmir. I don't think we've come to the stage where the government feels bad about it.

I mean in terms of denying history and denying self-determination.

The government is not denying its cruelties in Kashmir. The press doesn't report much and doesn't know much, but are proudly parading how we are dealing with the terrorists, even among people in India. There is a proud owning up to that killing in Gujarat: "This is what these Muslims deserve." So it's quite interesting, the psyche of these things. When you deny something, inherently that denial is the acceptance that it's a terrible thing, which is why you're denying it. But in Gujarat it's not thought of as a terrible thing right now. It's thought of as a great thing.

You continue writing your political essays. What about fiction? Have you returned to it?

I'm trying to. As I said, I don't really want to continue to do the same thing all the time. And I feel a bit of a prisoner in the footnotes department right now. One is constantly being co-opted. I could be forever on mainstream TV in India debating people and putting across my point of view, but eventually you're just adding to the noise. That is part of the racket here right now, this wonderful, messy, noisy, argumentative, cutesy stuff that's going on.

I'm not denying the fact that we need very incisive nonfiction, but personally, as a writer, I feel that much of my writing has been for myself, to understand something. And now, if I were to write, it would be a reiteration of my understanding. I want to do something with that understanding rather than just collating it. For me, fiction is that place. I want to surprise myself. I want to see what comes out without knowing in advance.

What was that comment you made about fiction and truth?
That fiction is the truest thing there ever was.

CHAPTER 8

Terrorism: No Easy Answers

You've been spending time in Kashmir. There has been a series of elections over the last couple of months that have been heralded, at least by the mainstream press in India, as a great referendum for freedom and democracy and a rebuke for the separatists. What is your understanding of what happened?

The thing I worry most about is losing the language with which to describe what's happening in Kashmir. It's almost as though you need a deep knowledge of what's going on in Kashmir to understand the elections. In August, even then I was there, there was an incredible spontaneous uprising, with hundreds of thousands of people on the streets. This time I was there in the silence, and still I could hear that noise in my head, *"Azadi, azadi, azadi!"* The fruit sellers were weighing their fruit, chanting, *"Azadi, azadi!"* The people on the buses, the children on the streets. It was as if the sky was chanting that.

Azadi means freedom.

Azadi means freedom. Azadi means a lot of things, including freedom in a very nuanced way, because that in itself is a very contested term in Kashmir. And then that nonviolent uprising was actually presented to the "leaders" of the separatist movement by the people. It wasn't that the leaders led the movement, but the

---

This interview was conducted in New Delhi, India, on January 1, 2009.

people came, dusted off the mothballs, pulled the leaders out onto the street, and presented them with a kind of revolution.

The Indian government's response to this was the harshest curfew ever imposed in Kashmir. Days and days and days together. Razor wire, steel walls. People were prevented from moving between districts and villages. Many Kashmiris were killed. There are between 500,000 and 700,000 Indian security personnel in the valley of Kashmir. They are spread out and are patrolling all the time. So, to put down this uprising wasn't hard for them in a military sense.

That was August. Then there was a big debate about whether or not to call elections because everybody feared there would be a complete boycott of the elections, which have been more or less boycotted in the past. The separatists called for a boycott. And to everybody's shock and surprise, there was a huge turnout in the elections. Nobody could understand exactly what had happened. Where had that sentiment gone? Where was that outburst of a desire for freedom that was being expressed from the street? How did it suddenly disappear?

The way in which the election was called was very interesting. A couple of districts in Jammu are Hindu-dominated. The Bharatiya Janata Party has never been in power there, but still there was a sort of political divide between these districts in Jammu and the Kashmir valley. Then there is Ladakh, Doda, and Kishtwar. And there are some parts of the Kashmir valley that are under the boot of the army.

If you travel in Kashmir, you see that there the army controls the inhalation and the exhalation. It controls everything. The way the elections were called was pretty brilliant, if you look at it from the Indian government's point of view. These places where traditionally the army's fiat rules went to the polls first. Without wanting to get into too much detail for an audience that's not familiar with this, the point is that there was a big turnout. Except in the cities. The turnout was low in almost all the cities and towns, but the turnout was very high in the villages.

I went back to Kashmir just now just to understand for myself what it was all about. The last stage of the polling in Srinagar was due to happen, and so the police put me under house arrest, which revealed more than it hid. They're so frightened of anybody who has a point of view different from that of the Indian state seeing anything. Before the polls happened, they conducted a massive round of arrests. They arrested not just the leaders of the Hurriyat separatist group, but all the workers, activists, and young people who were seen to have led these protests. Hundreds of people were put into jail.

Many liberal Indians say that the polls were free and fair. The first question you have to ask is: When you have that kind of a densely deployed army, can you have free and fair elections? Is it possible? Election observers and liberal Indians went to Kashmir, and they didn't see people being pushed to the polling booths at the end of a bayonet, so they said there was no coercion. But the people of Kashmir have internalized what it means to live under an occupation and how to deal with it. And they do have a long-term view because they have to survive. One of the things that happened was that the main party, the National Conference, which is now coming into power, campaigned very openly, saying that these elections have nothing to do with azadi. They're just about bread and butter issues.

Sarak, pani, and—what was the slogan?

Sarak, pani, bijli. It means roads, water, and electricity. I think that quite explains the fact that in urban areas, where they are more secure, people didn't feel the need to vote, whereas in rural areas, it's not actually sarak, pani, and bijli so much as a thin layer of protection from the occupation. For example, when the dreaded Special Operations Group picks up somebody, you need somebody to appeal to. And that somebody is the politician. So, for example, people were telling me there is one particular member of the legislative assembly who keeps getting voted back to power. Just before the elections, his modus operandi is to have the army to pick up five or six young men from that area. Then the people go and petition him. Then he gets them released, and earns their eternal gratitude. These are all sort of invisible things that happen.

There are many other reasons. For example, just now the stories are emerging that in this election, more than in any other election, there were hundreds of candidates who were fielded. Each of them, in a slightly feudal area, has a certain number of relatives and friends who vote for them. Because the main thing in these elections was that the government was very keen to encourage turnout, regardless of what happened, to show that this is a democracy. In fact, the day I left Kashmir, all these defeated independent candidates were having a press conference in a restaurant called Ahdoo's, talking about how they had all been offered money by the Intelligence Bureau to stand for election, and then some of them weren't paid, so now they are disgruntled.

There are other issues. For example, there is this group of renegades known as Ikhwanis, former militants who turned into very dreaded killers working for the government. Some Ikhwanis and sometimes their sons stood for election. And people went out to vote against them.

So there are a number of factors. But people did come out and vote. The way I see it is that people realize that they're lying on a bed of nails, and the elections are like a thin layer of sponge over the bed of nails, a way of getting by, a way of continuing to live. They are not in any way going to permanently solve the problem of Kashmir. What the Indian government has done over and over again is crisis management. Sweep things under the carpet, and then hope that it will go away. Then it resurfaces in a different form. I was in Kashmir when the sort of "free and fair" press of the mighty government of India arrived to gloat over these elections— people who knew nothing about Kashmir, who were coming there to give commentary, saying the most absurd things about how this was the end of the freedom movement.

To me, the saddest thing was that Kashmiris I spoke to, without exception, said, "We've done this to ourselves." And

I felt that this sort of psychological war on them—this lowering of their self-esteem, forcing them to participate in tactics of survival, which eventually make them despise themselves—was really the deepest form of colonialism. Someone said, "We feel like Shias at Muharram. We whip ourselves and draw our own blood, and then the Indian propaganda machine puts salt in our wounds."

It's very difficult to understand the full extent of this, but what people really want is being thwarted again and again and again. Everybody is speaking on behalf of the people. As a citizen of India, I feel uncomfortable with that. I feel that we can't gloat about doing this to somebody. Of course, India will always be able to manage it because it's a small valley. But, then again, I don't think this will always be possible. The price of holding down the Kashmir valley, which was being paid mostly by Indian soldiers, who are mostly poor people from India who don't count, is suddenly being paid by the Indian elite in five-star hotels in Bombay. That puts a totally different spin on things.

You write that "[t]he Indian military occupation of Kashmir makes monsters of us all." What do you mean by that?

It makes us complicit in the holding down of a people by military force. It makes us complicit in the propaganda. It makes us complicit in the lies. And eventually it makes us people who are unable to look things in the eye.

If you were to question the average Indian, the only thing they know is that there are terrorists in Kashmir. They wouldn't be able to tell you that sixty or seventy thousand people have died in this war. They wouldn't be able to tell you about the dubious morality of India holding on to this place. They say Kashmir is an *atut ang*, which means an inseparable limb of India.

And there are also close to ten thousand people missing.

That have disappeared. The point is that it doesn't seem to occur to anyone that Kashmir was never a part of India. It was an independent kingdom. So even today, when they gloat about elections, if you say, "Why don't you have a referendum, as was promised by the United Nations?" they say, "Things have moved on from then."

You say that it allows Hindu chauvinists to target and victimize Muslims in other parts of the country.

When the elections were rigged in 1987, the movement in Kashmir become militant. Young men were taking up arms and crossing the border to Pakistan to train and then return. One of the fallouts of that was the exodus of the small community of Kashmiri Pandits, or Kashmiri Hindus, from the valley. The king who signed the accession document was a Hindu ruler over Muslim subjects, so this small minority of Hindu Kashmiris was a powerful minority. But because they feared for their safety, rightly so, and because the governor, Jagmohan, quite unforgivably said that the government couldn't protect them, they facilitated the exit of these Hindu Pandits from the valley. The poor among them ended up living in refugee camps in Jammu. They still live in refugee camps in Jammu.

This was at the time of the Taliban coming to power in Afghanistan, the BJP leading a *rath yatra* toward the demolition of the Babri Masjid, and the rise of Hindu chauvinism. These Kashmiri Pandits were wielded like a club by Hindu chauvinists in India and used to whip up this anti-Muslim sentiment. Of course, that orgy of hatred, that whole manifesto of hatred of the BJP, eventually led to the destruction of the Babri Masjid, the coming to power of the BJP, the genocide against Muslims in Gujarat, the bombings in Bombay in retaliation for Babri Masjid, the genocide in Bombay against Muslims by the Shiv Sena, and the rise of this ugly, divisive politics.

What do the people you spoke to in Kashmir think of Pakistan?

When I was there in August, along with chants of *"Hum Kya Chatey? Azadi!"*—which means, "What do we want? We want freedom!"—I heard in equal measure *"Jeeve, Jeeve, Pakistan!"* meaning, "Long live Pakistan!" Yet if you question people, there are many reasons for that. If there were a referendum in which people were given the option of India, Pakistan, or azadi, I imagine that an overwhelming majority would say azadi. If they were given only an option between India and Pakistan, it's not my place to say this, but my gut feeling is that Pakistan would win hands down.

India says Pakistan is fueling terrorism in Kashmir. I think people see Pakistan as somewhat self-serving, yet a very important support for the freedom movement in Kashmir.

And there is awareness also that the state there is not only exploding but imploding.

I think that there is awareness of that. But what people have experienced is the brutality of the Indian state, so that is foregrounded for people in Kashmir at this point. It's a bit theoretical to say, "Maybe it will be worse for them." They say, "Then that's our problem. Why are you worried about our problems?"

It's been a very difficult time for Muslims in India. So, to imagine that Muslims would be longing to be a part of India when they don't have to be is a hallucination. Indian Muslims have a completely different problem from Kashmiris. Indian Muslims have a different issue here because they have to live here, and they have to find peace in this almost fascist atmosphere. But Kashmiris see themselves as people who have a choice. They don't have to put their heads down and kiss ass. If you go around Kashmir, people ask you, "Have you come from India?" They don't consider themselves Indians.

Let's talk about the attacks in Mumbai that began on November 26, 2008, which in India is referred to as "26/11." I was in Islamabad, Pakistan, by the way, watching this on television. It struck me that it was like a three-day serial. You would go to bed at night and wake up in the morning, turn on the television, and it was continuing. The out-of-breath commentary and reporting were quite stunning. You've talked about the media coverage of the Mumbai attack, but initially, you were very reluctant to even write about it. I know you're working on a novel, and you want to focus on that, but people came up to you on the street to ask, "Are you going to write something?"

It was a difficult decision for me to write about 26/11. There was a lot of ugliness in the air. People who were prepared to tolerate the people like me were already straining because of my views on Kashmir, which are just not acceptable in India. And then to write about Mumbai. . . .Yet it became much harder not to write about it than to write about it, because the elite had cornered the TV channels, and there was this spiraling ugliness and this baying for war. And then there was the way in which it suddenly appeared as if this was the first time that such a thing had happened in India because it was the first time that the golden heart of India, the absolute elite, had been targeted, which raised a lot of very interesting things to write about.

Predictably, people annoyed with what I've said have twisted my views to say, "She justifies it" or "She thinks it's okay for rich people to be killed," which is absolutely not what I'm saying. But what does it mean in this country where it really doesn't matter what happens to poor people? It doesn't matter that well more than 100,000 farmers have killed themselves. It doesn't matter as long as only poor, impoverished soldiers are paying the price to hold down Kashmir. But when your best and most beautiful citizens are paying the price, then what?

Living in this country, watching and reading the news, there was dead silence about the elephants in the room. One of the terrorists, Ajmal Kasab, spoke about Kashmir, Gujarat, and Babri Masjid. But it was as if he hadn't. It was as if those were not the issues at all. This was just some mad pathology. So that effort to push everything away and say this was a text without a context was something that became very, very dangerous.

Yes, it's true that I tried not to write about it, but I was literally pushed into it. People on the street would come up to me and ask, "What are you thinking?" I think that's because I'm not just writing as a lone individual. I don't want to claim some unique voice. Actually, outside the mainstream media, if you read what was being written on the Internet and what was being said on the streets, there was a remarkable maturity in the response.

There was a clamor to link 26/11 to the terrorist attacks in the United States on September 11, 2001. This was "India's 9/11." And now there has been significant legislation passed as a result. A new agency has been created called the National Investigation Agency. What has been the political upshot of this in terms of civil liberties and human rights?

This is a very important question, which I have no doubt that you understand in a very nuanced way, being an American, but there is a difference, which is that there is a completely different set of reasons for why the government and the elites are pushing for these laws. It doesn't have to do with the fear of terrorism only.

What is really happening in India right now has to do with the other battle, the battle that's not on television. The battle that's being fought in Chhattisgarh and Jharkhand. The battle of the poor against displacement. The battle of the Maoists against mining—which is actually a far bigger battle. This is where these laws come into use. Binayak Sen, a medical doctor and human rights activist in Chhattisgarh, has been held as a dangerous terrorist in prison now for almost two years with no evidence whatsoever, and no bail. Those laws are really for people governments don't like and who have nothing to do with terrorism. Nor do they really have centrally to do with the fear or desire to prevent terrorism. But they have to do with giving government power to criminalize democratic space. The aim is to criminalize the democratic space, to prevent people speaking, working, and organizing a mass movement. This is what is going on beyond the floodlights in the rest of India.

The magazine India Today *has named "The Terrorist" as its "News-maker 2008." The accompanying article has photos of accused terror-ists, all of whom are in Pakistan. How does one address the issue of terrorism? You have people who seem to have total disdain, not only for the lives of others, but for their own lives. How can you reach them? It's as if they're in another zone entirely.*

That is the problem. Those particular individuals have ob-viously departed to another station, and communication links have been cut. So if you try and look at whatever policies you make as some way of stopping terrorism forever, you're bound to fail. The only thing you can do is to look at the conditions in which more and more anger, more and more despair, and more and more resentment are being created. How do you change the chemistry there?

India Today has pictures of all the various Muslims whom they see as terrorists. All of them are under trial. But a whole lot of Hindus who have been accused of bombing and killing people, including a senior serving officer in the Indian army, are on trial as well. None of them are pictured.

Lt. Col. Srikant Prasad Purohit was implicated in the Malegaon blast.

Malegaon and the Samjhauta Express blasts. I think it's very important to say that the attack on Mumbai was the most recent in a series of attacks there and in Delhi, Jaipur, Bangalore, and Ahmedabad. All the people that police have held as suspects in these attacks are Indian nationals, Hindu and Muslim. Initially they were all Muslims.

There were several very big loopholes in the investigations, which some of us pointed out. L. K. Advani, who sees himself as the next candidate for prime minister, went around campaigning against us by name, saying that we were "anti-nationals" and it was suicidal to question the police and so on. And then the Ma-harashtra antiterrorism squad arrested this Hindu *sadhvi*, God woman, Pragya Singh Thakur, and a few self-styled Hindu priests, and Purohit, a senior serving officer in the Indian army. And then Advani himself began to campaign against the Maharashtra anti-terrorism squad, saying they were acting "in a politically motivated and unprofessional manner."

The fact is that we in India today have a very murky history of these attacks. Many people, including myself, have exposed how the police fabricate evidence, how the media fabricate evidence, how the courts work in ways that make any kind of due process ridiculous and redundant.

L. K. Advani, the BJP leader, has mentioned you in public talks. Turning to the media, the television anchor Arnab Goswami, one of the leading voices on Times Now, *also had something to say about you during his coverage of the Mumbai attacks.*

About me and Prashant Bhushan, who is a leading lawyer. "I hope Arundhati Roy and Prashant Bhushan are listening. We haven't invited them to our show because they are disgusting."

To believe that citizens should just sit quietly while all this happens, that there is no need for a debate, and that there is no need for questions feeds into this terrifying atmosphere of nationalism and fascism. And I don't use the word *fascism* lightly. I started to use the term after what happened in Gujarat, when two thousand people were slaughtered in broad daylight in the streets of Gujarat as the police watched, and in fact participated, that those who participated were then promoted, that those who killed then appeared on television to boast about how they killed and how they were supported. And then those who killed and supervised the killing were voted to power twice. The entire democratic machinery colluded with the courts of India. And the people. Let's not leave out the people. The people who knew these things happened voted for the killers, saying, "This is what Muslims deserve."

You make some connections between 26/11 and US foreign policy in South Asia, and you refer to "the detritus of two Afghan wars."

In a way, at least in the corporate media, there is a sort of coy silence about the role of the United States in what has happened in the subcontinent. Pakistan was the crucible in which America conducted an experiment in its jihad against the Soviet Union. Pakistan was the recruiting agency and the recruiting ground for mujahideen fighters from Chechnya, Saudi Arabia, and elsewhere to come and fight the Soviets in Afghanistan.

People were simply recruited, given Stinger missiles and AK-47s, and told to go and fight. People were indoctrinated. People were brainwashed into fighting that desperate war in which more than a million people died. Once you've released those Frankenstein monsters into the world, you can't whistle and hope they will come back like trained mastiffs. When John McCain, Condoleezza Rice, and Gordon Brown say Pakistan is the heart of evil and the founder of terrorism, it's like scientists blaming their crucible for an experiment that's gone wrong.

There are no easy answers to the problem of terrorism. Certainly, there was no easy answer to 9/11. The fact that the US re-bombed Afghanistan into the Stone Age didn't help them. And now to assume that you can bomb Pakistan to sort out the problem is absurd beyond belief. We are living in a very, very dangerous era, and more than anything, you need brains to sort it out. That seems to be a very scarce commodity.

You also commented about the United States, "A superpower never has allies. It only has agents." The Indian government and elites are lining up with the Americans, but ultimately you suggest that it will backfire.

It will. Does anybody care to study the history of former allies of the United States and what happens to them when they're kicked over like an empty pail? The world is full of these examples, whether it's Iraq or Pakistan or Chile. The list goes on and on and on. I don't think anybody should have illusions about how much America loves India.

It's interesting now how Israel is now part of this equation—Tel Aviv, New Delhi, and Washington. Anand Patwardhan recalls a time when Indian passports were stamped with "invalid" for two countries in the world: one was apartheid South Africa, and the other was Israel. The situation today is completely different.

I think about the fact every morning we wake up and have this national pride rammed down our throats—when actually there is no pride. There was a time when India stood for something, when it was part of the nonaligned movement, when there was a sort of moral dignity. So, the more we are told that we should feel national pride, in fact, the more you actually ought to be ashamed, because you know that this country stands for nothing except the self-interest of its elites now.

On the other hand, people throughout India are involved in environmental movements, in displaced people's protests and agitation. That side of India is alive and thriving—and full of fire and dignity. I feel a great deal of pride in that. I am in awe of the fact that it is a country where people are not taking things lying down and people are fighting with so much imagination. Yet the world of official power and diplomats and armies and weapons and governments, we have humiliated ourselves while trying to force people to feel national pride.

The year 2009 marks the twenty-fifth anniversary of two crucial events. One is the Bhopal Union Carbide gas leak. I was just in Bhopal. Thousands of people have died. Many thousands continue to suffer. I visited a clinic and talked to some survivors. Children are being born with birth defects because the aquifer was contaminated by chemical leaks. Nothing has happened to Union Carbide, which is now owned by Dow Chemical, a huge US chemical corporation, also infamous for making Agent Orange in Vietnam. The second is the massacre of thousands of Sikhs in the wake of the assassination of Indira Gandhi. To date, no one has been brought to book in either of these cases.

The Indian government didn't ask for the extradition of Warren Anderson, the head of Union Carbide, who was protected by the US government. And the government in power in India today still shelters people who killed Sikhs and burned them alive on the streets of this city and has denied justice to those people all these years.

This kind of poison never goes away. The Congress Party did nothing to hold the people who participated in those killings accountable. They kept quiet over the killing of Muslims in Gujarat.

The killing of Sikhs didn't spark wider outrage because Sikhs are a small, localized community. But everything in India is like this. Everything is swept under the carpet. You never get to the bottom of anything. The Godhra train was burned. Who burned that train? The pilgrims died. Who did it? We still don't know. Who attacked the parliament on December 13, 2001? We still don't know. Who were the killers in Gujarat, in Bombay? Why wasn't the Srikrishna Commission report implemented when the Muslims were killed in Gujarat? You never get to the bottom of it.

These things don't go away. They grow and become something. They poison the bloodstream and inform the politics of what's going on. And eventually, you can't push it away, because there comes a stage when people simply won't take it anymore. Whatever spin you put on it, people know what's going on eventually.

Let me ask you about the new president of the United States, Barack Obama, and the promise of hope. People say he will change America's image in the world, which has been damaged under the Bush regime. What was your response?

It's difficult to say. I watched the night that he won. And I wasn't so concerned about who he was as much as to see the happiness on people's faces and to know that, whatever will be given to them, they wanted a change. That they wanted something else means a lot, because the last time they wanted the same guy back, which was devastating for the rest of the world.

The 2004 election of George Bush.

When he was reelected, yes.

We don't say that, necessarily, in the States. Selected the first time, elected the second.

That election hardened a lot of people's hearts, including mine, because I had been one of those people who said there is a difference between the government and the people in the United States during the occupations of Afghanistan and Iraq. And how with Obama winning, the fact that he has been utterly quiet on the bombing of Gaza. The fact that he has recruited so many of the old guard. I haven't seen anything on the ground that makes me feel it's going to be all that different, even if the fact that people wanted a change makes me feel better about the people.

CHAPTER 9

Revolts and Rebellions

The summer of 2010 was one of the bloodiest yet in Indian-adminis-tered Kashmir. It was the summer of the stones and the stone throwers. What are those stones saying and who are the stone throwers?

As usual, powerful states and powerful people tend to believe their own publicity. And they believed they had somehow managed to break the spine of the movement in Kashmir. Then suddenly, for three summers in a row, there has been a kind of street uprising, similar to Tahrir Square in Egypt. We see a sentiment for freedom that keeps expressing itself in different ways.

During the last twenty years, the establishment has geared itself to deal with militancy and some sort of armed struggle but now finds itself facing young people armed only with stones. And with all this weaponry that the Indian government has poured into Kashmir, they didn't know what to do with those stones.

Couple this with the fact that one of the other great weapons of the Indian occupation has been the manipulation of the Indian media. This big, noisy dam of misinformation has been breached through Facebook, Twitter, and YouTube. So stories were coming out of Kashmir that hadn't before.

Kashmir is crisscrossed with a grid of army camps, interrogation centers, prisons, guard posts, bunkers, and watchtowers. It has now

---

This interview was conducted in New Delhi, India, on February 21, 2011.

earned the dubious distinction of being the most militarized zone in the world. What is living under occupation like for Kashmiris?

I think a good thing is that Kashmiris have begun to write and speak about that themselves, so I don't think it needs someone like me to tell that story. You and I don't know the story from personal experience. We are not the people who would be stopped and humiliated at check posts, slapped or beaten up, and casually humiliated.

The Indian government has waged wars on the edges of this country—in Kashmir, in Manipur, in Nagaland, in Mizoram, in Assam—ever since India was independent. Kashmir is not the only place where there are check posts and bunkers and killings and humiliation. But war has now spread to the heart of this country.

The Indian state doesn't want to consider or address the conversations that are coming out of Kashmir, or read the messages on those stones. But the rest of India is becoming Kashmir in some ways. The militarization, the repression, all of this is spreading to the whole country.

Why isn't Kashmir getting more international attention?

That's a good question. When the uprisings happened in Egypt, and when people moved into Tahrir Square, being somebody who has followed the ways in which the international media reports various events, I wondered why does it choose some uprisings and not others? Because the bravery of people—whether it's in Egypt, in Kashmir, or the Congo, wherever it's going on—one is not questioning that. But why will the international media, and Western media in particular, shine a light on one and switch the lights off on the other? That's really the question.

As we saw in Egypt, you had breathless reporting about this uprising for democracy. Why will they talk about Egypt and not talk about Kashmir? It's just your politics, isn't it? Egypt is so important for the Americans and the Western establishment to control, because without Egypt, the siege of Gaza doesn't exist. And you know that Hosni Mubarak was dying. There had to be a replacement. There was going to be a real problem during the handover of power. I don't think that it will necessarily succeed, but I think the attempt was to use and direct peoples' energy in a sort of controlled-fission experiment. But so far as Kashmir goes, right now the Afghanistan, Pakistan, India equation vaults over Kashmir.

The situation in Kashmir is not something that the world of corporations, the world of markets, the world of even strategic geopolitics sees as threatening the status quo. Deals are being made. The West needs Pakistan very badly. It cannot do anything with Afghanistan unless Pakistan is on board. And yet it needs India badly for two reasons. One is its huge market. And the other is as a very willing fallback for a US presence in South Asia, given the rise of China. India is seen as a stable and willing ally right now. So to annoy India by bringing up Kashmir is not something that strategically suits Western powers right now.

A week before candidate Obama was elected in 2008, he announced that Kashmir would be among his "critical tasks." How was that comment received in Delhi? And what has Obama done since then to follow up? He was in India in November 2010.

That comment was treated with absolute and righteous outrage by the Indian establishment. And I think it was made very clear to him, or to anybody who says anything about Kashmir internationally, that the Indian establishment will use everything in its power to make sure people back down. And Obama backed down. He came here at a time when the streets of Kashmir were full of young people calling for azadi, when already many people had been killed. And he said nothing.

I'd like to ask you about other postcolonial states. For example, Frantz Fanon, who was active in the resistance in Algeria to oust the French, argued that we needed fundamental changes in the structures of power, not just to exchange white policemen for Brown or

Black ones. And he wrote about the ways Algeria, after independ-
ence, evolved into a tyrannical state, not the state that the revolution
dreamed of. One of the characteristics of postcolonial states is the ma-
nipulation of oppressed minorities. For example, Kashmiris are sent
to police and patrol in Chhattisgarh, and people from the northeast
are sent to Kashmir to do the exact same thing.

Just like Indians were sent to Iraq and all over the place to fight
Britain's wars for it. India acts just like a colonial state. You see
the unknown Indian soldier buried all over the world, fighting
for empire. And even within India, if you look at it historically,
look at 1857—some call it a mutiny, some call it the first freedom
struggle—that's exactly what happened. How many British soldiers were there in India? Not many. But, for instance, in 1857 the
Sikhs fought on the side of the British in the ransacking of Delhi.
But today India does that. It sends Nagas to Chhattisgarh, Chhat-
tisgarhis to Kashmir, and Kashmiris to Odisha.

Given the level of opposition to its rule in Kashmir, what keeps India
there?

A whole lot of things. One is that both India and Pakistan
have a great vested interest now in keeping Kashmir on the boil.
To have 700,000 soldiers there, you can imagine the sums of
money poured into that occupation and what's happening with
that money—property, concertina wire, petrol, vehicles, power.
The power to control a population like that. The business deals
with the collaborators and the local elites. It's like running a little country. Why would anybody want to give that up? That's
one thing.

The other thing, oddly enough, is that it's just become such a
question of the national ego that to rethink this position when
you're so far down into the tunnel would require a great amount
of vision. Then you have a situation where political parties in India are vying with each other. If the Congress Party, which is in
power now, would do anything that remotely resembled something progressive in Kashmir, the Bharatiya Janata Party would

immediately try to capitalize on it. So this democracy doesn't have any space to maneuver in that sense, because it's a democracy, and the other party is just waiting to capitalize on poisonous publicity to keep this machine going.

And yet today I think that one of the really big problems that the state faces is that, after very many years, there are fissures in the consensus among Indians, and those fissures have come because people have seen the undeniably mass democratic unarmed protest day after day, year after year, in Kashmir. And people are affected by this. They're not easily able to say, "These are militants," or Islamists, or Taliban. So there has been a fracturing of the old consensus. And in the case of the wars in Chhattisgarh, Odisha, Jharkhand, and Kashmir, and even Manipur to some extent, the state is very well aware that the old consensus is a bit shaky. There are serious cracks.

A journalist in Kashmir told me that top Israeli military and intelligence officials have been visiting Kashmir. What are they doing there?

I think that the United States understands that Pakistan is on very shaky ground. We know it's a nuclear power. We know that the whole adventure in Afghanistan is on the skids. They don't know what to do. They don't know how to get out. They want to get out, I think, but they don't know how to get out, even now. You have the rise of China. You have a huge stake in the gas fields of Central Asia. And you have Pakistan, an old ally that's also on the skids, partly because of the US history of intervention or, I would say, almost wholly because of that.

Ever since it became a country, Pakistan was never allowed to administer its own affairs or develop democratic institutions. At least India was allowed to, and now it's kind of hollowing them out, but Pakistan was never allowed to. The United States needs to step back onto surer ground. It needs a new frontier because the Pakistan frontier is collapsing. And I think that's what's going on. How do they now build a retreat in Ladakh, in Kashmir, in these areas as a fallback plan?

And the Israeli involvement?

That's the same as the American involvement. There is no difference between them. The Israelis and the Indians are now thick.

The US conducts more military exercises with India than any other country in the world. When Obama came here in November of 2010, the New York Times *said the country "is rapidly turning into one of the world's most lucrative arms markets." And Obama arrives here with two hundred top US corporate executives in tow, signs a deal for Boeing C-17 cargo planes worth $5 billion, and there are many more arms deals in the offing. All to sate what the* New York Times *calls India's "appetite for more sophisticated weaponry."*

India's appetite certainly has grown. Partly that appetite has to do with pleasing the masters. Because I want to know when the last time was that they used any of these sophisticated weapons? And who are they going to use them against? Can they use any sophisticated weapons in a war against China or in a war against Pakistan? They can't. Because these are all now nuclear-armed countries. The great irony is that the more sophisticated the weapons the military-industrial complex develops, the less the real threats are from conventional warfare. The threats that from terrorism cannot be addressed with sophisticated weapons, with tanks, with torpedoes, with any of that.

Certainly all countries—I'm sure India is right on top of the pile—have a huge appetite for weapons of surveillance and spying. But the greatest use that conventional weapons for conventional warfare have been put to is to parade up and down Rajpath in New Delhi on Republic Day as a sort of narcissistic show rather than for any practical use. India is a country that spends billions and billions on these weapons while eight hundred million people live on less than twenty rupees a day.

Twenty rupees a day is about fifty cents in US currency. In fact, the India that is essentialized, the one that the West identifies with, is lauded and praised as new billionaires are added to the Forbes list. But Utsa Patnaik, an economist at Jawaharlal Nehru University in New Delhi, says there is "a deep agricultural depression" in the country. Farmer suicides because of indebtedness are at unbelievable levels, and there has been, correspondingly, a sharp decline in grain output and grain consumption. The Republic of Hunger is actually the title of one of Utsa Patnaik's books.

India has more poor people than seven of the poorest African countries put together. And we have this litany of farmers who have killed themselves because they've gone into debt. You have increasing ecological and environmental crises. You have wars breaking out. And yet this kind of cabaret goes on.

I actually spoke to some correspondents of major Western publications who told me they have strict instructions not to write bad stories about India, because India is the finance destination for the rest of the world. So you have people looking to India to revitalize their economies, and you have an Indian government that has become so servile that it doesn't any longer know what's good for it.

Leaving aside these wars in Kashmir and Manipur, which are a different kind of war—they're battles for identity and nationhood—you have a battle within India that concerns the rest of the world. Because it's not just a battle for survival of millions of people. It's also a battle for ideas of the future of the world and what it's going to be.

Take P. Chidambaram, the home minister, formerly the finance minister, from Harvard Business School, saying that he visualizes an India in which more than 85 percent of its people live in cities, which is something like five hundred million people that he expects should be on the move. They cannot be moved unless it becomes a military state. And then a couple of years later that same minister says that the migrants in cities are the root of crime there and "carry a kind of behavior which is unacceptable in any modern city," so they have to be policed.

There isn't any place for poor people to plant their feet anymore. You have judges and all these kinds of people basically sanitizing India against the poor. We're not talking about a minority. We're not talking about the few. But here we're talking of a majority of people in this country who have no place in the country. They have no place in the imagination. They have no place in the institutions. They have no place in the law. They have a few bones thrown at them, like the National Rural Employment Guarantee Act, but that also generates a kind of capital that middlemen siphon off. So you're really heading for a kind of crisis that I don't think any of the people who are in charge of this country have a handle on.

In your essay: "The real power has passed into the hands of a coven of oligarchs—judges, bureaucrats, and politicians. They in turn are run like prize racehorses by the few corporations who more or less own everything in the country. They may belong to different political parties and put up a great show of being political rivals, but that's just subterfuge land, telecommunications, education, health—no matter what the consequences."

Remember that I wrote this before the exposé of the Radia tapes.

The recorded conversations between corporate lobbyist Niira Radia and various politicians and businessmen leaked in 2010.

The Radia tapes were the taps on the phones of Niira Radia. She is the sort of PR person for Mukesh Ambani of Reliance and for the Ratan Tata Group, two of the biggest corporations in the country. The tapes reveal the fact that they are running everything. They are deciding who the ministers should be.

The Radia tapes are like a physician's diagnosis that is confirmed by an MRI. Now we're in a very interesting phase in India where the corporations are battling each other and therefore leaking news about each other to the press.

Radiawas also involved in what's called the 2G scam. Telecom spectrum was sold by the government to these companies at absurdly low prices, despite being worth billions of dollars. The same thing is happening with India's natural resources—at an enormous human cost.

What's happening in India is not unlike what has happened historically in Africa or in Latin America. But now you have India colonizing itself. You have India developing its own idea of civil rights and yet committing a kind of slow genocide on its people. You're not lining them up and killing them, but you're starving them, you're slowly cutting them off from their resources, you're encircling them, you're calling in the army. It's not one country doing it to another country but the elites of one country doing it to its own poor.

But today everybody knows that it's banditry. The divisions are only on what you're prepared to do about it and how you're going to fight it. Those are the divisions that exist between people.

So they're tactical, not strategic?

No, they are tactical and strategic, not ideological, at least not in terms of what you're opposing. So the resistance movements, ranging from the Gandhians to the socialists to the Maoists, are all fighting the same things, even if their strategies of resistance are different. And surely their ideologies are different. But a lot of the difference has to do with the geography of the site of resistance. You can't fight in the jungle the way you fight in an open plain, in the villages, and so on.

Your essay "Walking with the Comrades" recounts the time you spent in the forests of Chhattisgarh with people who are called Maoists or Naxalites. What kind of fundamental change are they proposing in terms of restructuring society?

They are pretty straightforward in that they're Communists. They believe in overthrowing the Indian state with violence. They believe in the rule of the proletariat. But right now the place where they're fighting from, 99.9 percent of them are Adivasi people. By Adivasi I mean indigenous people, tribal people. And that brings a different color to the nature of this battle. Many of them have never been outside the forest. They've never seen a bus or a train or a small town, let alone Delhi or a big city. So I would say that the battle right now is that in these huge areas where the indigenous people of this country live, the government, quite against its own constitution, has signed hundreds of memorandums of understanding to turn that land over to private corporations for mining bauxite, iron ore, and every kind of other mineral.

Even though ultimately they believe in a different society—and they do have a pretty conventional idea of the nation, which I don't share—the contours of the battle right now is really a battle to stop those lands from being taken over, to stop the annihilation of a way of life that today is the only way of life that can have any claims to being sustainable. It's in great threat. People are starving, people are ill, people have malnutrition. But that is because there has been such endless assaults on them. But they still have the tools and the wisdom to teach us something about how to live— and how we are going to have to live in the future. It's not that we all have to become tribal people, but we have to learn to relearn what civilization means.

I can hear television anchors and the other critics who carp at you saying, "There goes Arundhati again, romanticizing tribals."

It's interesting. If you read what I've written about my experience walking with the comrades, you'll see that I did not go in there and say, "This is a perfect society and they're so egalitarian and they're so beautiful, and let's all be like this." When you're threatened by arguments and by actual war, you have to find ways of undermining people, you have to find ways of labeling, of delegitimizing. This charge of romanticization is all a part of that.

What struck me most during my time in the forest was the relationship between men and women within those tribal communities. Today, 45 percent of the People's Liberation Guerrilla Army consists of tribal women. I spoke to many of them. Many of them joined because they were reacting to the patriarchy of their own very conventional communities. Historically the tribal people, especially tribal women, have been considered the natural trophy of forest department officials, government officials, police, who just go in there and pick up who they like and rape who they like. Today that cannot happen. So in that sense they've already won. They've already won huge victories of dignity.

Operation Green Hunt is the government military operation to crush the Maoist rebellion. You say that Operation Green Hunt actually did a "favor" by clarifying the situation for people. Could you elaborate on that?

To go back to what I said earlier, we know about the exploitation of indigenous people that happened in Africa in the early parts of the last century. We know about the slaughter and the genocide. But today you have to do things quietly. You can't be as brazen as people were in those days. So now you have measures in our constitution that are trying to make up for the completely colonial attitudes toward tribal people in postindependence India. So you have a new law, for example, called the Panchayat Extension to Scheduled Areas Act, which disallows the government from taking over tribal land and handing it over to companies. This smokes up the mirrors. But Operation Green Hunt clarified things to local people. It is very, very clear. Here is the policeman. He has a gun. He wants your village, he wants your land, and he wants your house. Do you want to give it over or do you want to fight? I'm being very schematic, but in a way that clarifies things.

You found an anonymous quote from England in 1821: "The law locks up the hapless felon who steals the goose from off the common, but lets the greater felon loose who steals the common from the goose." This kind of encapsulates much of what you've been describing.

This line is from a poem written at the time of the enclosure of the commons. Here it's the enclosure and corporatization of the commons. It's not just the enclosure, but the enclosure and the destruction of the commons simultaneously that's going on. I think even the middle class, which has so far benefited greatly from the opening up of the markets, is now very slowly beginning to feel an unease about this destruction. People know that eventually you're soiling your own nest. That's not going to get you very far.

And that, I think, is why we are in such an interesting time. A few years ago these were things that a handful of us were saying. Now, with the exposure of the Radia tapes, everybody knows it. What we were yelling about earlier is street talk now. I almost feel like I can think about doing something else.

The case of Binayak Sen has attracted a lot of international attention. Forty Nobel Prize winners have called for his release. What does he represent? In a country where there is so much injustice, why is his particular case worthy of attention?

I think it represents the fact that the rot and the injustice and the fear that just stalked a certain class has now breached a barrier and it's coming into middle-class drawing rooms. Who is Binayak Sen? He is a doctor trained at the prestigious Christian Medical College in Vellore. He is a person who an ordinary middle-class Indian would think has done a great thing by giving up a lucrative career to work among the poorest of the poor. And if you're going to go after him, who else are you going to target?

As far as the state is concerned, clearly it's sending out a signal. I keep calling the Binayak Sen case the urban avatar of Operation Green Hunt. The Indian military know how to deal with the Maoists in the forest. They know how to fire into crowds of unarmed villagers protesting in small towns or villages. How are you going to deal with the middle-class person who disagrees—and who has the ability, the power, the education, the communication skills to make other people, powerful people, status quo-ists, look at things in another way?

Binayak Sen was the first person to blow the whistle on the Salwa Judum, the government militia that was unleashed in the forests of Chhattisgarh at the behest of the government and some corporations, to clear the ground—building what the British general Harold Briggs called "strategic hamlets" when they were fighting the Communists of Malaya. This means terrorizing populations, making them move into roadside camps, and clearing the land. That's what the Salwa Judum was doing in Chhattisgarh. Binayak was one of the people who raised an alarm and spoiled things for them. That's why Operation Green Hunt was announced.

In spite of all you've been saying about the depredations of the Indian state, the shrinking of public space for dissent, you write, "Here in India, even in the midst of all the violence and greed, there is still immense hope." Where do you find that hope?

I find it in people. Look at what's happening. I mentioned the massive numbers of memorandums of understanding that were signed with multinational companies for mineral exploitation in 2005. It's 2011. The protests have increased. They have been repressed. There are hundreds of people in jail. But they're not managing to actualize most of these projects. I don't think there are many places where the world's richest and biggest corporations, with a state that completely colludes with them, have been unable to get what they want. Through all the disagreements and arguments within resistance movements about violence and nonviolence and armed struggle and Gandhian protest, eventually, between them, they have stopped powerful forces. It's a very fragile standoff, but it's real. And we have to salute it.

And I hope that it coincides with a time in which people all over the world are beginning to understand that things can't go on like this. And if they do go on like this, there will be a complete collapse. But at least we'll go down fighting. At least we'll go down saying that we'll do everything to stop this. I think that is a tremendously hopeful thing.

Are the solutions to the problems created by the masters going to come from the masters?

They're not. I gave a lecture at Harvard recently. It was called "Can We Leave the Bauxite in the Mountain?" Part of me was sort of thinking that the real effect I would like this lecture to have is to make the masters of the universe who were there feel sort of deprived and helpless, because the solutions are not going to come from the people who created the problem in the first place. I'm not saying everyone in Harvard has no imagination, but it is the sort of pinnacle of the establishment in some ways.

I think that this whole idea of how you look for a solution, too, needs to be talked about, because there can be a very imperialistic understanding of this. You have an imperial vision that created the problem, and you want an imperial vision that comes up with an imperial solution. It's not going to happen. You have to be able to look at the world in fractured ways. You have to pay respect to the fact that different ecosystems and different people and different kinds of situations will have different problems. The solution is not going to be a broad-spectrum antibiotic. And surely it's not going to be a solution that voluntarily comes from some climate-change conference in Copenhagen. It's not going to happen. It's going to have to be forced on people.

The beginning of that for me has to be a fight to protect places and cultures physically, especially places where people have a new imagination—or an old imagination that could become a new imagination without going through the horrors of what we call civilization.

You've become, whether you like it or not, the de facto chronicler of dissent from Kashmir to Chhattisgarh. A lot of people are interested in how you work. They ask me to ask you, what is her writing routine like? How does she organize material? Do you have a process that you follow?

None whatsoever. Someone asked me this question recently. They asked me, "How do you go about doing the research to write your pieces?" And I said, "I don't do research to write my pieces. I just keep myself informed in order to get over the indignity of living in a pool of propaganda. Then, when you understand what the real story is, you're so angry that you have to write something." I don't research things in order to write.

I think it's just something that's in my DNA, maybe, the idea of how do things connect up. I don't think that you can just assume things like the people are always right, resistance is always wonderful, and peoples' movements are always great. Because they're not. You can have greatly unpleasant and almost sometimes repulsive peoples' movements. The largest peoples' movement in this country in recent times is Bajrang Dal and the Vishwa Hindu Parishad.

Those are right-wing Hindu nationalist formations.

Yes. And recently there was a march of millions of them through Christian and tribal and Muslim areas in Madhya Pradesh, warning people that this is the new way. The truth is that some yogi or some obscurantist person can attract one million people to learn a yoga position, and not that many are listening to us. So we can't flatter ourselves either.

It seems, as a trained architect, you've brought some of that discipline to the work you're doing today in terms of deconstructing things and then putting them back together.

I don't know. I try not to comment on my own work in terms of what I'm trying to do. Eventually it's there in what I write, and hopefully my writing manages to communicate a certain urgency. I remember in one of the earliest interviews we ever did, you talked about the danger of being a tall poppy, of standing out, being visible, and fighting the silence. "You've attracted tremendous animosity and hatred."

You forgot to mention love.

How could I have forgotten to mention love? Are you ever worried or do you find yourself inhibited in any way because of fear?

That's a good question. Am I worried? I would be stupid not to be worried. I would be stupid not to be aware of what's going on. So I won't say that I'm not worried.

To come back to the idea of how these things play out when you're pretending to be a democracy, in many ways the upper infrastructure of democracy has been rented out to the corporates, and the lower infrastructure has been rented out to the mob. So now, wherever I go, wherever I speak—I've been traveling a lot and speaking a lot to rather huge audiences—the Hindu right always makes sure there is some kind of protest. People physically threaten me. And then there are others working to ensnare you in a sort of legal morass, with various court cases against you. But so far nothing serious has happened.

Nothing serious has happened in legal terms, but your house was attacked in New Delhi.

I mean nothing serious has happened in legal terms. But there is this constant threat. Right now there is this attempt to charge me with sedition, but the police themselves are reluctant to go ahead with it because there's a trade off. If you do that, you're going to internationalize the Kashmir issue in a way. So we are playing for high stakes, and it's not something we should be blasé about.

At the same time, when you see what ordinary people are going through—the horrors of people's prison experiences. The poorest people in this country living from hand to mouth being jailed. How are they ever going to get a lawyer or get out of prison. How are their families going to survive? If you take one small look around, you get a little steel in your spine, and think, Come on, let's not feel sorry for ourselves.

CHAPTER 10

India: "The World's Largest Democracy"

It's nice to see you here in the world's second largest democracy. You, of course, being part of the world's largest democracy.

It's a race to the bottom.

Talk about the northeast and the state of Manipur. Harsh Dobhal has edited a book titled Manipur in the Shadow of AFSPA. *AFSPA being the Armed Forces (Special Powers) Act. He says in his introduction, "The northeast of India has always existed on the periphery of the nation's consciousness, and in the footnotes of the narrative of growth, progress and development. In a region where lawlessness, rape, murder, army excesses, arbitrary detention, torture, and repression are the order of the day." We hear very little about this in the United States. What is going on in that region?*

AFSPA was first promulgated in Manipur in 1958—in some particular districts that were declared "disturbed." Since then, it has been expanded all across the northeast (Manipur, Mizoram, Nagaland and, of course, Kashmir). People who live there don't like the term *northeast*, by the way. They would prefer you to be a little more specific about what we mean.

This interview was conducted in New York, New York, November 20, 2011.

And now, while they pretend to debate repealing AFSPA, which allows a noncommissioned army officer to kill on suspicion—basically it gives the army complete impunity to do what it likes—they want the army in central India and Chhattisgarh. The army isn't going to go there unless it has an AFSPA, but that act has been receiving a lot of bad press recently. My guess is that they will pretend to repeal it and then use its provisions in some other law.

But in Manipur, Nagaland, and at one time Assam—now it's less so in Assam, you have a rule by the Indian army with complete impunity. These are occupied territories. Very few of us really know what's happening in Manipur or Nagaland, and I include myself, because I haven't been there. But they don't do body counts. And from whatever little I've read and can figure out, I think many more people have been killed in those places than even in Kashmir, where the figure is something like seventy thousand. This is a part of the Indian colonization process that still remains hidden in the shadows.

The tragedy is not that there isn't news about Nagaland and Manipur in the United States. The tragedy is that there isn't news about it in India. Increasingly, people are being left to fight their own battles.

What about the case of Irom Chanu Sharmila, who is now in her eleventh year of fasting to protest AFSPA?

Sharmila has become a sort of icon in Manipur. She is being force-fed. It's interesting to compare the reaction to her hunger strike to Anna Hazare's. All the television channels in the entire nation were so excited when Anna went on a hunger strike for a few days. You have to ask why. Why did one hunger strike cause that reaction, and why did the other one just become a circus exhibit? I know this is a cruel thing to say, but that's how people use Irom Sharmila. It's because what she's asking for is far more radical, and Anna is asking for something backed by the middle class.

Kisan Baburao "Anna" Hazare is an advocate of the anticorruption Jan Lokpal bill being debated in the Indian parliament. "Anna" means elder brother, in Marathi—you've done some research into Hazare's background. He's been presented as a kind of reincarnation of Gandhi, a very simple man, doesn't have a lot of personal wealth. But his politics are another matter.

Others did the research, which I wrote about. It's interesting that, for a person who calls himself a Gandhian, every time he's posed with a question about Kashmir or even corruption, his first response is "Hang them" or "Cut off their hands" or something else terribly violent.

It seemed, at least on the surface, that whatever he was saying touched a nerve in some part of the Indian body politic. People are fed up with corruption.

Yes, of course. What is interesting is that that movement rose on the back of a massive corporate corruption scandal, the selling of telecom spectrum worth billions of dollars. It's an old story. The government sells something to a corporation much cheaper than it ought to have for a kickback or a bribe to some minister, and then the corporations realize a huge profit. What happened with the 2G spectrum is nothing, really, compared to what's happening in the mining sector, for example.

With the 2G scandal, for the first time since India began its romance with the corporate free market, corporations were on the mat. The revelations exposed the nexus among the media, the corporations, and politicians. But the odd thing about this anticorruption movement that rose from there was that the very same media and the corporations shouted the loudest and supported it the most. All the anger was focused on the government. And many of the media houses, which were giving it twenty-four-hour coverage on television, and the print media were asking for less government discretion, more privatization, more corporatization. You didn't find a single anticorporate slogan. So it was almost the exact opposite of what's happening with Occupy Wall Street.

And, yes, there were a lot of people, a lot of poor people, too, who would go there to give their support. But what they were expecting and what that actual bill was about were two different things. Very few people actually read the Jan Lokpal bill, the people's anticorruption legislation that they were trying to push through. I found it an absolutely regressive thing, because what they were asking for was more police, a huge sort of centrally administered organization with something like thirty or forty thousand more police, with powers to tap phones, power over the courts, over the prime minister. There was no way of knowing how those people were not going to be corrupt themselves.

When you talk about corruption, I think the most important thing is that any notion of corruption in the accounting or in the legal sense has to be pinned to a legal framework that is acceptable. That's what the middle class in India want. Because the majority of the poor, whether the rural poor or the urban poor, live outside that legal framework. An anticorruption law would allow the middle class to say, "Look at these slums. They are there because corrupt politicians allow them to be there so that they can get votes. They should be kicked out." Or, "Look at these vendors on the street. Kick them all out. Look at these poor people filthying up a nice neighborhood. Keep them out." Or, "Look at these tribal people. They don't have documents to say that they really have the right to live in that village. Kick them out." So this process of legalization and digitization of a culture is like the enclosure of the commons.

Lest it sound as though I'm supporting corruption, I'm just saying that nobody has cared to define very closely what we mean by that. And a narrow accountant's definition only serves the middle class. It's important to ask the question, "What do you mean by corruption?" Corruption has something to do with the concentration of power and powerlessness. That's the currency. So instead of actually structurally addressing the fundamental issue of power, when you start just talking about corruption in the imagination of an accountant or a lawyer, rather than politically, it becomes very regressive.

Does Anna Hazare have any connections with the Hindu nationalist Rashtriya Swayamsevak Sangh or with the Modi regime in Gujarat?

Early on, one of the first things he said was that he really admired Modi as a development chief minister, which was a rather shocking thing for somebody to say. But, of course, historically he has always been a person the RSS has admired. He's been a person the World Bank has admired. It's interesting, if you look at Africa, you will find that the World Bank has run a huge number of anti-corruption programs there. It's a way of sort of allowing capital to penetrate at the grass roots.

Why did Prashant Bhushan, who has defended you and is a well-known advocate of human rights, become a supporter and part of this Team Anna?

Prashant is a lawyer who spent a lot of his time unraveling corporate scandals and arguing against the corporates in court. I think he was just so frustrated at the level of corruption, in the proper legal sense of the word, that he probably thought that we need a pure and great authority to sort it out. I don't think he was thinking of it politically.

Many people were so impressed with the crowds that were turning up, so impressed with this corporate media that ignores every kind of people's movement. There have been larger gatherings of people in Delhi that the papers have never mentioned. And people didn't stop to ask, "Why are these corporate-funded media, people who always ignore resistance movements, so excited suddenly? What is it that's exciting them? What is making all the CEOs sing Anna Hazare's praises? What is it that's exciting the middle class, which is normally so hostile? What is it that is making the Hindu right—perhaps the most violent people's movement, if you want to call it that, in recent times—flock to this movement?"

It was very frightening. But after a while, the movement began to unravel. People are seeing it for what it is.

Prashant was beaten up for saying the wrong things about Kashmir. What happened to him?

A lot of the people that are in this Anna Hazare movement have been talking about what they call "direct democracy," where people are allowed to recall parliamentarians they vote for and intervene in decision making directly. Again, this is something that needs to be thought through very clearly, because in a majoritarian country, it can lead to a kind of fascism. Particularly in a country with such a complicated system of caste, which nobody knows quite how to interpret outside of India. Caste is the engine that runs Indian politics.

Prashant was at a press conference, and somebody asked him, "Since you advocate direct democracy, what if the Kashmiris asked for direct democracy? What would you say to them?" And he said that they ought to have a plebiscite in Kashmir and that they do have the right to self-determination. He said quite clearly that he wasn't speaking on behalf of the Team Anna platform. But it just was met with outrage from the right, and ended in his being physically assaulted in his office.

And you have stated that Kashmiris have the right of self-determination.

Well, it's the same people, in fact, who disrupt everything I do. Everywhere I speak in India, they show up. They disrupt public events of mine all the time.

You said in a recent interview, "The country that I live in is becoming more and more repressive, more and more of a police state. . . .India is hardening as a state. It has to continue to give the impression of being a messy, cuddly democracy, but actually what's going on outside the arc lights is really desperate." How does a writer like you, an individual citizen, navigate that hardening of the arteries?

Just by traveling, I think, and seeing what's going on. By talking to people. By keeping in touch. Not just having six thousand researchers but having real friendships with people who do not belong to the society of those in the arc lights. It is very frightening to see what's happening in Odisha, Chhattisgarh, Kashmir, Manipur, and Nagaland. That's been going on for a long time. But everywhere is becoming a sort of surveillance society. Phones are obviously tapped, emails are tapped. They're trying very hard to control the Internet.

I could tell you horror story after horror story of what's going on in India. But that's not the point. It's important for us to understand structurally what the game is and see how to navigate that. That's what I do as a writer. Sometimes it's not easy. For example, when the Anna Hazare movement was happening, it wasn't easy going against the grain of some of my closest friends. But I didn't think they were seeing the situation very clearly.

When I travel around India, the level of pushback and resistance is remarkable. And it is particularly high among the most disadvantaged. The word poor doesn't begin to describe their economic situation. In Odisha there's a struggle right now over a proposed South Korean steel mill. It's the largest single foreign investment project in India's history—more than $12 billion. They're securing their own private port where they can then export directly to East Asia. There has been a tremendous amount of resistance there. Roads have been blocked. People have been able to at least slow down and in some instances stop various projects like this.

Amazing things are happening in India. But I just want to add a caveat to that. If you look at what was happening in India in the late 1960s and the early 1970s, why did the Naxalite movement arise? It arose demanding "land to the tiller," saying that the Indian government, when it won independence, had promised the end to zamindari, the system of huge landlords with serfs tilling the soil for them. But that land distribution hadn't happened.

The Naxalite movement was crushed in the late 1960s. And then you had a more reactionary sort of movement arise, Jayaprakash Narayan, saying "Sampoorna Kranti," which means "total revolution," but again asking for redistribution. From then to now, look where we've come. From demanding land for the landless, today we are fighting just for people who have a little bit of land to be allowed to hold on to it. The masses of displaced people, the masses of people of lower castes who have been rendered landless, who live in the cities in these squalid conditions outside of radical politics today. So we mustn't ever forget that the people who are fighting, who are putting up a resistance, still have some land. The Adivasi community still have their own lands. They are fighting not to allow the corporates to take over. But the idea of saying that there has to be justice—the idea of taking back from the expropriators and land to the tiller—has more or less disappeared.

So before we feel too good about ourselves, we have to realize that we really have been pushed against the wall in so many ways. I don't know when that bubble is going to burst—or how. But it will not be political necessarily. It very likely will be lumpen and criminal. It's very difficult to organize the poor in these huge cities, where they live working like slaves—some of them laboring twenty hours a day, seven days a week. Where is the time for politics? Where is the time for organization? It's extremely difficult.

And where is the space for dissent in India? I'm thinking of Jantar Mantar, a place where you are allowed to demonstrate. It's a little sliver of sidewalk, like an island, right off Connaught Place in New Delhi. And here in the United States we also see cordoned-off "free-speech zones" that the police assign for dissent. There seems to be a shrinking of space.

I've been to Occupy Wall Street in New York. I've spoken there. The idea in the establishment, both in India and in America—and, I'm sure, in China and everywhere else—is to deny people physical territory where they can assemble, unless they belong to the middle class. The people who are demanding any kind of radical change are not going to be allowed to assemble. So how do you gather and scatter and gather and scatter? Because everything is under surveillance. There are cameras everywhere, there are police everywhere, they are watching your communications. It's a frightening situation.

Yesterday I was at a talk, and somebody asked an interesting question. They said that the slogan of the Occupy Wall Street protest is "We are the 99 percent," but when you look at the rest of the world, that 99 percent is the 1 percent in terms of privilege, compared to the poor of India or Africa. And how has that privilege been accumulated? The United States has always stimulated its economy by manufacturing weapons and exporting war, whether indulging in war itself or supplying India and Pakistan with billions of dollars of weapons. When I think about the struggle here being about jobs in some way, I hope they're not going to be those kinds of jobs. Come and make some missiles for us, come and make some Black Hawk helicopters for us.

Politics has to be understood in a different way, not country-wise anymore but in other kinds of solidarities.

The Indian state, like other states, seeks to control the message. They want to frame discussion on their terms. This is quite understandable. It's nothing revelatory. There seems to be, at least in the case of India, an attempt to limit dissent by limiting access to the country, even inside the country, where it is sometimes difficult for Indian nationals themselves to travel. Gautam Navlakha, a journalist and human rights activist, was sent back from Srinagar airport. A US academic, Richard Shapiro, was denied entry into India in November 2010. In September 2011, May Aquino, human rights activist from the Philippines, was denied entry. In late September I was denied entry—

A dangerous man.

—at New Delhi's Indira Gandhi International Airport. This has a chilling effect. So what's going on? Is this a new development, where the borders are being controlled in such a way?

I don't think it's new. It's been a while now that if you're a businessman, if you want to buy or sell a mine or organize a shipment of iron ore, you don't need a security clearance. But if you're an academic or a journalist or a writer or a scholar, then you need security clearance. Obviously, journalists as well as NGOs are in India on the sufferance of the government. That has been made clear all the time. You have to walk this delicate line. You have to keep deciding how far you can push things, how much truth you can tell and how much you should keep quiet.

I've been told by foreign correspondents that their own desks from newspapers outside of India have said, "We want good news. The bad news is boring." The real reason is that India is a finance destination, so there's no need to disrupt this by talking about all the cruelty that's going on.

It's almost as if the Indian government acknowledges Kashmir is a different country, because they stop people from going there. They send them back from the airport. You can't easily go into Chhattisgarh now. It's dangerous. Police have basically said, "We shoot to kill beyond the Indravati," the river that defines Maoist territory for the police. So you go at your own risk.

What I find quite interesting is while all this silencing is going on, the kind of noise that the government would like to hear is building. So almost every weekend you have a literary festival with international publishers and authors. I don't think they need security clearance. They come as visitors. They don't really disturb the grass, and they go from Jaipur to Goa to I don't know where. Every newspaper has a literary festival. Many of these festivals are funded by these very corporations that are underneath the silencing. They even wanted to have a festival in Kashmir.

You were deported because they were frightened you were going to write about the discovery of the mass graves. You can have a literary festival in Kashmir, but David Barsamian can't write about the mass graves. What sort of literary festival will it be? What will Kashmiris be allowed to say? If they say something wrong, will they be taken directly to the army camp or will they be allowed to go home to change their clothes first?

I find this simultaneous orchestration of noise and silencing very interesting.

In December 2009, the "Buried Evidence" report was issued by a group of human rights activists. It documented the many graves containing thousands of bodies in Kashmir. That was recently actually verified by a state commission, which felt obliged, because of public pressure, to conduct its own investigation. So there have been two reports now about these mass graves. What has ensued in terms of investigation? Because anywhere from eight to ten thousand Kashmiris have gone missing since 1989. Could these be some of those people in those unmarked graves?

They could be. I suppose it's distressing to those who still hope that the missing are alive for us to assume the missing are the dead. One doesn't know until DNA tests are done. The important thing is that these graves are in only three out of many more districts of Kashmir. So what is happening to the other graves? Are they being desecrated and quickly removed? Are they going to be limited to this?

Nothing ever happens to any army officer who has committed a crime, either a summary execution, which is known as a "fake encounter" in India, or mass execution, or rape. Nothing ever happens. The army has complete impunity.

So what will happen? I don't know. The disappearances and the mass graves build anger. But the government knows how to short-circuit this. How do you allow people to vent their anger and calm down? How do you create a collaborator class that has huge stakes in the Indian occupation? How do you divert debate?

I will say this for the Indian occupation of Kashmir: it's a brilliant occupation. The world should learn from the detail with which it operates, the alternating of violence and rewards, the cajoling of the media. If the way the world is headed, as I think it is—if you want to maintain the system of capitalism that allows a few hundred people to own half the wealth of the United States and one hundred people to own assets worth a quarter the gross domestic product in India—then you are going to need to control societies militarily. And if you want a PhD in how to do that, come to India.

When I was in Kashmir in February 2011, I interviewed Khurram Parvez of the Jammu Kashmir Coalition of Civil Society. He told me about the level of surveillance and how detailed and sophisticated it is. He said, "Every small thing in Kashmir is monitored. I've done human rights work for the last twelve years. Over that time I have forgotten a lot of things. But the files maintained in the interrogation centers and intelligence bureaus are complete. They can give me the details of what I did on what day. They tell us sometimes, 'You met such-and-such person on such-and-such date.' We would have forgotten, but they keep a record for us. The surveillance is extensive. Our emails and phone calls, even with family members, are monitored. A lot of people here have voice trackers. Their voices are being tracked on any mobile they use." Not only is Kashmir the densest militarized zone in the world, but it is maybe also the most heavily surveilled. Think about the psychological aspect of that, knowing that when you're talking to a loved one or a close friend, everything is being monitored, emails are being read.

What does this do to a population? We know what it does. We know the exponential rise of people with psychiatric disorders and suicidal tendencies in Kashmir. But it's not just the state that is spying on its subjects. This whole network of informers is as well. People in your own house can be spying you. It's a bit like the Soviet Union. If somebody in your circle was arrested, then you had to denounce them or you would be arrested. It's a kind of slow poison dripping into a society which is completely unforgivable. And for what? What is this idea? What is this map that you have in your head? You have this map of India in your head, which is somehow sacred, regardless of what you do in parts of that country.

When West Pakistan was committing a kind of genocide in East Pakistan, it was morally okay for the Indians to go in and liberate it. So you have this morality that curls in on itself and becomes implacable.

Why is it so hard for people to see that between the debacle in Afghanistan, the expansion of the war by Obama in Pakistan, where drones are killing civilians with no accountability, and a situation in which both Pakistan and India have nuclear weapons and both countries have crazy religious radicals, Kashmir could actually be a buffer? Pakistan has acute internal problems. It is committing atrocities in Baluchistan. None of these states are moral states. If you criticize India, that doesn't mean you're pro-Pakistan. No. Very similar kind of things are happening in Balochistan as in Kashmir.

Parvaiz Bukhari, an independent Kashmiri journalist, told me something rather startling. One of the reasons the Indian government offers to justify its occupation of Kashmir is the fear that some two hundred million Muslims living in India would then be subjected to a Hindu backlash if Kashmir becomes independent. That speaks volumes to the insecurity and the vulnerability of this huge minority inside of India.

Whether or not Kashmir becomes independent ought to have nothing to do with what is happening with the Muslim population in India. What is happening with the Muslim population in India is terrible. They, along with Dalits, have been pushed right to the bottom of the social scale. But Dalits at least are rising up, at least in terms of demanding political representation. You have Mayawati and Lalu Prasad Yadav.

Kumari Mayawati, who is chief minister of Uttar Pradesh and president of the Bahujan Samaj Party, the Majority People's Party, and Lalu Prasad Yadav, the former chief minister of Bihar and president of Rashtriya Janata Dal, the National People's Party.

All of this is going on. But the Muslims are being pushed down without representation. They live in ghettos. In Delhi they live in Sha Shahjahanabad, a ghetto. In Gujarat they live in ghettos. Even in West Bengal, Kolkata, the state ruled by the left for so many years, they live in ghettos. So what is happening to the Muslim community and the terror under which it lives has nothing to do with Kashmir. It has to do with the rise of radical right-wing Hindutva ideology and a kind of majoritarianism that often shades into open fascism, as we see in Gujarat. But I don't think we should link those two things.

Many people were expecting that there would be even more protests in Kashmir in the summer of 2011. Why that didn't happen?

I don't know. I'm really not equipped to say. I think that perhaps there's a lot of thinking going on right now. You don't want to enter a situation where so much energy goes into an uprising, people are killed, young people are jailed. And then what happens next? It gets short-circuited, and you go back into that cycle.

So perhaps people are thinking through what comes next. What kind of azadi, what kind of society, what kind of constitution, what is it that we would like? Because it's not fair to expect young boys to just be on the streets braving bullets, getting their heads blown off, without a political plan.

When India was fighting for its freedom and the British said the natives are not ready for democracy, there were so many ways in which communities were divided, particularly between Hindus and Muslims. The violence of Partition was a result of that. Now the Indian state is trying to divide Kashmiris, pit them one against the other, the Ladakhis and the Jammuites, the Gujars and the Shias.

I understand that it's very difficult for people to have an open discussion when there are so many AK-47s aimed at your head. So really, initially they need to be allowed to think, to argue with themselves. Argument is not always unhealthy. They need to work out what the next step is going to be. I hope that that is what is going on. Because questioning what people want, when that questioning comes from the occupier, is mischievous. Yet people who are occupied need to have some hard debates. There were hard debates between Gandhi and Nehru and Ambedkar. Those debates do need to take place. And perhaps that's what's going on. I don't know.

A November 2011 report from the Pentagon to the Congress observes, "The relationship between the United States and India—what President Obama has called one of the defining partnerships of the twenty-first century—is a priority for the US government and for the US Department of Defense. The United States and India are natural partners, destined to be closer because of shared interests and values and our mutual desire for a stable and secure world. A strong bilateral partnership is in US interests and benefits both countries. We expect India's importance to US interests to grow in the long run as India, a major regional and emerging global power, increasingly assumes roles commensurate with its position as a stakeholder and a leader in the international system." Further on it says, "Relationship building between US and Indian defense personnel is one of DoD's highest priorities for the US–India defense relationship." We also learn that US Special Operations Forces interact with their Indian counterparts. So, clearly, the US government and military see India in a very particular way. I'm interested in their comment that partnership will benefit "US interests," but the interests are not spelled out. What might those interests be, and what do you think about this emerging alliance?

I could bet you that there's exactly the same kind of document between India and Israel as well. It has to do with many things. Recently there was a US sale of something like $5 billion worth of military aircraft to India. But I think over the next five years India is going to be one of the biggest purchasers of weapons. I think the budget is something like $45 billion.

If you look at what's happening globally, all of it has to do with countering China now. The United States is sending troops into Africa. As Afghanistan is becoming unmanageable and Pakistan is not behaving itself, the United States is stepping back into India. Not only does it have a huge market for consumer goods in India, but it has a huge market for military equipment and it has a geopolitical base to counter China. They must be so worried about Nepal now, seeing it as an ally of China. Pakistan is talking to China all the time. So India is going to be used as a pawn in this game. Apart from the fact that it's buying all China's outdated nuclear technology and allowing it to dump toxic waste, and is a traditional market in the sense of buying cars and cell phones and air conditioners and whatever, India, too, is competing with China, as well as the United States, for resources in Africa. It's a great game now.

I was looking at your 2002 speech in Santa Fe, New Mexico, and I was struck by its almost prophetic character. I don't know if it's fresh in your memory.

You're being like those policemen in Kashmir, pulling up my files.

Yes, I have your file here. In Santa Fe you said, "America's corporate heart is hemorrhaging." So you had a sense then that there was something seriously wrong with the US economy and the structures here.

How could it be otherwise? I'm not an economist, but you don't have to be an economist to see what's going on.

So do you think that that murmur is a little bit louder now, of the goddess saying, "Another world is possible"? Does it seem more pronounced now than nine years ago?

I think it is. Both sides are saying, "Another world is possible." The other side is saying a world of military rule is possible, a world of complete surveillance is possible, a world of capturing the imagination of people and holding it down is possible. And we are saying that there are too many of us for you to hold down all the time. The recruitment is happening on both sides.

CHAPTER 11

Women and Resistance

In your Eqbal Ahmad lecture at Hampshire College in 2001, you compared India to "a hammerhead shark with eyes looking in diametrically opposite directions," and described one India "on its way to a glittering destination" while the other "just melts into the darkness." What's happened in the last dozen years since you made those comments?

The hammerhead shark has matured, and its eyes are even further apart now. We know these things about India. On the one hand, the country is called a superpower, with an accelerated growth rate, which is slowing but still. And on the other, you have more poor people in India than all of the poorest African countries put together. You have most of the world's malnourished children living there.

What is distressing is that it didn't take a genius to have said this then, and it doesn't take a genius to be saying the things that I'm saying now. The purposeful way in which this machine continues to work, churning out millionaires, on one end, and the effluent of the poor that just slough off into the sea, on the other, is so deliberate. Honestly, the crisis is no longer to recognize it, to talk about it, or even to describe it. The point is, what can be done about it?

This interview was conducted in Chicago, Illinois, March 17, 2013.

You've written about the "juggernaut of injustices" that exist in India and the spectacular struggles of popular movements "that refuse to lie down and die." What's the current status of some of those popular movements and resistances?

Even from the time that I started being associated and engaging with them, when I was writing about the anti-dam movement in the Narmada valley, again and again I see people saying, as I was, that if a government does not respect reasoned, nonviolent dissent, by default it privileges violence. And now what's happened, if you read the news from India, is that more and more armed struggle in forests or militant uprisings in other places are being violently put down by the state.

Noam Chomsky notes that people focus on "retail terrorism"—the terrorism of small groups, individuals, and gangs—but not much attention is paid to "wholesale terrorism," when terrorism is committed by the state.

We have to reimagine what we mean by the state in India. The state is being run by gigantic corporations. I think even in the United States you would be hard-pressed to find corporations like Reliance and Tata. Businesses in India have tremendous cross-ownership. Reliance have petrochemicals, they have natural gas, they have twenty-seven television channels. Tata owns everything from power projects, to vehicles, to TV, to broadband, to salt, to publishing, to bookshops. And you see increasingly in places like Odisha and Jharkhand that mining companies are running their own mafia. All the police work under their instructions. So what is the state?

Again, on perhaps widening the definition of terror, what does it mean when so many Indian farmers commit suicide because of financial destitution or that hundreds of thousands of Indian children die, for lack of water and food?

The farmer suicides. I think that the establishment rather admires farmers who commit suicide, because, after all, they're not suicide bombers, they're just quietly killing themselves. And then their families have to go around begging to be entered in the list of farmers. And the definition of who is a farmer and who isn't helps you get compensation or not. A lot of women, for example, would not be included in the official statistics, even though they are farmers and were trying to keep their families going.

But to understand what's going on in India, you need approach it from so many different angles. We are a society that has institutionalized inequality through caste. And I increasingly think that you can't understand India until you understand caste, when you understand that there are these sealed communities that then don't necessarily feel sorry for or remorse over something that happens somewhere else. I'm not saying that the farmers that killed themselves are lower-caste. They're not. What I'm saying is, why does not something like this cause anguish? Why doesn't it cause a scandal? It doesn't.

In fact, even today politicians are continuing with irrigation scams, fertilizer scams, and every kind of scam in those areas where the suicides are happening. There is a curious hardness that has set in. Increasingly I hear the middle classes saying, "India is poised to become one of the most powerful countries in the world. Every country that has become powerful has 'a past.' We can't progress unless somebody pays the price. And it can't be all sort of touchy-feely and human rights and sympathetic. Something has to give." When I say "we," I am talking about this class of people that has fused itself with the idea of the nation. People openly say that this is the way it has been in the past, and this is the way it has to be now.

So you hear these ugly statements. You hear people on TV trying to provoke war with Pakistan, openly talking about nuclear war, openly talking about the fact that the leading candidate now for the next prime minister in India is Narendra Modi, despite the fact that he was the chief minister that presided over the massacre of thousands of Muslims in the most brutal way in Gujarat.

So even people like us, who are political and who are writing politically, need to understand that evoking people's sympathy, describing horror, describing terrible things, it isn't necessarily reaching that moral listening space that you imagine exists. You have to keep doing it. You have to keep your foot on the pedal. But we also have to understand that we are up against something very, very ugly now, which is going to become more and more ugly as we run up to the next election, because what has happened is that the Indian shining economy, the people who are sitting in the aircraft ready for takeoff, that exhilaration they felt has turned into panic now. The economy is not moving at the pace they expected it to. And that panic is creating a lot of ugliness. It takes different shapes and forms, but you can see the violence and the anger in those same middle-class people that were so happy a few years ago.

The political parties don't know how to deal with that violence, that anger, that impatience, because it's new. They are trying to push it back into the old spaces that everybody knows and recognizes—communal strife or a war with Pakistan or some provocation in Kashmir. They know how to make those moves. Whereas this new middle class is aggressive. It knows that it can get media attention, and it's attacking the old idea of politics itself.

There has been a massive migration from the countryside into the megacities—Kolkata, Delhi, Mumbai, Chennai, Hyderabad, Bangalore.

People are being pushed out of their villages by development projects, mines, and dams, and they flock to the cities. But the violence that you're seeing in cities is not coming from those people. The violence is coming from the new rich, like people in Delhi who have sold their land to the malls and suddenly have acquired a lot of money because of political status, and a kind of aggression that comes with it.

Politicians are very quick to criminalize the lower classes and blame the unanchored poor—whereas they are the ones against whom tremendous violence is perpetrated in the cities by the police and by the building contractors. There are more than ten million people living on the outskirts of Delhi, working like slave labor in terrible conditions. But they are not the violent people. They have occasionally burst out, at the Honda factory or at the Maruti Suzuki factory. But they are really the victims of violence. They are the victims of lower and lower wages, of having to pay more and more because prices are rising so fast. And workers literally live in circumstances I don't think people could even fathom in America and Europe.

Every time something happens, like the gang rape on a bus in Delhi in 2012, you immediately hear, "We need more police stations, we need more surveillance, we need more cameras." That whole idea of the citizen as a criminal. But if you actually were to inquire into any case, I think the chances are much more likely that behind almost all criminal activity in most cities is the police.

Certainly that mid–December 2012 incident in Delhi garnered global attention. The BBC in a report said that the case raised questions about "how India treats its women." What kind of questions were raised in the aftermath of this attack and killing?

If anyone needs the background, a young girl was gang-raped brutally and then murdered on a private bus in Delhi. The rapists were caught—the murderers. But today, if you read the papers, it's only referred to as a gang rape. You would imagine that girl wasn't killed. "Delhi gang-rape victim" or "Delhi rapists." They are not called "murderers."

This shows you the kind of twisted social stigma that is attached to rape in India. There were huge and unprecedented protests about this, which was a very good thing, but it brings about certain anxieties in people like myself. It's hard to explain, but there are certain ways in which rape is used to maintain the status quo in India. The army has raped a lot of women in Kashmir. The

Armed Forces (Special Powers) Act, which gives them immunity, allows that to happen. So, too, in Manipur and Nagaland. In "Walking with the Comrades," I wrote about how many women in Chhattisgarh watched their sisters or mothers or children being raped and murdered. In Gujarat, when the 2002 pogrom against Muslims happened, women were openly gang-raped. Pregnant women had their stomachs ripped open. They were burnt alive. There was a horrendous incident in 2006 in a village called Khairlanji in Maharashtra where about three hundred upper-caste people surrounded the house of a Dalit family, raped and murdered a mother and daughter, and then killed the whole family. The media took more than a month to even report it, and even later the people were called Maoists.

So you start to wonder which rapes are going to attract the national and international media, and which rapes are we are going to accept as a matter of routine. To be fair, initially, when the protests happened in Delhi, women did begin to raise these issues, and it did expand into a much more political view of what was going on. And then, of course, the Criminal Law (Amendment) Ordinance was passed this year. But you will see that in the ordinance the government looked at rape as a security issue, which means that marital rape, the Armed Forces (Special Powers Act), caste, all of these were just pushed out of the picture once again.

It also relates to the phenomenon of these massive populations moving to the cities and young girls beginning to leave the home to become financially independent, to begin to break away from traditional behavior, which creates huge anger among traditional men. All of that is going on.

But did it spark a discussion about misogyny and patriarchy? Because if it's not contextualized, then it's simply reduced to miscreants, to people carrying out criminal acts.

It did, but I think the word patriarchy was being used by people who seemed to have just discovered the idea. What did it really mean? I think, unfortunately, an incident of gang rape on a bus is not the best way to begin discussions on patriarchy.

I think we have to go back to another question: What is it about the women's movement in India and in the rest of the world that has in some ways depoliticized it? You have feminist organizations in India that are happy to discuss certain important issues about gender. But they completely ignore the women I wrote about in "Waling with the Comrades." In the forests of Dantewada, ninety thousand women belong to the Krantikari Adivasi Mahila Sangathan (Revolutionary Adivasi Women's Association). What was happening to the women there and how they were organizing was eye-opening to me. And yet those women—who are fighting for their land, who have been fighting even within their own communities for a different life, for different rights, for different ways of being seen and described and defined—are not considered feminists by professional feminists. Why should that be so?

We have to examine the corporate funding and the NGO-ization of the feminist movement. I've written about this topic at length in the essay called "Capitalism: A Ghost Story."

These women that you met in the jungle in Chhattisgarh, they have moved from being passive victims to active agents, to doing something about their situation.

The history of women in the Naxalite movement, and then in all the various fragments of it, and today in the Maoist movement is interesting, fraught, challenging, sometimes very often depressing but also very inspiring. I can't say anything simple about it. However, when I went into the forest, I had assumed in a rather clichéd way that any movement that opts to pick up arms is eventually going to do violence to women. I was shocked when I found that more than 40 percent of the liberation guerrilla army were women.

If you look at the Narmada movement, the Niyamgiri movement, so many movements, you see that women are at the heart of these protests. They know that what waits for them in that other life that's been offered to them, when they're told to integrate into the mainstream, is a very frightening life, where they would lose everything. So they are fighting. The feminist movement has had those debates in the past, and other versions of them are being played out now.

Not all, and even the ones that are funded are sometimes doing important work, but there is a big divide between what is now formally considered feminist and the struggles these women are waging. Anything that actually threatens the overarching economic order is then not considered feminist. I think what you exclude constitutes a definition of what your politics are.

Does this participation of women in resistance movements extend to Kashmir?

Of course. Kashmir is a place where they like to put out a particular, completely false image of Wahhabi fundamentalists fighting this democratic state, with women wearing burqas and so on. But anyone who spends two days in Kashmir will see that's certainly not the case. It's as diverse a society as any, and the women are at the forefront now. You see them physically facing down police and facing down the army in incredibly brave and anguished ways.

In this discussion about violence against women, certainly dowry-related "accidents" in which many women are victims of fires in kitchens. Then countless female babies are aborted because of this obsession with having male offspring.

The killing of girl children in India runs into the millions. As I said when you were quoting the BBC question about India's treatment of its women, what do you mean by India and what do you mean by women? India is a country where I have seen the most remarkable, the freest women of almost any women I've ever seen anywhere. And then, as you said, you have female feticide and everything in between. You have such a huge spectrum of what constitutes the world of women in India. And you can't even divide it simply. For example, when the pogrom against Muslims was taking place in Gujarat, women were very much part of it. Women were very much behind it.

I just want to say one more thing about this issue. In India, when a girl is raped, because the stigma is so enormous, nobody is allowed to disclose her name. So all the various newspapers and media outlets, in their excitement, kept giving the girl murdered on the Delhi bus different names. So someone called her "Damini" and somebody called her "Nirbhaya," which means "the fearless one," though I don't know why they assumed that she was fearless. What a strange thing to do to a young girl who was murdered in this way.

John Kerry recently wanted to honor her on International Women's Day because he seemed so moved by this story, and posthumously presented her with the International Women of Courage Award. I found this so grotesque, in terms of what the Americans have done in the last few years to the women of Iraq, what they've done to the women of Libya. They've driven millions of women against their volition back into purdah, back into the most inequitable lives—women who were poets and writers and doctors and scientists. The situation created by these wars has pushed them back. And then you pick out a young girl who was raped and honor her, while you're pushing millions of women backwards and putting the hands of the clock back for millions of women. You come and pick up this one case, which is completely unpolitical. What happened to her was a criminal act. What happens to the women of Libya and the women of Iraq and the women of Afghanistan is political. You're not committing a criminal act on one person but a criminal act on countries of women.

It's easy to be virtuous about the Delhi rape and murder case as opposed to drone attacks on Pakistan.

Yes, it's very easy. I remember I was in Sharjah when President Obama won his second term. He came up on stage with his wife and his daughters and was talking about whether they should or should not have another dog. At the time, Reuters quoted a man from Pakistan saying, "I lost my wife in the drone attack and my children are injured. Whatever happens, it will be bad for Muslims. . . .Any American, whether Obama or Mitt Romney, is cruel."

There seems to have been one scandal after another in India, each one bigger than the previous one. Jayati Ghosh, who teaches at Jawaharlal Nehru University in New Delhi, wrote in the Guardian *about "the explosion of revelations about corrupt practices that point to the worst excesses of crony capitalism." She describes "Wild West–style economic dynamism: unfettered by adherence to any rule of law that treats all citizens as equal, and reliant on close relations of capital with the state to ensure high levels of surplus extraction." That kind of circles back to what you were saying earlier about this state-corporate collusion in the extraction of natural resources.*

Obviously, the anticorruption protests in India also had made quite an impact on the debates around India all over the world. For me, corruption is a very, very dicey subject to build a political movement over, because what do you mean by corruption? To me, obviously, there is never going to be a situation where you're in a corruption-free society. But how do you minimize it? Corruption is a function of a very unequal distribution of power. Unless you address that, you're just dealing with the symptoms.

Unless you put a cap on cross-ownership of businesses, and unless you put a cap on how much one person, or one corporation, can control a country, there's going to be corruption. You can't appeal to some sort of moral core. You have to address the problem structurally.

You've spent time in Tihar Jail in New Delhi. It's one of the biggest prisons in the entire country. There were two deaths in that jail, one in February and one in March 2013. They're kind of like bookends. One involved Afzal Guru, the other Ram Singh. Let's start with the case of Afzal Guru, who was hanged.

Let me try and explain it as briefly as possible. At the time of the 9/11 attacks in United States, the Bharatiya Janata Party, the right-wing Hindu party, was in power. The Islamophobia that the 9/11 attacks set off segued into the policies of the BJP vis-à-vis the Muslim community. They had already demolished the Babri Masjid, a fourteenth-century mosque. That's what brought the BJP to power. There was this whole desire to place yourself in the same sphere as the United States, as a victim of terrorism. That has been a constant theme in India.

On December 13, 2001, there was this very strange, botched "terrorist" strike on the parliament in Delhi, where five "terrorists" drove into parliament in this highly inept way in a white car with a big poster that said, "India is a very bad country." There were wires hanging out of the trunk of the car. When they were stopped, they jumped out and killed some policemen and a gardener. And then they were all killed. This became "India's 9/11." The government arrested four people: a professor of Arabic from Delhi University called S. A. R. Geelani, Afzal Guru, his cousin Showkat, and Showkat's wife, Afsan Guru, who actually was in jail when I was there. I met her.

There was a huge sort of media circus, where the media just said anything they liked about these four people. They had been sowing seeds of terrorism from Delhi to London, they were attacking democracy, and so on. Some of us were very disturbed by the entire incident. It just didn't ring true, neither the way the attack happened, because it was so unprofessional—and stupid, if you like—nor what was being said about these people.

Many people knew this young professor, Geelani, who had been arrested, and found it hard to believe that he really had anything to do with the events. So Nandita Haksar, a lawyer, put together this group calling for a free trial for Geelani. I was also part of it. The atmosphere was wicked at the time. The BJP-types were saying, "You must try these people, too. They are traitors." Anyway, what happened was that eventually the courts acquitted Geelani. They couldn't find any evidence against him.

But Afzal Guru had a different story. He had lived in Kashmir. In the early 1990s, when thousands and thousands of young Kashmiris had crossed over to Pakistan for training and came back as militants, he was one of them. But as soon as he came back, he surrendered, because he was very disillusioned by what he saw on the other side. Once you surrender in Kashmir, though, you're preyed upon by the security forces, as Afzal was for many years. I find it very hard to describe this in brief, because I've followed this case and I've done a lot of writing on it. We've even just brought out a book about it.

Afzal did not have a lawyer at the time of his trial in the lower court, which is where evidence is presented and where witnesses are questioned. The state appointed a lawyer for him. That lawyer said, I don't want to appear for him. But the court insisted. And that lawyer in fact accepted incriminating evidence against his own client at this stage of the trial.

At the end, when the Supreme Court finally sentenced Afzal to death, it said two things, in a very long judgment. It said that the only evidence it had was circumstantial. Many of us have written about how the evidence was fabricated, how witnesses lied, how the police lied. And oddly enough, in this strange act of bureaucracy, there is a sort of dualism in the judgment. The court is trying to be lofty and correct, actually write down that this evidence was fabricated, this cannot be on record, the confessions are extracted in custody and therefore do not constitute legal evidence. All of it is down in black and white in the judgment. And then it goes on to say that we don't have any direct evidence to prove that he belonged to a terrorist group. And then a little bit later it says, "The collective conscience of the society will only be satisfied if capital punishment is awarded to the offender." It's such a brazenly shocking thing for the Supreme Court of a supposedly great democracy to say.

You see how the media behaved. The antiterrorism cell of the Delhi police actually extracted many versions of the confession from him, some of them on video. The court says you can't use custodial confessions, but the media television channels, even supposedly secular and liberal channels, are showing this confession without saying it's in police custody. And you can see the jingoists commenting, "Hang him by the balls in Lal Chowk" and "Cut him into pieces and feed him to the dogs."

So in this kind of amphitheater of this "great democracy," with every institution playing a part, last month suddenly they just hanged him, denying him the rights it has given to all other prisoners who have faced the death penalty.

So it's caused a huge underground fury in Kashmir, because what was heroic about Afzal was that he was just an ordinary Kashmiri who had faced what tens of thousands of ordinary Kashmiris have faced, which is brutal torture.

Just the brazenness of doing this to somebody. You have a man who was tried not even for being the mastermind or anything, just for being a foot soldier, and hanged, while the court says there is no direct evidence. And everyone is saying, "Eleven years after Indian democracy was attacked, justice at last."

When thousands of Muslims called "illegal Bangladeshis" were massacred in Nellie in Assam in 1983, wasn't that an attack on democracy? When three thousand Sikhs were killed in 1984 under the Congress, after Indira Gandhi was killed, wasn't that an attack on democracy? When in 1993 the Shiv Sena massacred Muslims on the streets of Bombay, wasn't that an attack on democracy? When Narendra Modi was chief minister and thousands of Muslims were killed and raped and burned and driven from their homes, wasn't that an attack on democracy? Would you ever imagine that the Indian system would imprison Bal Thackeray or Narendra Modi for even a week, let alone for eleven years, or let alone sentence them to death? But Bal Thackeray, head of the Shiv Sena, who died recently, who has never, ever held public office, was given a state funeral. And Modi will be probably running for prime minister.

Elections in India are to take place next year. Are you concerned about what may be in the offering between what can only be described as a discredited and rather unpopular Congress Party and the BJP?

I don't know what will happen in the elections. But I think what is most worrying is that Congress, discredited as it is, and the BJP in shambles politically because of its infighting, are both trying to regroup. As I said, because the economy has somewhat stalled, there are millions among the new middle class whose exhilaration has turned into panic. This new middle class, its aspirations, its acquisitiveness, its aggression, doesn't accept politics as it used to be. And this is not necessarily in a progressive way. It's in a slightly frightening way. Whereas the BJP, Congress now want to uncork the genie of communalism.

The BJP's election slogan last time was: "The nation is ashamed because Afzal is still alive." So now they will have to find another slogan. The Congress was trying to sort of out-BJP the BJP. In trying to do that, the hanging was aimed at Kashmir, knowing full well that it would unleash outrage there, knowing full well that in 2014, when the United States pulls out of Afghanistan, the whole equation in that area is going to change. So everybody—Pakistan, India, Congress, the BJP—would be quite happy with a little war. But can you have a little war with two nuclear powers? Everybody would be happy with polarizing the Muslims and Hindus.

One of the things that many of us are frightened of right now is that one of the aggressive moves by the Indian government is the Amarnath Yatra in Kashmir. Hundreds of thousands of Hindu pilgrims go to this shrine in the Kashmiri mountains, and they are protected by the army. It's a very tense and aggressive situation. One of the worries is that now, as we know, there are these Hindu terror outfits that set off explosions and pretend that they are Muslim groups. Many people are very worried about the possibility that one of these Hindu organizations will attack the Amarnath

Yatra. The fallout of that would be to immediately polarize the population, and the Hindu vote would then likely unite behind the BJP.

People ask me, "When is Arundhati going to write another novel?" You started one a few years ago. How is that progressing?

That's what I am fully engaged in right now. It's difficult to know how long it will take. But whatever I've written about and gone through in these last years, to me, there is no direct way of expressing what I'm thinking and feeling. I need the subversion of fiction. I need the truth of fiction.

Can you hint at the topics you're writing about?

To me, novels are never about topics. Novels are about—I won't even say the human condition, because that would be small. I think novels should be about everything, in a way. It's not just about some subject, because that's what I've done with my nonfiction writing. But fiction has something so delicate and so beautiful about it. It isn't topic-driven.

Your political essays are characterized by a focused rage and crisp writing. Do you have any models who have inspired you?

There are so many writers that I admire, whether it's Eduardo Galeano or John Berger. Nowadays I'm reading *The Iliad*. I find it's so absorbing. To me, what is beautiful and real about writing eventually has to do with this: Does it stand the test of time? Because all of us can easily believe that what's happening to us now has never happened before. It's unique. But it is and it isn't.

Especially now, I think India is becoming very much like the United States, so self-absorbed. The Indian middle class is more and more arrogant, more and more insular. To me, it's very important to be able to write something that is true to the place but which also doesn't recognize those boundaries, which also resonates in the hearts and in the minds of people who are experiencing similar terrors, similar loves, similar fears. Similar but not the same. How do you join people up with that? Galeano and Berger do that.

The art of writing is one that's so artless in some ways, and yet it's something that takes up all my—a lot of my waking hours. How do I communicate this or how do I explain this? Not to someone in particular. Even the rage, it comes from love. It comes from believing that somebody should know—or somebody wants to know what this is about. I have said in the past that there's not such a great difference between fiction and nonfiction. But there is. When I'm writing now, I know that there is. And the play that you allow yourself in fiction is completely different. You don't have to be crisp and to the point and focused. You mustn't be. You must play.

CHAPTER 12

Fascism in India

Today is Bastille Day, a day of revolution, and there've been some interesting developments in a neighboring country to India, in Sri Lanka, where in the last few days the Rajapaksa regime has been overthrown.

It's a little premature to say that because Gotabaya Rajapaksa has fled but Mahinda, his brother, is still there. Also, his son, Manoj, is saying things about we have to resurrect our family image. And the fact is that Ranil Wickremesinghe is still there as prime minister and acting president. The protesters have been today persuaded to leave the official premises.

Things are very frightening in Sri Lanka. And nobody knows, as we learned in the Arab Spring, what is going to come in that place. Is it going to be military rule? Is it going to be some other form of authoritarianism? The people reached the end of their tether. But who is going to bail out the country? The International Monetary Fund. It's a brave display of protest by people, but we cannot call it a revolution by any means.

The economy is in shambles, and there's huge amount of debt, some of which is owed to China.

And the economy took a huge hit because of COVID. It's a tourism-dependent country. There was also a lot of mishandling by the Rajapaksa family. But to assume that things will improve

This interview was conducted in New Delhi, India, July 14, 2022.

is premature, because in these parts, we are not exactly witnessing the winds of democracy.

Do you think a Sri Lanka–type uprising, which ousted the Rajapaksa regime, could happen in India, toppling Narendra Modi?

Not any time in the near future. I don't want to make any easy comparisons with what's happening in Sri Lanka. Sri Lanka's a tiny country. The Indian economy is in a lot of trouble. The rage that kind of surfaces from time to time, whether it's the farmers' movement or whether it's the recent protests about the change in the laws for recruitment to the security forces, gets snuffed out very quickly. The anger is redirected into Hindu nationalist bigotry. So I think we're a long way from seeing something like that happening.

In fact, we are seeing the opposite. We are seeing state government after state government being bought or toppled by the BJP. We are seeing a consolidation, with the institutions of democracy falling into this ideological sort of tunnel. It's terrifying to watch whatever democracy remained being dismantled. We're seeing absolutely no movement, no airing of opinion possible in places like Kashmir. And you've seen a lot of violence on the streets. The regime has certainly captured the imagination of a vast part of this population, including the educated middle class. And of course, the media is completely captured. The courts are behaving in very troubling ways. I would say we are very far away from a Sri Lanka–type of situation.

Talk about the farmers' uprising. The year-long nonviolent action.

Nonviolent on the part of the farmers, not the state.

Hundreds of farmers were killed by state violence. You, as a journalist, went there. You talked to farmers. You found out what their demands were. What impressed you about that whole movement, and what kind of lessons can be learned in terms of coalition building beyond farmers? Or was this just a one-off, very spectacular, but not connecting to anything?

I don't think of myself as a journalist, first of all. I didn't go to the protest site as a journalist. In fact, I actually kept a little bit away from that movement, simply because I actually have known people who were involved in it for many years. I have spoken at meetings in Punjab, and so on. And the reason I wasn't going there much was because there was such a huge attempt on the part of the government to paint them as terrorists, as leftists, as extreme Maoists. And since every adjective has been used against on me, I was concerned not to allow the state to isolate that movement for its association with people who are recognizably part of other resistances.

I know them well. There were many farmers' groups, some of whom are ideologically far apart from each other, who came together in this protest. One of the reasons it was successful is because there was a large section of wealthy middle-class farmers there who had genuine staying power. And then you had coalitions of landless labor, Dalit workers of the land who, for example, have major conflicts with land-owning farmers. Yet everybody came together because they saw what was happening as an existential threat.

There's a thread that connects all of this. Whether it was the anti-dam movement of the Narmada valley. Whether it was the comrades in the forest in Central India fighting against the acquisition of indigenous peoples' lands by big mining companies. Or whether it was this farmers' movement that saw its own lands and produce falling into corporate hands. But in the anti-dam movement and the fight in the forests, you don't have a middle class active in the resistance in a way that can sustain a movement on that scale and keep it going. So, this was one of the great advantages.

And apart from actually forcing the government to actually rescind the three farm laws they were protesting, the farmers' movement also created a new kind of language on the street. A new language with which to address this ugly Hindu nationalist language that has become so acceptable now to the Indian media and to the supporters of the BJP. But the strength of the street does not translate into any kind of strength when it comes to elections in Uttar Pradesh or anywhere else, even in the Punjab. The electoral process has been captured and compromised. And now, whatever change will come, will come from the street, like it did in the farmers' movement.

Rukmini S., an Indian journalist, warns, "[I]t would be overambitious to hold up the farmers' victory as a sign of things to come. The space for dissent in India has shrunk markedly over seven years as the Modi juggernaut has rolled on and emboldened Hindu nationalism." One farmer leader, Balbir Singh Rajewal, said, "We need to transform our movement to remove corporate control of agriculture." And then he adds, "Without removing Modi, this is not possible. It's time to become a united force to save India." Those are fighting words.

Yes, those are fighting words. The trouble is that when you look at what happened in the Punjab elections, some of the people from the farmers' movement who actually stood for election lost their deposits. In U.P., too, there was a great hope that the farmers' movement would turn the tide against the BJP and Yogi Adityanath, but it didn't, even though one can raise certain questions about how that election took place.

Nevertheless, as I was saying, the problem is there are two different dynamics here: the street and the electoral process. And the electoral process has been captured in a whole lot of ways, beginning with the fact that the opposition parties have run out of money. They have run out of imagination. And they have been in their own time in power—I'm speaking of the Congress Party and many of the regional parties, as well—so corrupt that they are spongy with compromise. So, now they are being caught in the talons of the enforcement directorate. And they are, most of them, basically being blackmailed. And therefore, there's no opposition.

Secondly, there's a system of secret electoral bonds, which makes the funding of political parties a deeply opaque process.

You have the institutions that run the elections completely terrified and beholden to the BJP. And then you have a media, which is really like Radio Rwanda. It's just frenzied, bigoted, craziness going on. So, to actually remove Modi in an election any time in the near future looks difficult.

And now, we've come down to people just being given rations with Modi's face on it. Five kilos of atta, wheat, and one kilo of sugar, and so on. It's like watching a plane flying backwards in reverse gear.

And the plane is going to crash.

The point is we are also, because of the nature of peoples' beliefs in Hinduism and other kinds of spiritualism, a very fatalistic people who seem, so far at least, to be able to absorb this punishment in return for some mythic future that also lies in the past. I don't know when—or if—that romance will end. At the moment it's in full bloom.

You're seeing a crackdown. Activists, lawyers, poets, writers, journalists, intellectuals are being hunted down. They are being jailed for Facebook posts criticizing Modi. Even to pursue the normal paths of justice, appeals in court or asking for an inquiry, have become punishable offenses. It's a very dangerous time.

You mentioned Yogi Adityanath, who is a Hindu monk. He's the BJP chief minister of Uttar Pradesh, India's most populous state, which has a large Muslim minority. He is being mentioned as a possible successor to Modi.

Frequently.

He has been stoking anti-Muslim hatred. There have been killings and lynchings in Uttar Pradesh.

It's not just him. It's something that one could almost call a policy. In fact, one of the bizarre cases right now is that there's a young journalist and fact-checker called Mohammed Zubair.

He works for an organization called Alt News, which has been brilliant in just systematically debunking fake news, whichever political party spreads it. And Zubair is now being charged for creating enmity between communities because he called Hindu leaders who have openly called for the genocide of Muslims in the Press Club of Delhi and other places "hatemongers" on Twitter. For that, he was jailed.

This ferocity of hatred toward India's large Muslim minority is alarming. More than two hundred million Indians are Muslim. They could be an independent country, one of the largest Muslim countries in the world.

If you say something like that, it plays into a very danger-ous narrative. That's what the whole logic of hatred is. Why don't you go to Pakistan? Pakistan is for Muslims, and India is for Hindus. As if every Indian Muslim, from Kerala to Tamil Nadu, to Hyderabad, to Maharashtra, was part of the agitations for Pakistan. This isn't true, but that's what the Hindu right likes to suggest. You have your independent country, Pakistan. Go there.

Islamophobia has long been part of the Hindutva toolbox to mobilize its base, but it's recently added to its repertoire of violence the bull-dozing of Muslim homes and businesses. You've written about this in Al Jazeera.

That's not so new, but it's being revved up to punish Muslims, then they protest. For example, when people protested against the anti-Muslim citizenship law, Yogi Adityanath started identi-fying the people who are at the protests, and without trial, with-out proof, without anything, just sending bulldozers to demolish their homes. The citizenship law basically cut the ground from under people's feet. You're supposed to come up with a set of leg-acy papers, like the Nuremberg Laws in the 1930s in Nazi Ger-many. There was a huge uprising against that before it was cut short by COVID.

And recently, a similar thing happened to the people who came out to protest the comments about Prophet Muhammad by BJP spokesperson Nupur Sharma. We've seen mass killing, we've seen lynching, we've seen people being killed in fake police encounters, we've seen false arrests. But bulldozing is a spectacle in which the public participates. It's almost like some divine avenging mechanical god that arrives. People are watching. The police are there. The media are broadcasting. The courts are complicit. So it's a way of drawing all the institutions into the spectacle and performing fascism. Performing fascism in which nothing is illegal. Now you're showing that everything is at our command.

You've said that the ruling Bharatiya Janata Party has more money than any other political party in the world. Where is that money coming from? Is any of it coming from the diaspora Indian population?

The diaspora is hugely supportive of the BJP and the RSS, but, as I was saying, they have these rather opaque systems. Take the RSS, which is actually the most powerful organization in India. It's not an NGO. It's not a political party. You can't study its bank accounts. The BJP is the highest recipient of these opaque electoral bonds. While everyone else is being forced to being more and more transparent, and every bit of our privacy is now available for data mining, this process is becoming more and more secretive.

In 2016, November, when Modi suddenly announced his policy of demonetization, where suddenly, with no notice, 500-rupee notes were no longer legal tender. This devastated all the other political parties. It devastated the Indian economy. It was like shooting at the engine of a moving car. So, the economic trouble that they're in didn't start with COVID. It didn't start with Russia's invasion of the Ukraine. It started in 2016.

In that June 17 Al Jazeera piece you say, "To my mind," the bulldozing of homes and businesses of Muslims "marks the moment when a deeply flawed, fragile democracy has transitioned—openly and

brazenly—into a criminal, Hindu-fascist enterprise with tremen-
dous popular support." That's pretty stark language.

It is. What I find very disturbing is that I keep talking with
my friends in Kashmir about it. In Kashmir, there's a sense in
which you have a state, you have the army, you have the torture centers, you have the control of the media, and you have,
of course, many compromised people, but you don't have this
overwhelming sense that a large section of the population supports all this. In India, we have that sense now that this fascist,
criminal enterprise does have a lot of popular support. We can't
deny it.

And it makes you think all the time, how does one live under
these circumstances? What is the moral way to live here? What is
the way to write about India in this moment? Because your love
for the place, for the people, is suddenly colored by this horror
that people are willing to actually participate in the crushing of
another people? Whether it's Christians, whether it's Muslims,
whether it's people on the left, whether it's writers. The hatred is
so palpable. So, there is a fear, too, because people are called out.
People are targeted. People are made to understand that we have
laws, but those laws are applied differently depending on your
religion, your gender.

How did Germans go on giving their children piano lessons
and sending them to school and ballet classes, while the unthinkable was unfolding? That hasn't happened here. It's not that. Even
though they are building huge detention centers, and even though
two million people are being struck off the citizenship list in Assam, and even though the very foundations of who belongs to this
country, and who has rights in this country, and who doesn't, is
being questioned. But people who've seen this coming from a long
time are now subsumed in it, drowning in it.

Prime Minister Narendra Modi, now elected twice, his many fol-
lowers refer to him as Vishwa Guru, the guru of the whole world.
What's the secret of his attraction to so many millions of Indians?

I don't want to use the word *charismatic*, but when he speaks at political rallies, he has this howling, sneering, threatening appeal. He was called Hindu Hriday Samrat, the Emperor of Hindu Hearts, after the Gujarat massacre. It is important to remember how he stepped onto the national stage. In October 2001, soon after the 9/11 attacks, with the global spread of Islamophobia, the RSS saw its moment. Modi was appointed chief minister of Gujarat—not elected, but appointed. Within a few months, you had the horrible burning of a train in Godhra. Sixty Hindu pilgrims were burned to death. And following that, you had weeks of this pogrom, this massacre of Muslims in broad daylight in the streets in the towns and villages of Gujarat.

Modi was the chief minister. Huge questions have been raised about how the state machinery seemed to have stepped back and allowed this to take place. But soon after the massacre, Modi called for elections. The election commission, at the time, didn't allow it. But as soon as they allowed it, he won with a huge majority.

Is it known what caused the train fire?

There are lots of different theories about it, but I'd say, assuming it was an act of arson, because these pilgrims were returning from Ayodhya, where the mosque had been demolished.

The Babri Masjid.

And there was a lot of belligerence. There was supposed to have been some altercation on the station platform, and things got out of hand. But the point is, whoever did it, you cannot justify beating and killing thousands of Muslims, and burning their homes and shops for that. And the fact is the rhetoric of hate in the country at that time had been built up to such a level that one incident was enough for everything to burn. And that's what happened.

What happened on August 5, 2019, when the Indian constitution was abrogated and what little autonomy Kashmir had was nullified?

On August 5, arbitrarily, the Indian government abrogated Article 370, and basically turned Ladakh, which was a part of Jammu and Kashmir, into a union territory. It's not that Kashmiris just lost their autonomy, they don't even have the right to vote for a local government now.

While this was being done, thousands of people, including former chief ministers, were locked up. The internet was cut off. For months and months, the valley was just locked down with no communication. No phones. Nobody knew what was going on.

And now you have a situation of complete terror. Any kind of dissent, any disagreement, any sharing of the horrors that people are enduring is just smashed with an iron fist. People are in jail. Journalists are threatened. I don't know how long you can have six million people living in a situation like that.

What about the possibility of settler colonialism?

Part of abrogating Article 370 also had to do with revoking a law that made Kashmiris stewards of their own land. So Indians can now just flood in. It's difficult, because despite all this, they haven't really managed to completely control the area. Despite all this power, and all this iron-fistedness, it seems India has not been able to smash the place and secure it.

We've talked about the anti-Muslim violence and attitudes that are so prevalent in Modi's India today. But you also pointed out in a recent University of Texas lecture, "Alongside the Muslims of India and Kashmir, Christians, too, are on the front line. . . . In this last year alone, there have been hundreds of attacks on churches, statues of Christ have been desecrated, priests and nuns physically assaulted." I suspect many people don't know that the minority Christian population, as well as Muslims, Dalits, and others, is under the gun.

There were more than four hundred attacks last year on Christians. The Christians are much more vulnerable because they're a much smaller and poorer minority. And so they are very terrified.

Much of the Christian population is deep inside the forest. So attacks on them don't even often make it to the news.

Your family background is Christian. Does that give the Hindu right another kind of x-mark against you?

That has always been the case. They're a little puzzled by me. First of all, my mother's family comes from Kerala. The Syrian Christians are a very elite community there. They're not the community that's under attack, at all. As I have written in *The God of Small Things*, they're landowning and very casteist. I don't have that much sympathy for them. Three generations of my father's family individually converted to Christianity. So, yes, there is that continuous theme of "she's not a Hindu—that's why she's like this." But my name is not a Christian name. So I'm of such a mixed provenance that even I don't know exactly what I am [laughs].

Let's talk about the pandemic, which devastated India, probably resulting in several million deaths. No one knows the exact figure. How did India's billionaire class make out during the pandemic? Did the Ambanis, Mittals, Birlas, Andanis, and Jindals do okay?

They increased their wealth several times over. But again, what happened in the pandemic, it's like Modi treats Indians as an enemy that needs to be ambushed. Just in the same way as he ambushed us with his announcement of demonetization, he ambushed us with his announcement of a COVID lockdown with only four hours' notice. And then the whole world saw that biblical movement of millions of people walking thousands of miles home, stranded workers in the cities, people getting crushed by trains, people dying of thirst, people in a panic. That was the first wave. The second wave was when the hospitals had no oxygen, and people were dying on the streets and being cremated on the sides of the road, even in Delhi.

I traveled to Uttar Pradesh. You saw bodies floating down the river and you saw thousands of shallow graves. And many people said, "Well, if Modi hadn't been there, it would have been worse." So, we are dealing with a situation in which everything, whether it's good or bad, works out positive for this regime. I don't know when a point will come when people address their own suffering and examine the reasons for it. But right now, people on the left don't understand this. The very cut-and-dried arguments about hunger and unemployment don't work. People are living in some other realm right now.

I was deeply affected by what happened during the COVID catastrophe in India. I lost my sitar teacher of many years, Debu Chaudhuri, and his son, Prateek Chaudhuri.

It was just unthinkable what was going on. People's parents died in their homes. People not knowing what to do with the dead bodies. The cruelty of it. People were on Twitter, begging for those oxygen machines, and they were being arrested for showing India in a bad light or spreading "false information."

There's a constellation of organizations under the rubric of Sangh Parivar.

The BJP is the front desk of the RSS. And then, you have a whole lot of other organizations like the Bajrang Dal, the Vishwa Hindu Parishad, and other organizations, which are loosely affiliated. There's a sort of division of labor.

The RSS is the most powerful organization in India today. The most powerful. You have foreign diplomats going to RSS headquarters to pay their respects. The RSS has millions of members. It has a militia. It has women's organizations, farmers' organizations, indigenous peoples' organizations. It has publishing. It has schools in which millions of children study. It's a nation within a nation, ready to step out and take its place in the world. In fact, 2025 will be its hundredth year, and perhaps there will be a declaration of India as a "Hindu nation."

In your essay "Democracy's Failing Light," you ask, "Could it be that democracy, the sacred answer to our short-term hopes and prayers, the protector of our individual freedoms and nurturer of our avaricious dreams, will turn out to be the endgame for the human race?"

That was written in 2009, before the BJP and Modi came to power at the center. But you already saw in India that this kind of completely uncontrolled capitalism was washing through the institutions of democracy, conflating democracy with the free market. You saw the devastation of rivers and forests, of mountains, the plundering of land. You saw a country colonizing itself, in a way, in order to live the dreams of Europe and America. The idea that democracy has been just reduced to elections. Elections are compromised everywhere. So, yes, we are in trouble.

It's a very fragile moment, both here and there and all around the world. In an essay for CNN, you wrote, "The damage to Indian democracy is not reversible." But one might be able to say that about the United States as well.

Climate chaos poses an existential threat to everyone, from New York, to New Delhi, to New Zealand. Floods, droughts, storms, fires, and record heat waves are almost commonplace, with more in the offing. The word unprecedented has kind of lost its meaning when it comes to extreme weather events. What are your views on what can be done in the time remaining? Clearly the clock is ticking.

Everything I write, in some way, is about the climate crisis—whether it's leaving the bauxite in the mountain in Chhattisgarh, or dams, or roads that are being blasted into the Himalayas, glaciers that are melting.

Every battle one fights always ends up with a deep loss even though people know they shouldn't be doing it. You know that you shouldn't be cutting all the forests and mining. You know that you shouldn't be building a dam. You know that you shouldn't be ruining the drainage of a whole plateau. But somehow the danger of climate change is so vast that it doesn't register in our little minds.

So, for me, changing this can only be achieved through legislation of a certain kind. You can't make people feel guilty about driving SUVs if you keep providing them the SUVs. You can't expect some moral principle will suddenly come and overtake humanity, and everyone will behave themselves. That's not going to happen.

What does every single one of these projects do to our imaginations, as well as to the actual place? That is the question I am trying to raise in my writing.

People in this part of the world have been fighting those battles because they're existential ones. They're not theoretical battles. In Europe and elsewhere, they'll soon become existential battles as well. But how many years have people been fighting in the forests, in the valleys, in the rivers? Yet they were not considered climate activists or environmental activists. Even if they were, they were sneered at.

We are celebrating the Howard Zinn centenary this year. He was born in Brooklyn in 1922. I recall seeing a painting of Howard in your home. Is it still up?

Actually, it got soaked because my roof started leaking buckets of water.

You knew Howard. You did some events with him.

Yes. Just days before he died, I spoke to him, and I told him, "Howard, I have this really beautiful portrait of you hanging on my wall, because you've got to know that I have a big crush on you." And he said, "Arundhati, I take that sort of thing very seriously" [laughs].

People frequently ask me about your personal safety, the dangers you face. I assume you take precautions. But what about that issue of danger?

Well, look. In my case, when I'm talking about all the people who are in jail, all the people who've been arrested, who've been attacked, and being on the A-list of antinationals, people will wonder how I am not in jail. It's a dance. What are the costs and benefits to the regime of going after somebody like me? And while one should not be incautious, I think when they want to do something, they'll do it. So, there's no point in being completely colonized by this fear of what is going to happen. I feel it's very important for us not to hunch our shoulders, not to become paranoid. To be careful, not to be stupidly brave or anything. To be careful, to be strategic, but to continue to hold our position.

You told an audience in Vancouver that your formation as a reader and then as a writer began because of a library.

I grew up in a little village in Kerala called Ayemenem, a village on the banks of a river. It's where *The God of Small Things* is set. It's in Kerala. It wasn't like a village in North India. This was Kerala, with my Rhodes Scholar uncle, making pickles. But there was nothing there. There were no shops. There was no cinema, there were no restaurants, there was no TV. There was nothing. We had to make our own toys, our own fishing rods, and spend our hours by the river.

And of course, there were no books. There were no libraries, no bookshops. So my mother somehow managed to get in touch with the British Council Library in Chennai, Madras. They would send us one hundred books in a parcel, and we could read them and return them after three months. That used to be just the most exciting day of your life, when this box would arrive. And you were so excited, you didn't know whether to open a book or to run to the loo.

Your essay "Come September" has spread far and wide. You conclude it with "The time has come, the Walrus said. Perhaps things will get worse and then better. Perhaps there's a small god up in heaven readying herself for us. Another world is not only possible, she's on her way. Maybe many of us won't be here to greet her, but on a quiet day, if I listen very carefully, I can hear her breathing." Can you still hear her breathing?

I have to listen really carefully.

I have to say, that was a time when I felt that the injustices and the craziness and everything was up on the surface. I felt more hopeful then than I feel now. I don't want to be that person who is just being hopeful because that's the position that you take. I go through periods of very deep despair. But I also know that sometimes you have to just reduce the scope of the lens you are looking through. And you see people being so brave, and so funny, and so defiant.

I feel that it's not just the fascists, and it's not just the Hindu fundamentalists and the nationalists that we have to look out for, but even ourselves. There's been so much unpleasantness, division, everyone locking themselves up into little silos, locking themselves in and then rattling their cages. The loss of the ideal of solidarity. These are really terrible things. I feel that we have also participated in flying the plane backwards.

I occasionally give public talks, and I sometimes conclude with that passage I just read—"The time has come, the Walrus said. . . ." Every time I read it, and even now, I choke up, because it's so beautiful.

Fundamentally, I'm a fiction writer, and I feel that poetry, literature, the way you build a story, the way you tell a story, the way you construct a sentence, these are all more indestructible than almost anything else. So to insist on beauty. To insist on the fact that you are going to spend a lot of time trying to create something that presents the world as different from the way people want you to see it. That you notice things that people don't want you to notice. These are acts of resistance for me. They're not sloganeering acts of resistance. They're not marching acts of resistance.

If I were to take our conversation into a different space, I would say that I listened very carefully, and I heard her breathing. I wrote my novel *The Ministry of Utmost Happiness* because that is her breathing. That is the other world that's possible—not because you have to create it, but because you have to notice it. Because it already exists. Right here. You just have to look for it.

The Ministry of Utmost Happiness, as one review noted, "is crammed full of misfits and outsiders, the flotsam and jetsam of India's complex, stratified society. The novel is inhabited by cohorts of others: hijras, political rebels, the poor, women who will not 'know their place,' and abandoned baby girls."

It's also inhabited by people in power—intelligence officers and mainstream journalists. It's not a world just about mavericks and misfits. It's also about the army, the police, the intelligence services, the structures of government, and how these things interlock.

What can people do, particularly outside of India, in the face of the authoritarianism that Modi and the BJP represent?

That's a very broad question, and I can only answer it by saying that, just as we need to understand what's happening in the United States, people everywhere need to understand what's going on in the world, and not participate in this notion of India as this democracy with Bollywood, yoga, and all these touchy-feely things. It's a dangerous place. And if India goes into chaos, as it might, it will have implications for the world.

At the same time, I think things have come to a point that we can't call it back. We have to go through it. So, all one can ask for is an intelligent understanding of what we are going through. And we should provide an intelligent understanding to others and try to understand what they are going through.

AFTERWORD

Arundhati Roy: Word Warrior

Naomi Klein

On March 7, 2003, two weeks before the United States invaded Iraq, Arundhati Roy sent me an essay she had just written. The subject line was "My Last Words: A Submission in Anger." It arrived at the perfect time: despite the unprecedented outpouring of opposition to the attack, the cable stations were giddily counting down to war as if it were New Year's Eve. If there was ever a moment when the world needed a dose of Arundhati Roy's rage and wisdom, it was now.

It took one sentence before I realized that the article was a fake, not written by Roy but by someone out to discredit her. The giveaways were phrases like this: "zombie fascists" to describe the citizens of the United States, "the greatest artistic performance in modern history" to describe the September 11 attacks on the World Trade Center.

My heart broke for Arundhati when I read those words. All a writer has is her voice, her words. And here was Roy's precious voice being stolen, violated, made to espouse views she pours her life energy into resisting. But the counterfeit was also strangely instructive: when Roy's enemies set out to destroy her, they do so by trying to rob her of the very thing that makes her powerful—her unfailing humanity, her refusal to give in to easy hatreds, her clear and furious condemnation of all forms of terror.

With her writing and her actions, Roy has placed herself in opposition to anyone who treats people as collateral damage—of a mega-dam, a terrorist attack, or a military invasion. As the attack on Afghanistan began, she wrote: "Nothing can excuse or justify an act of terrorism, whether it is committed by religious fundamentalists, private militias, people's resistance movements—or whether it's dressed up as a war of retribution by a recognized government." And Roy has chosen the very moments when the US government is engaged in its most barbaric acts to reach out to the people of the United States, to make clear distinctions between citizens and states, to try to understand the fear—of outsiders, of each other—that bestows on US politicians so much undeserved power.

Unable to goad her into a politics of hate, Roy's political opponents have resorted to faking it, inventing Arundhati Imposters to do their dirty work. But there's a hitch: Roy's enemies can't write, a serious liability when trying to imitate one of the finest writers of our time, and I have yet to meet a single person who fell for the fake.

I have described Arundhati as a great humanist, but that, of course, is only part of the story. Roy's generosity has its limits— and thank goodness for that. Because if she were only about peace and love, the world would be denied one of its great pleasures: watching Arundhati Roy wage a bloody war of words against US president George W. Bush. He says, "You are either with us, or you are with the terrorists"; she says that we don't have to choose between "a malevolent Mickey Mouse and the Mad Mullahs." He says, "We're a peaceful nation"; she says, "Pigs are horses. Girls are boys. War is peace." He says the invasion of Iraq was right and just because we caught Saddam Hussein; she says that's "like deifying Jack the Ripper for disemboweling the Boston Strangler."

I don't know how Arundhati comes up with these killer one-liners, but I'm grateful. Each one is a gift, capable of transforming fear and confusion into courage and conviction. In Roy's hands, words are weapons—weapons of mass movements. But Roy's essays and speeches are not propaganda, quite the opposite: they are attempts to name our world as it is, exactly, precisely, perfectly. It is for this reason that I sometimes fear that Arundhati will be driven mad by George Bush and the violence he inflicts on the English language. Recently, Roy wrote that she imagined Noam Chomsky watching an American cable news show with an "amused, chipped-tooth smile." I imagine Roy watching that same program with a great roll of tape, picking up the words George Bush has ruthlessly severed from their meanings—peace, evil, war, democracy, truth, good, innocent, justice…—and carefully, urgently, taping them back together again.

The conversations in this book span three years, a period in which Roy invented a new way to be a political activist, not only in India, where she lives, but also in the heart of empire itself, the United States. As Roy tells David Barsamian, it is usually white people who travel south to tell Black and Brown people who they are. When the travel flows are reversed, the voices from the South are usually personal testimonials about poverty and suffering back home. Roy, however, is occupying a very different cultural space; she is, in her words, a "Black woman from India speaking about America to an American audience." Elsewhere, Roy has claimed this right because the United States is not merely a country but the hub of empire. "[M]ay I clarify that I speak as a subject of the US empire? I speak as a slave who presumes to criticize her king."

It is Roy's deep understanding of the mechanics of power that is her greatest contribution to movements against neoliberalism and war. Again and again, Arundhati has used her gifts as a novelist and trained architect to help us visualize the invisible architecture of modern empire. Crucially, she has helped us to understand how powerful interests that seem to be in conflict—the nation-state versus corporate globalization; religious fundamentalism versus US capitalism—actually serve to strengthen and protect each other, and join forces to lay waste to democracy. In these pages, Roy describes the Indian elite's embrace of corporate globalization and the rise of Hindu nationalism as "a pincer action. With one hand they're selling the country out to multinationals. With the other they're orchestrating this howling cultural nationalism."

According to Roy, all imperial projects—whether political, economic, or religious—share a logic, the logic of bigness. In her essay "The Greater Common Good," she writes of "[b]ig bombs, big dams, big ideologies, big contradictions, big countries, big wars, big heroes, big mistakes." It is this tyranny of scale, Roy tells Barsamian here, that systematically seizes power away from communities and delegates it to centralized governments, and further away still, to global institutions like the World Bank and the World Trade Organization. "The distance between power and powerlessness, between those who take decisions and those who have to suffer those decisions, has increased enormously…. . The further and further away geographically decisions are taken, the more scope you have for incredible injustice. That is the primary issue." Our job, Roy tells us, is to narrow the distance, to bring power and decision making closer to home. For me, this simple mission has become a kind of barometer for my activism: our opponents hoard power, we disperse it.

The press is forever dwelling on Roy's beauty and poise, but she describes herself in less precious terms as a "hooligan." I never believed it until I met her, but it's true. Roy is a natural anti-authoritarian, not only in theory but also in practice: she is incapable of deferring to authority, whether to George W. Bush or to India's Supreme Court (a crime which landed her in jail for "contempt"). It is this total absence of deference that Roy's power-worshipping enemies find so endlessly maddening, and that the rest of us find so limitlessly inspiring.

At the 2003 World Social Forum in Porto Alegre, Brazil, Roy delivered a now legendary speech titled "Confronting Empire." At the end of her talk, Roy played with the forum's slogan, telling the crowd of tens of thousands that "another world is not only possible, she's on her way…. [O]n a quiet day, if I listen very carefully, I can hear her breathing." That stadium has never heard silence like that. For weeks after, all of us—from the most hard-core anarchists to the most staid socialist politicians—were firmly under Arundhati's spell, convinced we too could hear that quiet breathing, and utterly determined to turn it into a global roar.

One month later, we did just that: on February 15, we filled the streets of our cities with the largest and most unified rejection of war the world has ever seen. These demonstrations "really stripped down empire," Roy tells Barsamian. "It stripped off the mask." But by the final conversation in this book, readers will notice that Roy is getting impatient. While we are straining to hear our other world, our opponents are building theirs with terrifying determination, employing whatever weapons are required, whether the IMF's checkbook or the Pentagon's cruise missile. There is value to this brazenness, Roy says: it lets us know that the time is past for simply unmasking empire, it's time to take it down, "to dismantle its working parts"—starting with the illegal looting of Iraq. "Enough of being right," she says. "We need to win."

Thank you, Arundhati. As usual, the road ahead is being lit up by your bright and furious words.

—January 2004

Index

AZADI
ARUNDHATI ROY

The chant of 'Azadi!' – Urdu for 'Freedom!' – is the slogan of the freedom struggle in Kashmir against what Kashmiris see as the Indian Occupation. Ironically, it also became the chant of millions on the streets of India against the project of Hindu Nationalism.

Even as Arundhati Roy began to ask what lay between these two calls for freedom – a chasm or a bridge? – the streets fell silent. Not only in India, but all over the world. The coronavirus brought with it another, more terrible understanding of Azadi, making a nonsense of international borders, incarcerating whole populations and bringing the modern world to a halt like nothing else ever could.

In this series of penetrating essays on politics and literature, Arundhati Roy challenges us to reflect on the meaning of freedom in a world of growing authoritarianism. Azadi, she warns, hangs in the balance for us all.

'A startling collection of essays . . . The passion and beauty of her voice is unabated'

Guardian

'Arundhati Roy is one of the greatest writers of our time'

Naomi Klein

MY SEDITIOUS HEART
ARUNDHATI ROY

My Seditious Heart collects the work of a two-decade period when Arundhati Roy devoted herself to the political essay as a way of opening up space for justice, rights and freedoms in an increasingly hostile environment. Taken together, these essays trace her twenty-year journey from the Booker Prize-winning *The God of Small Things* to the extraordinary *The Ministry of Utmost Happiness*: a journey marked by compassion, clarity and courage. Radical and readable, they speak always in defence of the collective, of the individual and of the land, in the face of the destructive logic of financial, social, religious, military and governmental elites.

'Unflinching emotion as well as political intelligence . . . she continues to offer bracing ways of seeing, thinking and feeling'

Time

'Arundhati Roy calls for "factual precision" alongside the "real precision of poetry". Remarkably, she combines those achievements to a degree that few can hope to approach'

Noam Chomsky

THE MINISTRY OF UTMOST HAPPINESS
ARUNDHATI ROY

At magic hour; when the sun has gone but the light has not, armies of flying foxes unhinge themselves from the Banyan trees in the old graveyard and drift across the city like smoke . . .

Anjum lives in a graveyard, gathering around her the misfits and outcasts of Delhi's bustling streets. Tilo is a Kashmiri woman, brilliant and beautiful, fated to be loved by three rival men.

When Anjum takes in an abandoned baby, it is Tilo who claims the child as her own – and so begins a tale that will sweep across twenty years, crossing the cities and forests of a teeming continent . . .

'A sprawling, kaleidoscopic fable'

Guardian

'A great tempest of a novel [. . .] which will leave you awed by the heat of its anger and the depth of its compassion'

Washington Post